MW00658297

Everyday Media Literacy

In this graphic guide to media literacy, award-winning educator Sue Ellen Christian offers students an accessible, informed and lively look at how they can consume and create media intentionally and critically.

The straight-talking textbook offers timely examples and relevant activities to equip students with the skills and knowledge they need to assess all media, including news and information. Through discussion prompts, writing exercises, key terms, online links and even origami, readers are provided with a framework from which to critically consume and create media in their everyday lives. Chapters examine news literacy, online activism, digital inequality, privacy, social media and identity, global media corporations and beyond, giving readers a nuanced understanding of the key concepts and concerns at the core of media literacy.

Concise, creative and curated, this book highlights the cultural, political and economic dynamics of media in our contemporary society, and how consumers can mindfully navigate their daily media use. *Everyday Media Literacy* is perfect for students (and educators) of media literacy, journalism, education and media effects looking to build their understanding in an engaging way.

Sue Ellen Christian is a professor of communication at Western Michigan University. She was the 2016 Michigan Distinguished Professor of the Year and has received the highest honor for teaching from her institution. She is an award-winning former *Chicago Tribune* staff writer and the author of *Overcoming Bias: A Journalist's Guide to Culture and Context* (Routledge).

"*Everyday Media Literacy* comes at a critical moment in the life of the American mind; we've never had more facts at our disposal, and we've never been more acutely aware of how wrong they can be. This wonderful book, as contemplative as it is clear in its instruction, offers insight into the overwhelming tide of choices and encourages us to make our decisions mindfully. It is required reading for students of the storytelling crafts. But it's also for anyone seeking clarity and understanding of the world around them."

—Christi Parsons, senior editor, *The Atlantic*

"Researching like the scholar she is and writing like the journalist she was, Sue Ellen Christian has produced a perfect handbook for citizens in an information (and disinformation) age: Readable, informative and important."

—Kathy Kiely, Lee Hills Chair in
Free-Press Studies at the Missouri School of Journalism

"Prof. Christian takes on the critical issue of media literacy with an approach that is clear, accessible and well-researched, and that considers the subject from a global perspective. *Everyday Media Literacy* will enable readers to navigate the contemporary chaos of misinformation to distinguish fact from falsehood and become more engaged, informed citizens."

—Louise Kiernan, editor-in-chief, ProPublica Illinois and faculty,
Medill School of Journalism at Northwestern University

"This book is accessible, engaging and important. Read it to regain control of the news as it affects you and to protect our democracy. A lot of people are trying to twist the news. This book straightens things out again."

—Joe Grimm, editor-in-residence,
Michigan State University School of Journalism

Everyday Media Literacy

An Analog Guide for Your Digital Life

Sue Ellen Christian

Routledge
Taylor & Francis Group
NEW YORK AND LONDON

First published 2020
by Routledge
52 Vanderbilt Avenue, New York, NY 10017

and by Routledge
2 Park Square, Milton Park, Abingdon, Oxon, OX14 4RN

Routledge is an imprint of the Taylor & Francis Group, an informa business

Library of Congress Cataloging-in-Publication Data
A catalog record for this title has been requested

ISBN: 978-0-8153-8658-2 (hbk)
ISBN: 978-0-8153-8659-9 (pbk)
ISBN: 978-1-351-17550-0 (ebk)

Typeset in Warnock Pro
by Apex CoVantage, LLC

Visit the eResources: www.routledge.com/9780815386599

To my students

and

As always, to the home team:

Bob, Robert, Daniel and Amelia

Contents

Acknowledgments

Thank you:

To the media literacy pioneers who saw the need decades ago and dedicated their scholarship, research and creativity to show the way;

To Western Michigan University for the allowance of a sabbatical in which to complete this book. I'd like to specifically thank the administrators who signed off with their support for this project: Dr. Leigh Ford, Dr. Carla Koretsky and Dr. Susan Stapleton;

To Ryan Lewis, for starting on the journey with me, and to Madison Bennett, for ending it with me;

To Alexis Stubelt, for your committed work on graphics (and to Marie Lee, for introducing us);

To Julie Zimmerman, for your insightful editing and generous friendship;

To dear friends and family who provided support, encouragement and prayers.

Graphics and Illustrations

Alexis Stubelt created the graphics in this book unless otherwise indicated. She is a graphic designer from Portage, Michigan, who works for *Encore Magazine.*

Ryan Lewis created illustrations and graphics as noted in the text. He is an assistant professor of art in graphic design at Western Michigan University's Gwen Frostic School of Art.

Introduction

Why Media Literacy and Why You

Your first act of critical thinking, which is essential to media literacy, is deciding whether or not media literacy is even a "thing." Whether it is worth your while.

Media literacy is far more than a protective guardrail between you and your gaming console or a set of rules to strictly follow. It is a dynamic and hands-on discipline. Media literacy offers you tools and knowledge with which to equip yourself to live fully and mindfully in 21st century connected culture.

One of the tenets of media literacy is to question and critically consider messages (including this book), so what follows is my brief argument for why media literacy, and this book specifically, are worth your while.

WHAT IS THIS BOOK ABOUT?

This book aims to equip you with a framework for intelligently thinking about the media you consume and create. I give you theory and terms where it's needed to fully appreciate the themes at hand, but I am not doing a deep dive into the nuances; this is a book for all comers from all disciplines and interests. Because it is inevitable that some content will be dated nearly as soon as it's written due to the fast-changing digital media industry, the themes developed, I hope, are evergreen. These themes come with a lifetime warranty; that is, this stuff is useful throughout all your days on our media-rich planet.

WHY SHOULD *I* READ THIS BOOK?

You should read it if you're looking to be informed but not exhausted by news and information. If you like media and want to enjoy it while at the same time being attuned to choices made when you consume *and* create it. If you don't want to unknowingly allow tech companies access to your private data, but you don't have the time or energy to read all the blasted fine print on privacy waivers either. If you want to use media for positive purposes without being consumed by online life. If you believe in the power of information to change public and personal outcomes. If you'd like to be a relatively happy digital citizen who is in control of their use and creation of media. If you want media to serve you instead of the other way around.

Also, you are unique in our media history: Younger generations are the first immersed in this new era of plugged-in living, be that for good or ill. You are tech pioneers, and that is exciting and should also be a little unnerving. Even as I write, the technology of both devices and software is evolving in both empowering and troubling ways.

WHY SHOULD I READ *THIS BOOK*?

Use this book for four reasons. First, this book strives to be user-friendly, only a smidge preachy, relatively free of academic jargon and relevant. Second, the information presented is rooted in scholarly research and data and comes from credible sources. Third, the person who wrote this book (that's me) is an award-winning educator, author and former journalist; you are in capable (though not well-manicured) hands. Fourth, I have sought to seriously acknowledge and advocate for an inclusive and global perspective to media literacy, and to write a book that is not U.S.-centric. Media literacy can be a powerful vehicle for equity within society.

WHEN DO I NEED THIS BOOK?

The sooner the better. You need this book at the point in life when you are consuming media like you consume air: without thinking. Global media consumption is rising, not falling. Think of this book as a short-term, intense but fun training on how to think smarter about daily mediated communication.

WHERE DO I USE THIS BOOK?

Basically, anywhere. I made a book and not a digital thing (though I reference digital things constantly, and there is an online version with hyperlinks), so it is portable, largely unbreakable, doesn't need batteries or outlets and is waterproof-ish. Also, because in research studies the majority of students say they'd rather have a print text than an online one.

HOW DO I USE THIS BOOK?

This book is to be *used*, not merely read. Mark it up, make notes in it and share it with others. Scratch and sniff it if you like. How thoroughly, intensively and delightfully you use this book depends on you. Honestly, the best education in media literacy is to DO media literacy, not read about it, so don't cheat yourself and ignore the many resources and activities offered throughout these pages; those lead you to a full understanding of a media literate lifestyle.

When you see this icon, that means it's an ideal time **to discuss** with others the ideas being raised. The other icon you will see sprinkled through the book is an invitation **to do** something, be it read an article, watch a video snippet or write about a media experience. Each chapter has a *Vox Discipuli* box (Voice of the Students in Latin) (( )) that shares a relevant quote from media users who are past or present students. Their contributions are intended to help you see yourself in these pages.

The *Media Literacy Selfies* are occasional pauses meant to invite critical engagement with *this* text. It's my way of encouraging students to question their teacher/facilitator, as media literacy education necessarily is about collaborative inquiry.

I hope this book will be an introduction for you into media literacy as a mindset and an everyday habit.

A snippet (because that is all copyright laws allow!) from "Song of the Open Road" published in 1856 by American poet Walt Whitman sets us off on our journey. The words of this analog poet are surprisingly useful in confronting our digital reality:

> *From this hour I ordain myself loos'd of limits and imaginary lines. . .*
>
> *Listening to others, considering well what they say,*
>
> *Pausing, searching, receiving, contemplating*

1 Using How Your Time with Media Can Be More Intentional

Three out of four of you do the same thing as soon as you wake up in the morning.

It's not brushing your teeth, or petting the dog, or grabbing a coffee.

Nope, if you're ages 18 to 24 and living in the United States, the very first thing nine out of ten of you do within 15 minutes of waking up is reach for your smartphone. Six out of ten of you don't even wait 15 minutes; it's immediate.

Eyes open, and you're online and at the day's social media, emails and news updates, according to the IDC Research Report sponsored by Facebook (2013). Your smartphones are your alarm clock, your music to start the day, your orientation to what the world is up to and your update on what friends are

LEARNING OBJECTIVES

Terms: Media literacy, media message, third-person effect, uses and gratifications theory, hypodermic needle theory, intermittent reinforcement.

- Explain the five key concepts and questions of media literacy.
- Know the types of mass media.
- Identify key perspectives about modern media.
- Understand the basic trends in digital media consumption and creation.
- Recognize how the five purposes of communication relate to media creation.
- Describe the uses and gratifications theory and its categories.
- Explain how digital technology use can be addictive.

Share some of the reasons you use media each day. Are you satisfied with the ways you use media? Why or why not? What changes would you like to make?

planning and what the day holds. In fact, only about *two hours* of our days are spent without using our phones, which we don't often use for phone calls but as tiny computers that fit into our pockets. We see in our smartphones a device that connects us to friends, family, information, entertainment and productivity. Such perceived value makes today's smartphone very *sticky*. One in four of us cannot recall a time when our phones were not next to us or in the same room, the IDC report states.

Across this wide, connected world, people use all forms of media from the first moments of their day. For example, when it comes to getting the first news of the day, one in two people in Japan turn to the TV. In Ireland, almost four in ten people rely on the radio. In Finland, 80 percent of Finns read a printed newspaper every week, according to 2016 data (Jyrkiainen, 2019).

So, at the start of this book, I ask you to take just one day's worth of average TV time and devote it to reading an entire book (uh, that'd be this one). Average TV time in the United States in 2017 was about 238 minutes, according to eMarketer (2018), so that should get you at least through Chapter 9. By the way, that U.S. viewing time is 79 minutes *less* than average daily TV time in Romania, about the same as Slovakia and 100 minutes *more* than Norway (RTL, 2018). So, you folks in Norway: read fast. Ultimately, media literacy saves you valuable time, and it adds value to your time with media.

To start this guide to equipping yourself with media literacy skills, knowledge and mindset, this chapter looks at what media literacy is, and how and why we spend time with media. Worldwide, digital media use is rising. This is an invitation to think intentionally about our media habits, and why we seek out media in the first place.

WHAT IS MEDIA LITERACY?

Media literacy goes far beyond helping you avoid phishing scams or manipulation by advertisements. It addresses all forms of communication. The U.S.-based National Association of Media Literacy Education (2019) defines media literacy as the "ability to access, analyze, evaluate, create, and act using all forms of communication."

MediaSmarts, Canada's Centre for Digital and Media Literacy, defines media literacy as: "being able to *access* media on a basic level, to *analyze* it in a critical way based on certain *key concepts,* to *evaluate* it based on that analysis and, finally, to *produce* media oneself" (2019).

The Second European Media and Information Literacy Forum described media literacy this way:

> Media and information literacy empowers citizens with knowledge, skills and attitude to critically access information and media, to critically analyze information and media content, and to engage with media and other information providers for social, civic and creative purposes.
> (2016, Background section)

Media literacy requires the development of knowledge, skills and attitude to provide users with an essential framework for effective lifelong engagement with media messages. It doesn't matter what your area of study is, or what you plan to do in your career; media literacy is inherently interdisciplinary. Media literacy calls upon a breadth of skills and knowledge to develop competencies in critical thinking and cultural and contextual understanding of media. You can be from a farm in Minnesota or a cosmopolitan city such as London; media literacy tools are the same, but based on your background, culture and knowledge, you will use those tools differently. Plus, nearly anyone who consumes media is a media creator, and media literacy affects your media creation, too.

> Media literacy requires the development of knowledge, skills and attitude to provide users with an essential framework for effective lifelong engagement with media messages.

Why Media Literacy Matters When you understand how media works both for and against your purposes, you become a wiser consumer and creator of media—and you become a better citizen of the world. OK,

I get it; wherever you are in the world right now, being an engaged enlightened citizen is likely not tops on your agenda. Getting a decent grade, a good deal on a holiday getaway, a lift to work because it's raining—all likely higher-agenda items. But the bottom line is that media literacy matters greatly, and it goes far beyond helping you avoid phishing scams or manipulation by advertisements. Media literacy equips you with competencies to serve you in both highly personal and very public ways.

On the personal front, media literacy teaches you to express yourself by ethically creating media, both digital and analog. It encourages you to evaluate media messages' direct *and* implied meanings, and weigh those against your own principles. It sharpens your ability to access information from a variety of sources, not just your favorites, but those that challenge your worldview. When you encounter media messages that degrade or diminish, you as a media user can learn to quickly assess, evaluate, respond as needed and move on. (By the way, the word "message" in this book's context—as in, a "**media message**"—is a term used in communication scholarship to describe any piece of media *in whole or in part.*)

On the public front, media literacy asserts your right to information and expression, advocating for a digital world that is transparent and accessible to all citizens worldwide.

Media literacy sets standards for critical thinking that protect you from misinformation and disinformation. It equips you with skills to deconstruct a message to understand its meaning and references and develops in you an appreciation for other peoples' points of view when sending messages across cultures. It champions awareness and purpose in your public messages.

Democratic societies depend on media literate citizens who are equipped with accurate information, who understand how to mobilize using social media to exercise free speech and who can evaluate propaganda and see it for what it is (and propaganda comes in all shapes and colors, from an opinionated news broadcast to a beautifully-orchestrated movie that champions certain ideals).

Well-crafted media is enticing, engaging and persuasive. It is a powerful tool for entertainment and for information we need to survive and seriously progress. Critical competence in 21st-century digital communication and

MEDIA LITERACY SELFIE

This section has a lot of assertions and not a lot of support for the claims. That support, and specific examples and applications of media literacy, will come soon enough. For any media you consume, however, be on the lookout for sweeping language full of squishy verbs like "equips" and "encourages" and "champions" that don't follow with concrete data, illustrations or details.

media creation and consumption are essential. Here are five key reasons why media literacy matters:

- Media is our global language. It is pervasive and it is essential to our modern life.
- You can better use media for your own purposes as opposed to being used by it when you understand why, how, *for* whom and *by* whom a media message is created.
- You create media each day. Why not create it in the most effective, creative and intelligent way that you can?
- Media doesn't come with nutrition labels. Given all that you consume, it makes sense to know how to critically assess what you're feeding your brain.
- We aren't born with the skills to critically assess and understand media. We have to learn them.

MEDIA LITERACY KEY CONCEPTS

The California-based Center for Media Literacy provides a useful framework for thinking about media with these five key media literacy concepts and questions (2019). I will reference them throughout this book:

1. All media messages are "constructed."
2. Media messages are constructed using a creative language with its own rules.
3. Different people experience the same media message differently.
4. Media have embedded values and points of view.
5. Most media messages are organized to gain profit and/or power.

Five Key Questions Based on these concepts, the Center developed five key questions to ask ourselves when "doing" media. Again, they will guide our inquiry at many points in this book:

1. Who created this message?
2. What creative techniques are used to attract my attention?
3. How might different people understand this message differently than me?
4. What values, lifestyles and points of view are represented in, or omitted from, this message?
5. Why is this message being sent?

I created a handy guide inspired by some of these concepts to help you remember them. Take a screenshot of it and save it on your phone, make it your screensaver or create a reminder to look at it each week. However you manage to do it, keep these guidelines close at hand to get the most out of the time you spend with media every day.

ASSESSING MEDIA LITERACY

There is no better place to begin our work of critically assessing information than with the topic of this book. In short, is media literacy a tested and trusted intervention? Is it worth your time and money?

The answer is yes, but it's a qualified yes, as there is not yet a common and robust measurement tool for media literacy education and training. Like the variety of training regimens for athletes, each of which may target different outcomes (speed, agility, endurance), there are a lot of ways to reach media literacy fitness, and many measures of success.

Varied Approaches The difficulty in assessing media literacy's efficacy is in part due to the many definitions of media literacy that various researchers use. Another problem is that there are many ways that media messages affect us, so measuring just one or two potentially ignores many others. As one media literacy scholar/professional told researchers, the outstanding problem is "how to develop a cost effective and efficient measure of media literacy without oversimplifying or trivializing the robust competencies that we're trying to measure" (Schilder, Lockee, & Saxon, 2016, p. 45). Competence in media literacy knowledge and skills can be difficult to measure due

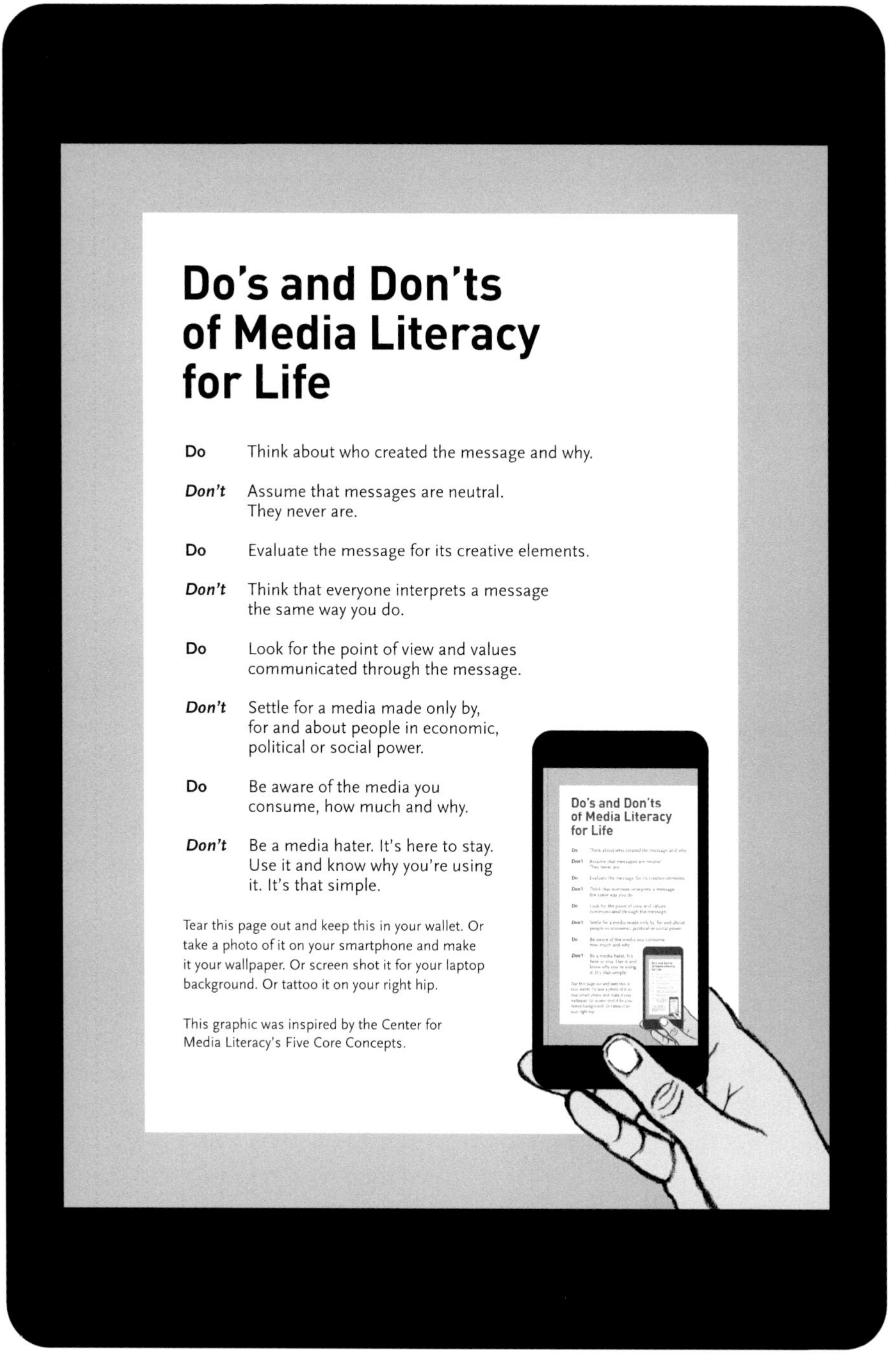

Do's and Don'ts of Media Literacy for Life

Credit: Ryan Lewis

to a number of factors, such as the cultural context in which assessment occurs, and the age and socioeconomic status of the participants.

Renee Hobbs of the University of Rhode Island's Media Education Lab is a pioneer in media literacy education, and she has long chronicled the various factions and interpretations within the media literacy community of scholars, educators and practitioners. She notes the tension between protectionists who want to curtail the negative effects of media on youth and those who focus more on empowerment to enable youth to actively use media to its full benefits (Hobbs & Jensen, 2009). "Media literacy in an urban public school is going to look different than media literacy in an affluent, well-resourced school, which will look different from a media literacy afterschool or library program. Chinese media literacy and Middle Eastern media literacy are going to look different than what we see in Brazil, Canada, Great Britain or the United States. There's no one right way to do it," she told an interviewer (Blumberg, 2019).

Positive Effects Media literacy education generally has a positive effect, concluded an analysis of 51 media literacy interventions spanning a variety of subject areas (Jeong, Cho, & Hwang, 2012). Recipients of media literacy education showed more knowledge about the media and its influences, and behaviors were also changed, such as reduction of risky health behaviors, the analysis found. In another study, students who took a college media literacy class were more likely than those in the control group to understand that media inaccurately portray gender and race as well as misrepresent and stereotype minority groups (Bergstrom, Flynn, & Craig, 2018).

One example of research that indicates the worth of media literacy education is a 2015 study by Erica Weintraub Austin and colleagues involving more than 2,000 U.S. teenagers; the study examined the impact of media messages that were sexual in nature. The study found that teaching young adults media literacy skills on how to evaluate the message didn't mean they didn't look at those messages or that they dismissed them outright. Instead, the study showed, *media literacy equipped users with the skills and knowledge to critically assess the messages,* which made those messages less influential in teens' decision-making concerning sex.

Third-Person Effect A different assessment, this one of the effectiveness of a media literacy class at the college level in making students more active and informed consumers of media messages, had one particularly interesting finding. Students who took the media literacy course were then wise to the idea that media does, in fact, influence them. The study found notable evidence that the course lessened the incidence of the so-called "third-person effect" when students were compared to those who didn't take the course. The **third-person effect** describes the (inaccurate) perception that people think that mass media messages have a greater influence on *other* people than on themselves.

"This is a key finding because one of the central obstacles to achieving higher levels of media literacy lies in students feeling that media have little influence on them as individuals because films, television, video games, Web sites, and the like are 'just entertainment'" (Duran, Yousman, Walsh, & Longshore, 2008, p. 65). The third-person effect is a bit like thinking that other people can't hold their alcohol, but by golly, you can. And, you can dance really well on top of it.

PERSPECTIVES ON MODERN MEDIA

Modern media affords a vibrant world of consumption and creation. It's a wonderland, truly, and each year brings innovations that allow us to do everyday life differently.

Here is a synopsis of just a few of the *many* perspectives on the role of media in our society as explained by scholars Hoechsmann and Poyntz (2013). As you read through these, try to identify specific media products or real-life events that are good examples of the perspectives described.

Media as Evil: Media is the source of inspiration for real-world violent acts, aggressive or overly sexualized behavior among youth, materialism, cyber-bullying, online surveillance, consumerism, dumbing-down of intellectual thought. Media even masterfully manipulates children with products and programs.

Media as Cultural Imperialism: Media offers a white-washed (literally) homogenized culture. Less developed or underdeveloped countries get stuck with America's movies, television shows, music and more. A one-size-fits-all culture of global aesthetics and values is foisted upon the world by U.S.-based corporations driven solely by growing markets so they can grow profits. Local culture, customs and color are trampled by the big feet of billion-dollar media producers. The result is a cultural sameness that robs humans of rich, homegrown expressions of art and culture in its many forms, media and otherwise.

Media as Dictator: We blindly follow what the media tells us to care about, talk about and think about. As consumers we respond to the agenda that media sets for us and tend to ignore those issues about which we aren't watching, hearing or reading.

Media as Empowerment: Media can be a source of creativity, expression, education and civic engagement. It offers agency and action, not merely passive reception.

Do any of these sound familiar to you? It's helpful to develop your own understanding of how media affects your life. Our understanding of media is influenced by ideology, history and culture; throughout this book, these influences will be discussed.

TYPES OF MEDIA

American adults spend most of their waking hours engaged with media or digital content in some form. As society has incorporated the latest technologies into daily life, the types of media have expanded:

Traditional media includes newspapers, magazines, books, television, radio, films, video, music, direct mail and billboards.

New media or digital media, is digitized. It includes any digital forms of the traditional media, as well as social media, the internet, video games, virtual reality and augmented reality. The content has been digitized into computer data called bits.

Mass media is defined as communication that reaches and influences a large number of people—these days, that can mean a global audience. That might take the form of a blockbuster movie, a popular podcast or celebrity vlog.

MEDIA USAGE

Media consumption is growing exponentially. As digital devices evolve to deliver media content efficiently, dynamically and nearly anywhere we go, media use has skyrocketed. The challenge is using media to meet our needs while still having healthy offline lives.

"With the constant possibility of connectivity, one of the things that I see is a very subtle movement from 'I have a feeling. I want to make a call' to 'I want to have a feeling. I need to make a call'—in other words, people almost feeling as if they can't feel their feeling unless they're connected," said author and media scholar Sherry Turkle (2010). "I'm hearing this all over now so it stops being pathological if it becomes a generational style."

U.S. Usage The average American adult spent an estimated 11 hours and 6 minutes a day using media in early 2018. Media use in the United States is on the rise in the areas of gaming and mobile apps. Radio and audio listening trends are stable or increasing, perhaps because you can do it passively, while doing other stuff, like your laundry (Nielsen, 2018).

Also, in the U.S. people 15 to 19 years old spent a little over an hour per day on average playing computer games, according to the American Time Use Survey (U.S. Bureau of Labor Statistics, 2017). The survey shows that reading time is way down: People over 75 read for personal interest for 51 minutes a day, compared to 6 1/2 minutes for people ages 20 to 34.

Global Usage Across the globe, people were forecasted to spend an average of 479 minutes with media each day in 2019; that's about 8 hours

Media Usage in an Internet Minute 2018

Source: Domo.com, 2018

(Zenith, 2019). According to the Global Web Index (2018), a sampling of what Millennials worldwide in 2017 did each day with their media time included:

- 158 minutes on social network sites
- 82 minutes on streaming music
- 78 minutes on online TV and streaming
- 66 minutes on online news sites

Worldwide, usage of the internet, mobile devices and social media is *increasing*. Smart Insights (2019) and We Are Social & Hootsuite and DataReportal (2019) tell us that:

- 4 billion people worldwide use the internet (that's 53 percent of the world's population)
- 5.1 billion use mobile devices
- 3.1 billion use social media
- 2.2 billion use Facebook
- 1.9 billion use YouTube

WHY WE USE MEDIA

At the heart of media consumption and creation is the desire to communicate. Note the purposes of communication and think about how each purpose applies to your media use. For instance, as a creator of media, you text a friend to inform him about where to meet you for some food; you express yourself through a Pinterest bulletin board of favorite things; you entertain your family with an Instagram story of photos from last weekend's birthday celebration; you write an email to a mentor to persuade her to write you a letter of recommendation and you interact with classmates on the class blog site.

Uses and Gratifications Do you ever ask yourself *why* you spend so much time with media? What are you seeking when you go on Snapchat? What are you looking for, literally and figuratively, when you log onto YouTube? What are your expectations when you decide to spend a couple of hours playing video games (besides to win, of course)?

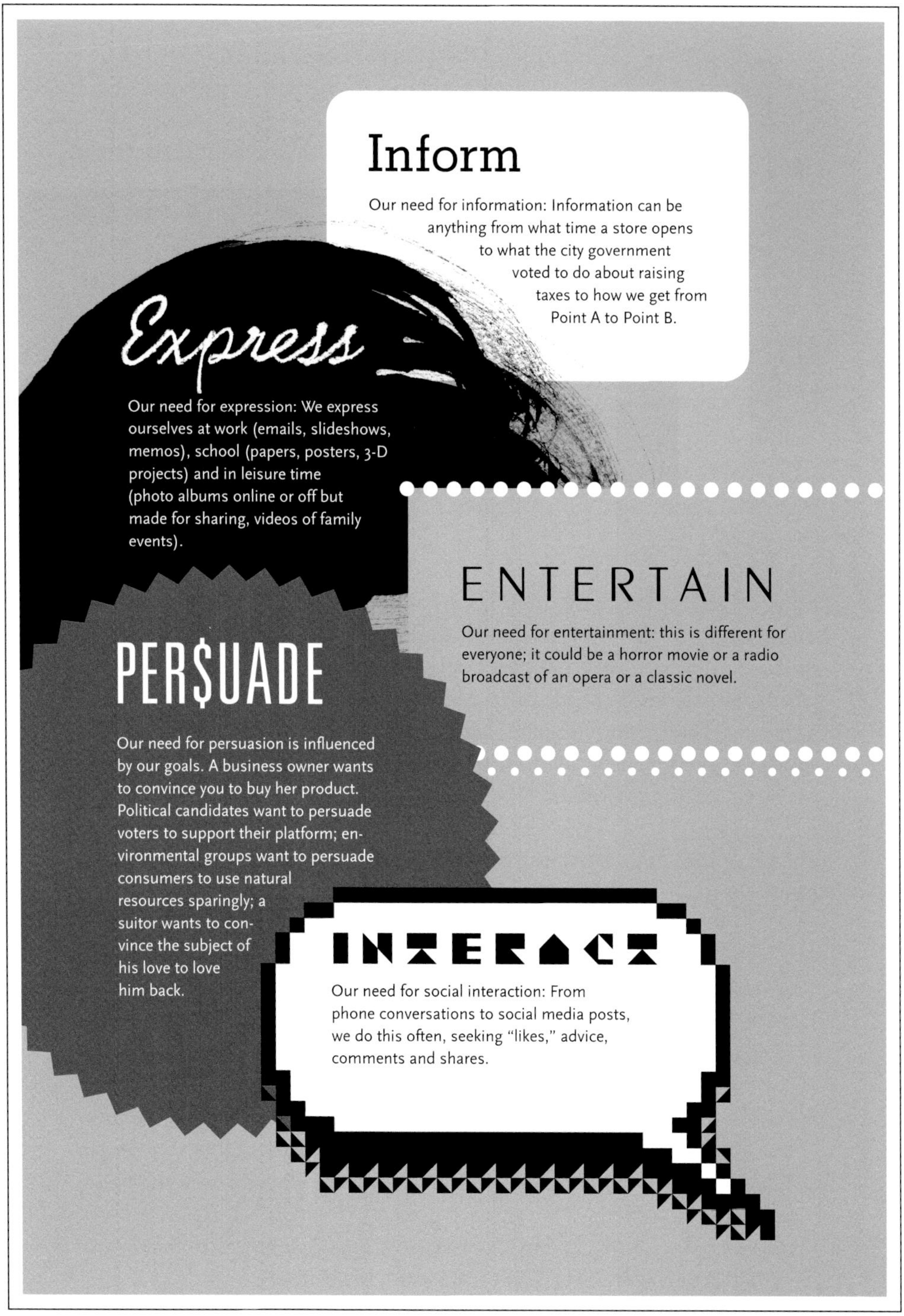

Purposes of Communication

Credit: Ryan Lewis

Identifying the reasons how and why we seek out media can help us to be more intentional about our usage.

Identifying the reasons how and why we seek out media can help us to be more intentional about our usage. The **uses and gratifications theory** of media is a user-centered theory that depicts media consumers as *active*, not passive, recipients of media messages. The theory describes the idea that people seek out media to satisfy their individual needs. Here's an example of uses and gratifications from Japan, where a 2018 survey of more than 2,000 social media users ages 15 to 39 found that more than half of them used social media because it was convenient to get access to helpful information (MMD Labo, 2018). Perhaps they made a query to their Tokyo-based social media followers: *I'm in the South Shinjuku neighborhood; where is a good place to eat?*

Thirty-eight percent said they used social media for real-time updates on the status of family and friends. And 36 percent said they used social media to discover new hobbies and to find new places to go. In other words, people used social media to meet a specific need, such as relaxation, entertainment, companionship, to pass the time, for information, social interaction, arousal or escape. The media that best deliver on those needs get used more often.

There are four main reasons that people use media, proposed researchers Denis McQuail, Jay Blumler, and Joseph Brown (1972):

- **Cognitive**: To learn, such as to increase their knowledge in a specific area by watching a documentary.
- **Affective**: To satisfy an emotional need, such as by watching a romantic movie.
- **Personal/social integrative**: Personal integrative, to focus on construction of your personal identity, such as to use social media to increase your credibility or social standing; and social integrative, to explore your social identity, such as interacting with family and friends on social media to connect with others.
- **Tension release/diversion**: Such as to use a violent video game as a catharsis or a sci-fi flick as an escape from reality.

Usage Differences People who use the same media may have very *different needs* met by it. For instance, while a couple might seek out the same TV show for their media needs, that TV show may fulfill very different needs between the two viewers. One might enjoy it for the intricate plot that challenges her mind and her partner might enjoy it for the escape from a boring day at the office.

Also, audience members may derive very *different meanings* from a message than what was originally intended by the creators. For example, a country music video might make you laugh aloud if you think it's poorly executed or has cheesy dance moves. Comedy is likely not what the creators intended! Another example: The American hip hop group the Beastie Boys made "Fight For Your Right" as a parody of rock anthems—but it was beloved by the very fans they were making fun of. On the other hand, a fan is a fan, so the creators get the attention, even if it is not for reasons they originally intended. Can you think of a time that you found a different meaning in a media message than the creators likely originally intended?

Part of uses and gratifications theory is the emphasis on the fact that we each seek out *different content* to meet our needs. It's worth noting, then, that audience members often select the media that most aligns with their viewpoints and values. For instance, if you're politically conservative, you're not likely to tune in regularly to watch long stretches of a liberal news broadcast, unless you like to yell at the TV screen. This theory also suggests that we as audience members are *highly selective* about what we consume.

Hypodermic Needle Theory Uses and gratifications theory is in diametric opposition to the **hypodermic needle theory**, which holds that media audiences are passive recipients of the media they consume. As the name implies, the theory asserts that audiences are injected with media messages and they have no choice but to be directly affected by it, as it's been inserted into their brains through listening and watching. (Cue the B-movie horror flick.) The concept focuses on the immediate and uniform response of audiences to media.

This theory has been debunked by scientific studies. But I mention it here because I think it serves as a useful contrast to the *active audience* concept that supports so many ideas in media literacy today. We have more choices, and we are highly selective in our media choices. So selective, we can pick and choose *only* the media content that aligns with our beliefs and viewpoints.

The hypodermic needle theory (also called the silver bullet theory) arose during the advent of mass communications in the United States in the 1930s to 1950s. U.S. President Franklin D. Roosevelt was delivering "fireside chats" over the radio to the American public, and Adolf Hitler was pushing the propaganda of his Nazi party on the German population. A good example of this theory in action is the widespread panic that erupted in the United States after the radio broadcast of H. G. Wells' *War of the Worlds* convinced a radio-listening public that Martians had landed in New Jersey. (And *then* the *Jersey Shore* reality TV series came along. . .). It's worth a listen to the *War of the Worlds* radio broadcast to appreciate its impact at the time; it's easy to find online.

Uses and gratifications is part of an active model of media consumption; it focuses on *why* people use media. The hypodermic needle theory is in the tradition of the media effects model of media consumption; it focuses on what media *does* to people. In the first model we are active users, and in the second model we are passive audience members.

Theories in media and consumption abound. Many books and articles are devoted to the topic. For our present purposes, we are best served in taking a step back from our media usage to examine our own reasons for our use; *why* we use media, *how* we use media, and *what* we get out of it and expect to get out of it. Being as intentional as possible in your use of media is a critical step in media literacy.

SMARTPHONE ADDICTION

A study in South Korea is exemplary of a nearly global problem: One out of five people in that country experienced excessive dependence on their smartphones in 2018. And the ratio is rising annually. Nineteen percent of people between ages 3 and 69 were either potentially at risk or were high risk for addiction to their smartphone, the study by the Ministry of Science and ICT found (Korea Bizwire, 2019). The study of more than 28,000 people found that many "experience physical and mental withdrawal symptoms during their everyday life and often put smartphone use as a top priority in their lives."

The ratio is increasing every year.

In Italy, 27 percent of respondents said they argue at least once a month with their partner or children about excessive smartphone use, and 22 percent had disagreements with their parents about it. Italians topped the ranks of Europeans in having these family arguments (Deloitte, 2017).

Sounds familiar, right? OK, so can you really be addicted to your smartphone and the media it serves up like an all-night buffet? A better word at this point, until there is more neurological research conducted, is that smartphone use can become *compulsive*. A current debate is whether the internet is a *medium* that feeds the addiction, which may be addiction to social media use, pornography or online shopping, or if the internet is actually the *source* of the addiction.

Wired for Social Either way, what we as users experience is real. We ache for our smartphones when they aren't on hand. Why? Because we are wired for it. The reward-based dopamine pathways in our brain become active when we are anticipating or experiencing a positive event, like eating a slice of good pizza, listening to your favorite song, connecting on our smartphone with a good friend or spending time with a romantic interest. Dopamine, an evolutionary tool to help us humans, motivates us to want more.

Cognitive research shows that dopamine pathways are lit up by social stimuli that are the essence of social media, such as laughing faces, expressions of maternal and romantic love, and positive emotional expressions (Krach, Paulus, Bodden, & Kircher, 2010). So we keep coming back for more.

Chamath Palihapitiya, a former Facebook executive and now CEO and founder of Social Capital, told an audience of Stanford University students that social media usage is harmful. "The short-term, dopamine-driven feedback loops that we have created are destroying how society works" (Haynes, 2017).

"If you feed the beast, that beast will destroy you," said Palihapitiya, who added that he has posted on his Facebook page maybe ten times in the past seven years. "If you push back on it, we have a chance to control it and rein it in. And it is a point in time where people need to hard brake from some of these tools, and the things that you rely on."

VOX DISCIPULI

It's what I call the "mindless login syndrome." A lot of times I just mindlessly log onto Facebook. I'd just grab my phone and go onto Facebook without even thinking about it, or I'd grab my phone to Google something or check my emails but end up on Facebook instead—that's not good. That's the main thing I wish I could change about my media habits. —J, 29

Intermittent Reinforcement What makes social media in particular at risk for compulsive smartphone use is this: the possibility of an amazing text or super-wonderful news coming through. It's called **intermittent reinforcement**, which is the unpredictability and the possibility of a random reward that keeps us coming back for more. The behavior of checking our phone is reinforced after an unpredictable number of occurrences in which we get a payoff such as a funny meme. It's like gambling. Or fishing.

This idea is based on the behaviorist researcher B. F. Skinner's famous experiments training lab rats. Skinner developed his behaviorism theory by training rats to hit a lever to get a food reward. The most effective training occurred when the animal only sometimes got the reward. It's called "variable ratio reinforcement schedule" and we live it each day when we keep checking our smartphones to see if there's a text, an email, a post, a follow, a like, a notification (Stafford, 2006). It usually is mundane stuff, but sometimes, we get something grand. So we keep checking for that media treat. Rats.

Take this smartphone compulsion test: https://bit.ly/2QtW4uE. It's one small indicator of whether or not you need to change your habits. By the way, this quiz is on the website of the Center for Internet and Technology Addiction. It's an informative and reputable site, with other interesting quizzes too, but it's also a business. The quizzes are one way to attract us to this resource.

Combatting Addiction Best advice: be intentional. We are always somewhere else when we are online. The internet transports us elsewhere. Instead, choose to be present in the here and now, and that means being offline. We need to get offline in order to recharge psychologically.

In his book *Digital Minimalism* (2019), Georgetown University computer science professor Cal Newport suggested going on a 30-day tech cleanse. He advocates going without any technology except the essentials for 30 days. This will declutter your brain and break your dependent relationship with your smartphone, social media and game controls, he asserted. After 30 days, slowly begin to add technology in a healthy, balanced and intentional way. Ask yourself if a particular technology is something that you value and then set rules for use, like limiting it to 30 minutes a day, or a certain time of day.

Try to identify five offline things you can do *this week* that can replace your smartphone use for even 30 minutes.

HOW TO BREAK A MEDIA HABIT

If you want to adjust something about your media use habits, be it a massive overhaul or a small tweak, here are tips on how to break a media habit (Devine, Forscher, Austin, & Cox, 2012; Jager, 2003; Greenfield, 2017):

1. **Identify the bad habit you want to change.** Knowing that a habit is having negative effects helps give motivation to change it. Be clear about what you want to change; set an alarm on your phone to remind you throughout the day, or write it on a sticky note and put it on your bathroom mirror. Start with a small, realistic goal. So if your ultimate plan is to use your smartphone a total of only two hours each day, a good place to start is with not checking your phone for 15 minutes. You can add 5-minute increments as you get better at your new "habit" of phone intermissions.
2. **Notice what triggers the use.** If you check your phone when nervous or in socially awkward situations, replace that tendency with a realistic alternative. Practice deep breathing exercises while waiting in the fast-food line. Work on your memory by trying to recall all the kinds of shoes people around you are wearing without looking at their feet. Look for others not on their phones and strike up a conversation– about not being on your phones. Learn to tolerate being bored.

3. **Change your routine.** This may help reset those automatic movements. Tips include: Don't use your phone as an alarm clock. Put your phone in the next room. Turn off notifications. Unfollow people who constantly virtually tap you on the shoulder for attention. Get an app to help you resist the temptation to go online. Get another to track your online time.
4. **Tell others.** Sharing your goal allows friends and colleagues to support you *and* keep you accountable. In the case of the goal of reduced smartphone use, tell your support team to reign in the mindless texts and bored memes.
5. **Expect setbacks but not failure.** You'll slip into the old "bad" habit because it's a habit. That's expected. But don't give up. Motivation is essential to changing a routine.
6. **Replacement.** Replace the media use with something *equally engaging* that isn't related to your habit. If you like to binge-watch streaming video after a long day, then anticipate this temptation to stream away the evening online and instead plan to go for a walk, play sports, connect with friends or try a new recipe. You could shock your BFF and read a book.
7. **Reward yourself.** After reaching your first small goal, treat yourself to a short-term reward. Download a new song as your ringtone. Get a snack with friends. Blow off your least-favorite chore.

Media Is Beautiful It's true that heavy media use has been linked to risks such as infidelity spurred by social media connections, depression and loneliness due to excessive online living and not enough offline living (formerly known as, simply, living).

That's why media literacy calls for intentionality in the ways you interact and engage with media of all kinds. Living offline improves the quality of your online life. It takes work, like eating right or exercise. But those good habits are worth it. The benefits to doing this are healthy relationships and a healthy life.

We use media because it is so *wonderful* in so many ways: We keep up with family and friends on social media. We discover new ideas on YouTube. We enjoy timely news updates thanks to online news sites. Virtual reality and augmented reality are exploring dynamic ways to tell stories and help us see life from another person's perspective. Immersive video puts us in a scene and allows us to explore it 360 degrees. Television programming is more inclusive and edgy than it has perhaps ever been, prompting opportunities for reflection, understanding and, sometimes, heated debates about lifestyles and values. Media offers humanity many rich outlets and opportunities to explore who we are and where we're headed.

CHAPTER REVIEW

- Apply one of the media literacy key concepts to a media message.
- Give an example of each of the key perspectives on the media discussed in this chapter.
- Identify an appropriate media message for each of the five purposes of communication.
- Contrast the uses and gratifications theory with the hypodermic needle theory.
- Describe how social media uses intermittent reinforcement.
- Identify ways to change a negative habit.

ACTIVITIES

1. Estimate your media use for one day, then track it. Use the Personal Media Log to record your findings. Write a paragraph or two about your estimate versus your actual usage.
2. Go on a digital media fast for 24 hours. No music, TV, streaming, gaming, radio, etc. No email or texting unless it's essential for academics or work. Analog books and magazines are OK. Warn your people beforehand that you'll be offline. Be prepared to feel anxious and unsettled; it is expected. Get others to join you on the fast for support and for partners in card games.

   After your media fast, write a one-page reflection paper about your experience. Questions to consider in your reflection: What media content did you miss the most? What surprised you? What did you do instead of being with digital media? How did you feel? Is there any habit you want to change in your digital media life?

Personal Media Log

Media	***Estimated* Time *(minutes)***	***Actual* Time *(minutes)***
Texting		
Social media		
Web searching and reading		
Gaming		
TV of any kind (streaming, live, etc.)		
Music		
Email		
Movies		
Print texts		
....		
....		
....		
TOTAL		

Personal Media Log

Credit: Ryan Lewis

REFERENCES

Austin, E. W., Pinkleton, B. E., Chen, Y. Y., & Austin, B. W. (2015). Processing of sexual media messages improves due to media literacy effects on perceived message desirability. *Mass Communication and Society, 18*(4), 399–421. doi:10.1080/15205436.2014.1001909

Bergstrom, A., Flynn, M., & Craig, C. (2018). Deconstructing media in the college classroom: A longitudinal critical media literacy intervention. *Journal of Media Literacy Education, 10*(3), 113–131.

Blumberg, F. C. (2019). Media literacy for the 21st century: Interview with Renee Hobbs, EdD. *Society for Media Psychology & Technology, Division 46 of the American Psychological Association.* Spotlights feature.

Center for Media Literacy. (2019). *Five key questions form foundation for media inquiry*. Center for Media Literacy. Retrieved from www.medialit.org

Deloitte. (2017). With whom do you argue at least once a month about your excessive smartphone usage? In: *Statista—The Statistics Portal.* Retrieved from http://bit.ly/32wzpQq

Devine, P. G., Forscher, P. S., Austin, A. J., Cox, W. T. L. (2012). Long-term reduction in implicit race bias: A prejudice habit-breaking intervention. *Journal of Experimental Social Psychology, 48*(6), 1267–1278. https://doi.org/10.1016/j.jesp.2012.06.003

Domo. (2018, June). Data never sleeps 6.0 (available on domo.com). In: *Statista—The Statistics Portal.* Media usage in an internet minute as of June 2018. Retrieved from http://bit.ly/2xVuzOB

Duran, R. L., Yousman, B., Walsh, K. M., & Longshore, M. A. (2008). Holistic media education: An assessment of the effectiveness of a college course in media literacy. *Communication Quarterly, 56*(1), 49–68. Retrieved from http://bit.ly/2NTOYyu

eMarketer. (2018). Daily time spent watching TV per capita in the United States from 2013 to 2020 (in minutes). In: *Statista—The Statistics Portal.* Retrieved form emarketer.com.

GlobalWebIndex. (2018). Millennials: Examining the attitudes and digital behaviors of internet users aged 21–34. In: *Statista—The Statistics Portal* (p. 9). Daily time spent with online entertainment among Millennials worldwide as of 3rd quarter 2017 (in minutes). Retrieved from http://bit.ly/2KPq01T

Greenfield, D. (2017). *Tips for electronic etiquette and mindful technology use.* West Hartford, CT: The Center for Internet and Technology Addiction.

Haynes, T. (2017, December 11). Former Facebook exec: Social media is ripping our social fabric apart. *Real Clear Politics.*

Haynes, T. (2018, May 1). Dopamine, smart phones & you: A battle for your time. *Science in the News.* Harvard University.

Hobbs, R., & Jensen, A. (2009). The past, present, and future of media literacy education. *Journal of Media Literacy Education, 1*(1).

Hoechsmann, M., & Poyntz, S. R. (2013). *Media literacies: A critical introduction.* Hoboken, NJ: Wiley-Blackwell.

IDC. (2013). *Always connected: How smartphones and social keep us connected.* IDC Research Report Sponsored by Facebook.

Jager, W. (2003). Breaking "bad habits": A dynamical perspective on habit formation and change. (n.p.) In L. Hendrickx, W. Jager, & L. Steg (Eds.), *Human decision making and environmental perception: Understanding and assisting human decision making in real-life settings: Liber amicorum for Charles Vlek.* Groningen: University of Groningen.

Jeong, S., Cho, H., & Hwang, Y. (2012). Media literacy interventions: A meta-analytic review. *Journal of Communication, 62*(3), 454–472. doi:10.1111/j.1460–2466.2012.01643.x

Jyrkiainen, J. (2019). *Finland: Media landscape.* Maastricht, Limburg, The Netherlands: European Journalism Centre. Retrieved from http://bit.ly/2y7FCVn

Korea Bizwire. (2019, February 13). 1 in 5 S. Koreans at risk of smartphone addiction: Poll.

Krach, S., Paulus, F. M., Bodden, M, & Kircher, T. (2010). The rewarding nature of social interactions. *Frontiers in Behavioral Neuroscience, 4*(22). doi:10.3389/fnbeh.2010.00022

McQuail, D., Blumler, J., & Brown, J. (1972). The television audience: A revised perspective. In D. McQuail (Ed.), *Sociology of mass communications* (pp. 135–165). Harmondsworth: Penguin.

MediaSmarts. (2019). Media literacy fundamentals: What is media literacy? Retrieved from mediasmarts.ca.

MMD Labo. (2018). Leading reasons why young people in Japan use social media platforms in 2018. In: *Statista—The Statistics Portal*. Retrieved from https://mmdlabo.jp/investigation/detail_1703.html

National Association of Media Literacy Education. (2019). Media literacy defined. Retrieved from namle.net.

Nielsen Company. (2018). *The Nielsen total audience report Q1 2018*.

RTL. (2018). Average time spent watching television daily in European countries in 2016 and 2017 (in minutes). In: *Statista—The Statistics Portal*. Retrieved from http://bit.ly/2LnRD1h

Schilder, E., Lockee, B., & Saxon, D. (2016). The challenges of assessing media literacy education. *Journal of Media Literacy*, *8*(1), 32–48.

Second European Media and Information Literacy Forum. (2016). *Background*. United Nations Educational, Scientific and Cultural Organization.

Smart Insights. (2019). Global social media research summary 2019. Citing data from We Are Social and Hootsuite.

Stafford, T. (2006, September 19). Why email is addictive (and what to do about it). *Mind Hacks*. Retrieved from http://bit.ly/2Shllpz

Turkle, S. (2010, June 29). Digital demands: The challenges of constant connectivity. *Nieman Reports*, 20–21.

U.S. Bureau of Labor Statistics. (2018, June 28). *American Time Use Survey—2017 results*.

We Are Social, & Hootsuite, & DataReportal. (2019). Most popular social networks worldwide as of January 2019, ranked by number of active users (in millions). In: *Statista—The Statistics Portal*. Retrieved from http://bit.ly/30BL52J

Zenith. (2019). Daily time spent with media worldwide from 2011 to 2021 (in minutes). *Statista*. Retrieved from http://bit.ly/2xPUdEM

2 Thinking

How to Protect Your Daily Allotment of Attention

This poor, poor page. It is at a *major* disadvantage to teach you anything, because it is not well equipped to get your attention.

It's not an in-person teacher, which is the best way to learn information.

It's also not video, which is one of the most successful mediums for audience engagement.

It's not a fantastic infographic that breaks down the concepts in a vivid diagram.

It's text. So the best options are an attention-grabbing headline, a story, or humor. I'll try the latter, as I personally adore a cheesy joke:

KNOCK, KNOCK.

Who's there?

LEARNING OBJECTIVES

Terms: Media multitasking; hyper-reading; automatic processing; controlled processing focused, sustained, selective, alternating and divided attention states; external factors; internal factors; filter bubble; attentive user interface.

- Analyze why attention is so valuable.
- Trace the history of media's attempts to gain our attention.
- Explain how the explosion of media devices affects attention.
- Detail the effects of multitasking on cognitive response.
- Understand various ways technology is changing our brains.
- Identify internal and external motivating factors for attention.
- Recognize the impact of filter bubbles on your information exposure.
- Describe ways to stay focused.

Think about what gets *your* attention. What keeps it? How do you allocate your attention? And are all forms of your attention equal? Describe when you are focused and why.

Icing.

Icing who?

Icing so loud the neighbors can hear.

I hope this chapter rings loud in your ears, too. It needs to get your attention (and the neighbors'). It discusses levels of attention, the inefficiencies of juggling our attention and how digital information is changing the way we process information.

COMPETITION FOR OUR ATTENTION

As technology becomes more mobile and real-time, we will find ourselves constantly interrupted by media and devices. By 2025, an average connected person anywhere in the world will interact with connected devices nearly 4,800 times per day—basically one interaction every 18 seconds, according to the International Data Corporation (Reinsel, Gantz, & Rydning, 2018). Also by 2025, IDC says, nearly 30 percent of data created will be in real time.

Twitch TV, which features live gaming and chats embedded in every streaming video, is just a taste of the interactive, mobile and real-time media that will continue to define our mediated existence. In particular, the eSports market continues to grow in popularity, with ESPN's College Esports Championship, and its broadcasts of the Overwatch League, an international league of 12 franchises centered on the first-person shooter game.

Bright colors, quick movement, powerful images, engaging music and catchy dialogue all attract our attention to media messages. (Remember this when you create your own media messages!) Multiple decisions go into producing a message and getting an audience's attention is among the most important. We'll learn more about the art and science of constructing media messages in Chapter 5 on Creating. For now, let's focus on media once its created and how it vies for our limited attention.

The Value of Attention Attention gets a whole chapter because it is that important, that undervalued and that essential to life in the 21st century. The sheer scarcity of human attention is what makes management of it so important. In the modern digital economy of interrupting pings and pop-up notices, attention is the commodity of the day.

Herbert A. Simon, an American economist, political scientist and cognitive psychologist, may have been the first person to conceptualize attention as an economic principle. He wrote that:

> In an information-rich world, the wealth of information means a dearth of something else: a scarcity of whatever it is that information consumes. What information consumes is rather obvious: it consumes the attention of its recipients. Hence a wealth of information creates a poverty of attention and a need to allocate that attention efficiently among the overabundance of information sources that might consume it.
>
> (1971, pp. 40–41)

In 2001, Thomas Davenport and John Beck coined the term "the attention economy." The idea of attention as commodity is a seminal principle of how media companies make money by selling consumers' attention. The pair wrote in 2000 that,

> Economics, by definition, is the study of how whole societies allocate scarce resources. . . . Attention is what's in short supply. And human attention certainly behaves like an economic good in the sense that we buy it and measure it. On an individual level, we're deeply aware when we don't have enough of it—which suggests the first lesson of attention management.

Money will follow where people are putting their attention. That is, where the attention is, the money is. According to digital culture expert Kevin Kelly, the co-founder of *Wired* magazine, a factor in users' decisions of whether or not to pay for material that they can get for free are *intangible* factors (2008). Among those abstract factors are *immediacy, authenticity, accessibility* and *findability*. Imagine you have 100 "attention dollars" each day. How would you spend them? List your expenditures, complete with dollar amounts, on the back of the envelope for your cell phone bill.

Media such as television and radio have long depended on advertisements to pay for programming. Our eyes and ears were the vehicles by which we paid attention to those mediums. With digital media, our hands and fingers are the vehicles by which we pay attention. In the digital world, our attention is measured in the form of clicks, screen scrolls, page views, posts, likes, shares and retweets. These are the currency of social media. Social media platforms sell our attention to advertisers. The more attention, the higher the ad rates and the greater the potential payoff for advertisers. (We will explore this topic further in Chapter 6 on Spending.)

The media industry has always—always—needed consumers' attention in order to make money.

The media industry has always—always—needed consumers' attention in order to make money. In that sense, today is no different than 50 years ago. Network television sold ads to pay for programming, and minutes' worth of ads were peppered across programming. We watched and the hope was by watching, we'd go buy the product or service advertised.

More Devices Today, what is pronouncedly different than in the past is the explosion of devices on which to show content in order to sell our attention to advertisers. For example, in the United States, 90 percent of households have at least one smartphone, desktop/laptop computer, tablet or streaming media device, with the typical household containing five such devices (Olmstead, 2017). With more modes of delivery, more media products are being created. No longer are there just a handful of movie production companies, for example; now Netflix and Hulu are creating their own movies, as well as television series.

The various social media platforms vie for our attention, and they are constructed to continue tapping us on the shoulder throughout the day to get that attention: Facebook offers notifications when a friend posts on your wall. Twitter will send a notice to your inbox, letting you know that someone you follow posted a news article you ought to read. Instagram will alert you when users comment on your photos. YouTube will keep suggesting other content you might enjoy. Email notifications flit across your screen or ping at you throughout a workday. HEY, by the way: Are you an online attention-seeker? Are you part of the problem of the daily deluge of digital material we receive? How do you decide when to forward or share an article, report, meme or image?

"Just Checks" We have become experts in superficial attention, the half-hearted watch. Author and Georgetown University professor Cal Newport (September, 2016) calls our media distractions "just checks," as in taking a moment to "just check" our email/texts/Facebook accounts/Instagram feeds/YouTube channels in case something important came through.

"Each one of those *just checks* shifts your attention," Newport wrote. "Even if this shift is brief (think: twenty seconds in an inbox), it's enough to leave behind a residue that reduces your cognitive capacity for a non-trivial amount of time to follow."

As I hope you recall from Chapter 1, the allure of the "just checks" is not because they consistently deliver rewarding content; it's the very fact of *inconsistency* that compels us to routinely "just check." That's the power of *intermittent reinforcement* (you know, what keeps you playing slot machines when you aren't winning, and what keeps anglers fishing when they aren't catching). How does variable reinforcement affect what you pay attention to? Identify specific recent incidences of doing a "just check" while trying to focus on a task.

Newport offered an enticing option to "just checks": If we could commit to long blocks of time without interruption, think how productive and sharp we'd feel.

MEDIA MULTITASKING

Media Multitasking **Media multitasking** refers to simultaneously engaging with different media, be it television, print, videos, music, social media, email or searching the Web. Can you effectively media multitask? Some of my students tell me they can easily media multitask. They chat with their roommate while keeping an eye on the show on television, occasionally texting a friend and listening to music through a single earbud. Oh, and they are typing their assignment.

Multitasking
Credit: Ryan Lewis

Easily multitasking and *effectively* multitasking are not the same thing. It might be easy to have three or more devices going at the same time, but it doesn't mean you are effective at any one of them. Not all tasks, including some work assignments, require single-minded focus. But some absolutely do.

Our Brains Can Manage Only So Much Research by neuroscientists Earl Miller and Timothy J. Buschman (2015) reported that we have finite neural resources; it's one good reason not to talk on a mobile phone and drive. Our brains just aren't built to do both well *and* simultaneously.

"Multitasking causes the new information to go to the wrong part of the brain," said neuroscientist Daniel Levitin, citing research by others (2015). "If students study and watch TV at the same time, for example, the information from their schoolwork goes into the striatum, a region specialized for storing new procedures and skills, not facts and ideas. Without the distraction of TV, the information goes into the hippocampus, where it is organised and categorised in a variety of ways, making it easier to retrieve" (para 7).

VOX DISCIPULI

If I could change anything, it would be cutting out the things that do not matter. What I mean is that social media apps allow for us to get invested into things and people that really don't do anything for us. I do not need to follow a ton of celebrities and reality stars, but I do, and I think cutting down would allow my feed to be more personal and allow me to see what's going on in the lives of the people that I care about. —Madison, 25

Inefficient Thinking Think of your neurochemical resources as fuel. Each time we flit from one task to another, we use some of that fuel. Our brains cannot run all the motors of each task at once, as multitasking implies. Instead, when we turn our attention from one task to another, we are quickly switching each motor on and off, and that burns fuel. Before we know it, we've exhausted our brain's ability to keep focusing. We have scattered thinking. It's not efficient or effective.

"Innovative thinking, after all, comes from extended concentration, i.e. the ability to follow an idea of thought down a network of new paths," said neuroscientist Miller (2016). "When you try to multitask, you typically don't get far enough down any road to stumble upon something original because you're constantly switching and backtracking" (para 3).

It is hard to train ourselves to focus for long periods of time, and these days, 15 minutes of cognitive focus is a thinking marathon. Distracting technology is hurting our capacity to focus even as work that requires serious concentration is increasing in demand (Newport, 2016).

High concurrent levels of usage result in stress, overstimulation and scattered thinking (Levitin, 2015). As we learned previously, unfortunately, we are working against our natural composition, as we are addicted to the reward system in our brain that lights up when we accomplish something as mundane as sending an email. It's the more fruitful but less immediately rewarding deep thinking of our prefrontal cortex that we need to hold out for, but often don't.

To summarize, switching tasks degrades brain functioning. Media multitasking slows our brains down and increases the number of mistakes we make. Researchers (Ophir, Nass, & Wagner, 2009; Leroy, 2009) tell us that when we are media multitasking we are:

- Less able to filter out distractions.
- More likely to be preoccupied with irrelevant information in memory storage.
- Less efficient when switching from one task to another.

HOW TECHNOLOGY IS CHANGING OUR BRAINS

Experts agree that technology is changing our brains; that fact is not in question. But *how* technology is changing our brains is in question. It's not all bad or all good when it comes to technology and its effects on our brains. As three researchers found in their excellent survey of current study on the question, "some products designed to benefit cognitive development actually hinder it, while some products designed purely for entertainment purposes lead to long-lasting benefits" (Bavelier, Green, & Dye, 2010; Causes for Optimism and Concern section).

"In the same way that there is no single effect of 'eating food,' there is also no single effect of 'watching television' or 'playing video games,'" they wrote. "Different kinds of media have different content, task requirements, and attentional demands and thus lead to different behavioral effects" (Content Matters section).

For instance, baby DVDs/videos in some cases *decreased* language development in babies 8 to 16 months old (Zimmerman, Christakis, & Meltzoff, 2007). However, action video games, which are maligned in many homes as time-sucking, mind-decaying black holes, are actually proving to have many benefits. (Can you hear the cheering teenagers?)

Bavalier and colleagues provided this summary of various research that shows measurable benefits of action video gaming:

> A burgeoning literature indicates that playing action video games is associated with a number of enhancements in vision, attention, cognition, and motor control . . . For instance, action video game experience heightens the ability to view small details in cluttered scenes and to perceive dim signals, such as would be present when driving in fog. . . . Avid players display enhanced top-down control of attention and choose among different options more rapidly. . . . They also exhibit better visual short-term memory . . . and can more flexibility switch from one task to another.
>
> (When Bad Turns Out Good section)

Changes are happening to our brains due to media, but it's not a "one size fits all" phenomenon.

"Attention and cognition are the foundation on which all our capacities depend—our ability to think, to concentrate, to solve problems, and be present with each other," stated the U.K.-based Centre for Humane Technology (2019). "Technology's constant interruptions and precisely targeted distractions, which have been designed to keep us more engaged with tech products, are taking a major toll on these critical functions" (2019, Attention page; Introduction).

Reading One area under intense study is the way that we read online. On a screen, we read for highlights, not details. To help us quickly sort through the quantities of material we get online, we have adopted the technique of **hyper-reading** to quickly decide if we want to give something more time. Communication professor James Sosnoski (1999) introduced the notion of hyper-reading, describing it as "reader-directed, screen-based, computer-assisted reading" (p. 167). It involves selective reading, skimming content, and yet worse—"pecking," which is random, out-of-sequence reading that robs the reader of any cohesion in a text. Do you find yourself reading that way online?

MEDIA LITERACY SELFIE

Textbook layouts unintentionally promote "pecking," as they highlight key terms. When you are doing your required reading, don't you simply skim for the colored, **bolded** or *italicized* text to know what to focus on? If you do that, you miss all my jokes. I know—that's the point.

As online readers, we direct our attention to a message, scroll down as needed, our eyes scanning for useful tidbits. We are looking to grab highlights and move on. The fact that we have screens to scroll down and manipulate is critical to this new form of reading. While hyperlinks embedded in text might seem a good thing, as they provide more data and direct sourcing of material, actually, the results are mixed, depending on whether comprehension or complexity is the goal (DeStefano & LeFevre, 2007).

TYPES OF ATTENTION

How much of your media use is automatic? That is, how much of your media use is done without thinking, such as watching the next video that pops up on YouTube, even though the one you sought out is done? How much of your media use is purposeful and self-directed, such as seeking out news sites to learn more about a breaking news event?

We encounter a lot of media in a mode called **automatic processing**. If we are exposed to the message, if we're close enough to see and hear it, but we don't really focus on it, then that's automatic processing. Automatic processing is involuntary, unintentional and without effort. And it's a good thing. It allows us to filter all the thousands of messages coming at us throughout a day, from logos on T-shirts to billboards to background music at the grocery store.

However, when we decide to focus on a media message, we are using **controlled processing**. Controlled processing is purposeful and requires effort. We are *psychologically* engaged with the message, either in part or in whole, such as when we are working through a difficult passage in a book. It's not just sensory exposure, meaning that we see and hear it but it doesn't really register in our brains. No, controlled processing means we are paying attention to it *at some level*.

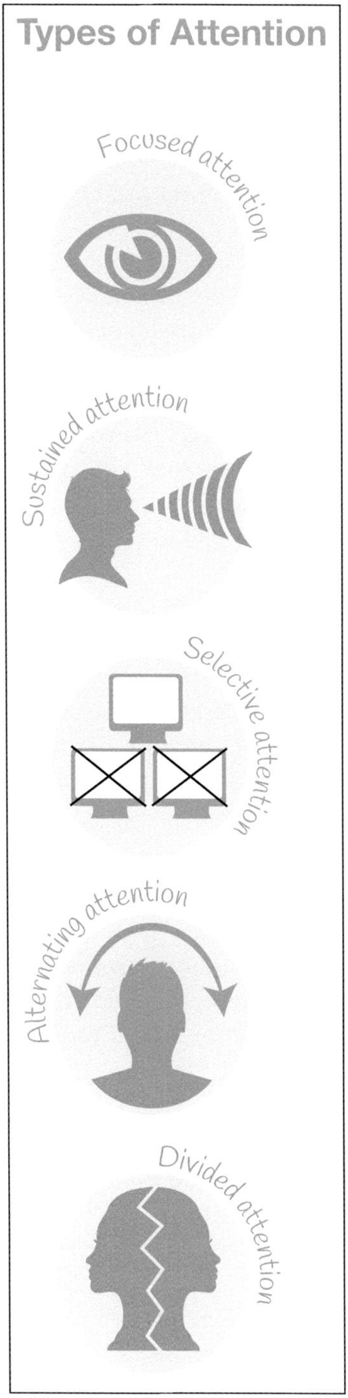

Here are the types of attention (Commodari, 2017; Sohlberg & Mateer, 1989):

- **Focused attention** is responding individually to a specific visual, auditory or tactile stimulus, such as responding to a question from a classmate.

- **Sustained attention** is the ability to maintain focus over an extended period of time. Sustained attention processes enable us to be vigilant and to exert continuous effort. When we listen closely and take notes on a lecture or speech, we are showing sustained attention.

- **Selective attention** is focusing on one particular item, feature or task and ignoring distractions and competing stimuli, such as reading a book while people in the same room are talking and laughing. Selective attention chooses some information to process over less-relevant information.

- **Alternating attention** is moving between tasks or stimuli that require different kinds of cognitive engagement, such as doing homework while listening to music.

- **Divided attention** describes attempting to respond simultaneously to two or more tasks. They may have different cognitive demands, such as sorting silverware while singing a song.

Attention Choice Another aspect to consider is whether we are giving our attention *voluntarily* to some media that is attractive to us, or whether our attention is *compulsory*, meaning that it is compelled, or required; that is, a boss/teacher/parent/significant other has given you something to address.

When we do elect to pay attention to something by *choice*, external and internal factors play a part in our focus.

External factors such as the intensity, size, repetition, duration, movement, contrast, change and novelty of an object influence our attention. More of all of these increases the odds of getting our attention and keeping it. A billboard with a nearly-naked, very attractive person will get your attention. Pictures attract more than words. A screaming siren, an explosion onscreen, a pungent smell—these all get our attention because they are intense. Repetition is important to getting one's attention. Repetition is important to getting one's attention.

Internal factors that influence our focus include our innate interest in the object, our desire for it, our motives for pursuing it, our end aim or goal, our habits, our past experiences with it, our aptitude at focusing and our attitude toward the task and our mental disposition and temperament. This explains why you want to listen to all nine episodes of your favorite podcast on gardening but your friend can't get through the first 15 minutes; he isn't remotely interested in the flowering Japanese andromeda.

FILTER BUBBLES

A **filter bubble** is a term coined in 2011 by Eli Pariser, internet activist and CEO of the website Upworthy, to describe situations in which internet users encounter only information and opinions that conform to and reinforce their own beliefs.

Filter bubbles come about due to algorithms that, while not by design, do result in amplification of ideological segregation because they push content we are likely to agree with and like—and share. These algorithms on social media and in search engines send us news and information that we tend to agree with and the results isolate us from opposing viewpoints. We get in a safe bubble of belief and belonging and don't get challenged with other ways of thinking and being.

While filter bubbles are a concern, researchers have found that they are not as alarming as initially forecast. One study concluded that "the vast majority of online news consumption mimicked traditional offline reading habits, with individuals directly visiting the home pages of their favorite, typically mainstream, news outlets," a research study concluded (Flaxman, Goel, & Rao, 2016, p. 318). Directly visiting news sites allowed for "greater exposure to opposing perspectives."

Serendipity The danger of "recommended for you" articles and videos on social media platforms and online news outlets is that those recommendations are based on what you typically choose. The result is that you don't get exposed to differing viewpoints. One reason I love reading a print newspaper is for the unexpected; I'm scanning the pages for a particular story only to find my eyes diverted to another story, graphic or photo that caught my attention, and I learn something I didn't know I wanted or needed to learn. This sort of serendipity—a discovery by happy chance—is important to our development as democratic citizens.

Harvard Law School professor and author Cass R. Sunstein noted in a 2018 Facebook Newsroom post that citizens need to be "exposed to materials that they would not have chosen in advance." He continued:

> Serendipity is a good thing. Unplanned, unanticipated encounters are central to democracy itself. Such encounters often involve topics and points of view that people have not sought out and perhaps find quite irritating—but that might change their lives in fundamental ways. They are important partly to ensure against fragmentation, polarization, and extremism, which are predictable outcomes of any situation in which like-minded people speak only with themselves.

In our online and digitized social and informational world, we won't find information that contradicts our thinking if we cling to the usual platforms and news outlets. We will never be confronted with fresh thinking or different perspectives if we don't venture outside our laptop bookmarks and smartphone news apps to uncharted digital territories. The internet provides us with choice, and with that freedom comes a responsibility to extend ourselves.

To get you out of your ideological echo chamber, visit the "Blue Feed, Red Feed" webpage produced by the *Wall Street Journal* that shows liberal and conservative Facebook posts on similar topics alongside one another—it's updated regularly. Or, try *Read Across the Aisle*, an app that notices when you've accessed a lot of the same news sources on your phone, and will prod you to seek out diverse content.

HOW WE TRAIN OUR ATTENTION

We develop a media consumption habit first by having a goal we want to meet, such as when we decide to entertain ourselves by chilling out in front of the TV after a particularly rough day at work. Then, over time and with repetition, that goal-directed behavior, which was conscious and intentional, begins to morph into non-conscious and automatic behavior. We get in the routine, or habit, of chilling out in front of the TV after work whether we need to "chill out" or not. It's just what we do. Not helping matters is that advertisers and producers of mass media are expert at reinforcing our choices until they do become habits.

Communication scholar Robert LaRose's theory on media habits (2010), explained in the preceding paragraph, isn't an either/or proposition. It states that our media consumption habits are on a spectrum, with one end as conscious behavior regarding media use. At the opposite end is automatic processing regarding media use.

For example, if hearing your alarm in the morning means you grab your smartphone to check social media updates that you missed overnight, that wake-up routine may be automatic for you. You do it without thinking. But there is intentionality in the act as well—you intend to find out what you missed from friends while you slept. So that is purposeful behavior. The mix of automatic and intentional behavior peppers our media consumption. What prompts you to slip into automatic media consumption? Look for patterns in your media use; what places, things, people, moods and other stimuli trigger your media use?

Technology is teaching our brains to think superficially and not deeply. The brain is plastic—it is adaptable. This is a lovely trait of our brains, but it also means that the endless distractions of mobile devices and the media content they provide around the clock is retraining our brains, and not in good ways.

A study led by Columbia University psychologist Betsy Sparrow and colleagues (2001) suggests we are less likely to remember actual information and are better at remembering where we can find it—because we know we can find it on the internet at any time. It's our constant lifeline. "The Internet has become a primary form of external or transactive memory, where information is stored collectively outside ourselves," they wrote (p. 776).

Also, all these distractions make it hard for our brains to figure out what is relevant; we seem to be training our brains to be constantly distracted by the newest diversion (Ophir, Nass, & Wagner, 2009). It's kinda like a dog chasing after squirrels. There's one! There's another! Whee, yet one more . . . quick, get it!

- Turn off notifications on your computer, tablet, watch, and any other devices that ping, flash or vibrate.
- Go greyscale on your screen. It reduces the visual attractiveness. That makes it boring. Boring begets productivity.
- Remove all mindless apps from your home screen; only leave useful tools.
- Remove any social media from your phone. Or, install a website blocking app that limits your time on social media or other distracting sites.
- Devote 20 minutes at a time to each task.
- Anticipate and try to fend off all distractions.
- Stay committed to staying put.

Keep for **Reference!**

Tips to Get and Stay Focused
Sources: Akshay, n.d.; Nass, 2013

ATTENTIVE USER INTERFACES

As the number of devices with which we interact each day increases, technology experts are developing so-called "Attentive User Interfaces" (AUIs) that aim to support our finite attention by managing interruptions.

Microsoft researchers are working on technology to give our computers and communication devices the ability to sense our attention needs. Technology experts are exploring how to fuse together multiple streams of information from one's laptop, smartphone and tablet, for example, in order to reduce distractions and interruptions. The goal would be to increase our ability to filter incoming information and make it easier to sustain attention.

AUIs can measure whether you're at your computer, how close you are to a given screen, if you're facing toward it or away from it, if your spoken words are giving a hint as to what task you are planning to do next and where your gaze is directed. It's all in service to the scarcity and superficiality of our attention. Researcher Roel Vertegaal (2003) has likened these interfaces to a well-timed traffic light system that efficiently manages the flow of traffic by using sensors in the road to determine where users will go next. Research into AUIs forecasts a world in which AUIs will be programmed to do our routine tasks, so we can focus on insightful and innovative thinking—so we can direct our attention elsewhere.

CHAPTER REVIEW

- Understand why media companies need to attract our attention.
- Explain how media multitasking affects cognition.
- Contrast the types of attention states.
- Give an example of an internally motivating factor for attention.
- Compare automatic and controlled processing.
- Define filter bubbles.
- Give an example of serendipity in media use.
- Describe what an attentive user interfaces does.

ACTIVITIES

1. Identify your own triggers for distraction and try the "Tips to Get and Stay Focused" for a couple days. Then, pair up with a peer and take turns interviewing each other on camera about your success, challenges and reactions to the experience. Use your smartphone to do the recording, and edit it with a simple and free video editing app (such as Quik, Splice or Adobe Premier Clip).
2. Break up into trios and analyze a current popular TV ad for its use of attention-getting devices. Present your analysis to the group.
3. Go to https://bit.ly/2MwYZkf to see interactive graphics of political polarization in the United States; the images visualize the great divide between liberal and conservative ideologies on Twitter. Make a list of five specific things you can do to broaden your exposure to different viewpoints on social networking sites and on news and information sites.
4. Complete "The Past is Calling" exercise. Write your answers between the phone cords.

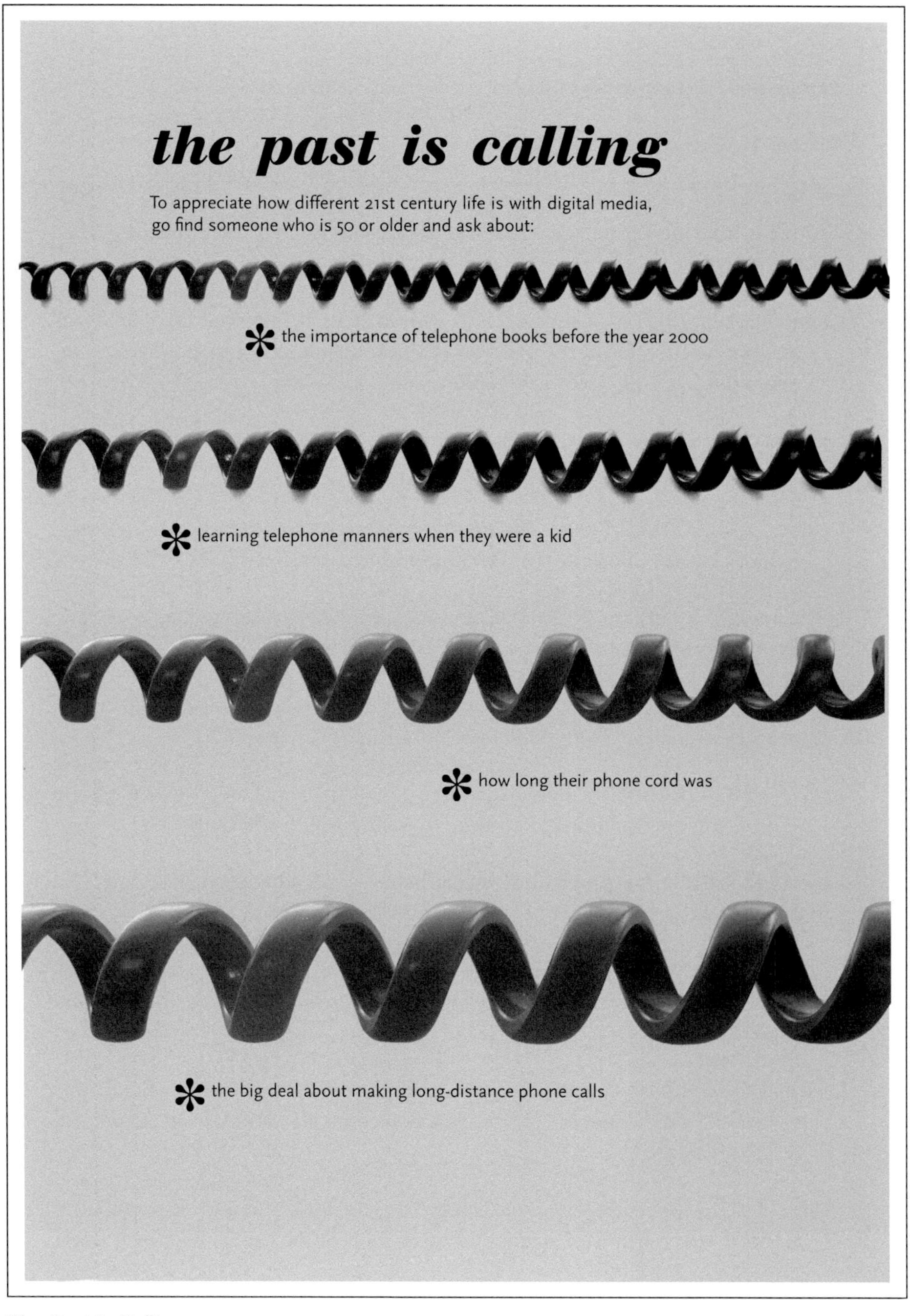

The Past Is Calling

Credit: Ryan Lewis

REFERENCES

Akshay. (n.d.) 9 crazy hacks to stay focused at work. *LifeHacks* website.

Bavelier, D., Green, C. S., & Dye, M. W. G. (2010). Children, wired—for better and for worse. *Neuron, 67*(5), 692–701. doi:10.1016/j.neuron.2010.08.035

Centre for Humane Technology. (2019). Ledger of Harms. Retrieved from http://bit.ly/2xVnaiy

Commodari, E. (2017). Novice readers: The role of focused, selective, distributed and alternating attention at the first year of the academic curriculum. *i-Perception, 8*(4). doi:10.1177/2041669517718557

Davenport, T., & Beck, J. (2000). Getting the attention you need. *Harvard Business Review.* Retrieved from http://bit.ly/32BCRJX

Davenport, T., & Beck, J. (2001). *The attention economy: Understanding the new currency of business.* Boston, MA: Harvard Business Review Press.

DeStefano, D., & LeFevre, J. (2007). Cognitive load in hypertext reading: A review. *Computers in Human Behavior, 23*(3), 1616–1641.

Flaxman, S., Goel, S., & Rao, J. M. (2016). Filter bubbles, echo chambers, and online news consumption. *Public Opinion Quarterly, 80*(S1), 298–320.

Kelly, K. (2008, January 31). Better than free. On his personal blog site, *KK.org.* In "The Technium" topic area. Retrieved from http://bit.ly/2LyOa06

LaRose, R. (2010). The problem of media habits. *Communication Theory, 20*(2), 194–222. https://doi.org/10.1111/j.1468-2885.2010.01360.x

Leroy, S. (2009). Why is it so hard to do my work? The challenge of attention residue when switching between work tasks. *Organizational Behavior and Human Decision Processes, 109*(2), 168–181.

Levitin, D. J. (2015, January 18). Why the modern world is bad for your brain. *The Guardian, The Observer.* Neuroscience section. Retrieved from http://bit.ly/2Y9YzFa

Miller, E. (2016, December 28). Here's why you shouldn't multitask, according to an MIT neuroscientist. *Fortune.* Venture: Tools of the Trade. Retrieved from http://bit.ly/2LpZlIc

Miller, E., & Buschman, T. J. (2015). Working memory capacity: Limits on the bandwidth of cognition. *Dædalus, the Journal of the American Academy of Arts & Sciences, 144*(1), 112–122.

Nass, Clifford. (2013, May 10). Talk of the Nation: The myth of multitasking. *National Public Radio*. An interview by Ira Flatow.

Newport, C. (2016). *Deep work: Rules for focused success in a distracted world*. New York, NY: Grand Central Publishing.

Newport, C. (2016, September 6). A productivity lesson from a classic arcade game. *Study Hacks Blog: Decoding Patterns of Success*. Retrieved from calnewport.com

Olmstead, K. (2017). *A third of Americans live in a household with three or more smartphones*. Washington, D.C.: Pew Research Center.

Ophir, E., Nass, C., & Wagner, A. D. (2009). Cognitive control in media multitaskers. *Proceedings of the National Academy of Sciences USA, 106*(37), 15583–15587. doi:10.1073/pnas.0903620106

Reinsel, D., Gantz, J., & Rydning, J. (2018, November). Data age 2025: The digitization of the world from edge to core. IDC white paper. Doc# US44413318.

Simon, H. A. (1971). Designing organizations for an information-rich world. In M. Greenberger (Ed.), *Computers, communications, and the public interest* (pp. 37–72). Baltimore, MD: Johns Hopkins Press.

Sohlberg, M. M., & Mateer, C. A. (1989). Clinical model of five levels of attention. *Introduction to cognitive rehabilitation: Theory and practice*. New York, NY: Guilford Press.

Sosnoski, J. J. (1999). Hyper-readers and their reading engines. In G. E. Hawisher & C. L. Selfe (Eds.), *Passions, politics, and the 21st century technologies* (pp. 161–177). Logan, UT and Urbana, IL: Utah State University Press.

Sparrow, B., Liu, J., & Wegner, D. M. (2001). Google effects on memory: Cognitive consequences of having information at our fingertips. *Science, 333*(6043), 776–778. doi:10.1126/science.1207745

Sunstein, C. (2018, January 22). Is social media good or bad for democracy? *Facebook Newsroom*. Retrieved from http://bit.ly/2NXUAIc

Vertegaal, R. (2003). Attentive user interfaces. *Communications of the Association for Computing Machinery, 46*(3), 30–33.

Zimmerman, F. J., Christakis, D. A., & Meltzoff, A. N. (2007). Associations between media viewing and language development in children under age 2 years. *The Journal of Pediatrics, 151*(4), 364–368.

3 Verifying

How to Find a Fact, and Know When You've Found One

MADE-UP NEWS

"Lottery Winner Arrested For Dumping $200,000 Worth Of Manure On Ex-Boss' Lawn."

That was the headline of a phony news story on World News Daily Report, a satirical website, about a lottery winner's revenge. It garnered the most Facebook shares, likes, comments and clicks in 2018, according to a BuzzFeed News analysis (Silverman & Pham, 2018).

More than 2.38 million people interacted with that bogus story!

The phony news story has a photo of the laughing "lottery winner" that in actuality is the mug shot of a man who in real life was arrested for suspicion of driving under the influence. A disclaimer on the World News' website states that, "it assumes . . . all

LEARNING OBJECTIVES

Terms: Fake news, clickbait, algorithm, motivated reasoning, confirmation bias, availability heuristic, illusory truth effect, bandwagon effect, truth, belief, post-truth, data void.

- Recognize the types of misinformation and disinformation.
- Understand why accurate information is important to a functioning democracy.
- Explain the reasons for the rise in misinformation and disinformation.
- Describe the common cognitive biases that help explain why humans fall for misinformation and disinformation.
- Explain why conspiracy theories are hard to disprove.
- Identify the various approaches to address misinformation and

disinformation by tech companies, government, news outlets and educational efforts.

- Know basic fact-checking techniques.

How concerned are you about unreliable news and false information? Why do you think it has become such a problem in our world today?

responsibility for the satirical nature of its articles and for the fictional nature of their content" (2019).

Though the word "satirical" means to make fun of, or parody, there was enough legitimate attention given to the story that a day after it was posted, the fact-checking website Snopes ruled the story false. (By the way, you can see the video of Snopes debunking of the lottery winner here: http://bit.ly/2YaJi4u.) Meanwhile, people on a subreddit, which is a forum dedicated to a specific topic on the website Reddit, debated the awesomeness of the fake lottery winner's bold and smelly move, as well as the veracity of the post; in other words, people kept the story alive. (Go ahead, take a moment to riff on all the puns for this phony story: It's b.s., full of crap, a stink bomb. . . .)

As you can likely tell, there is a reason hoaxes and false "news" get so much traction online; often, it's entertaining. But, it's also confusing to people. Sometimes, the information chaos hurts individuals, stirs up dissent that leads to violence, or wreaks havoc on election outcomes. In fact, one in two people (54 percent) across the globe are concerned about what is real and fake on the internet (Newman, 2018). Are you one of them?

This chapter takes a close look at the broad array of information in our media choices.

We examine our role as consumers, creators and citizens in relation to misinformation. We look at how to know a fact from a fake, why disinformation is on the rise and why humans fall prey to misinformation.

TYPES OF MISINFORMATION AND DISINFORMATION

In 2017, Collins Dictionary named the term "fake news" the word of the year. But the term "fake news" is a misnomer. **Fake news** is not news at all; it is deliberate misinformation designed to get attention and make money for the creators. There is nothing journalistic about the content.

Many people use the term "fake news" when what they really mean is news they don't agree with. See this partial list of fake news sites developed by PolitiFact and Facebook: http://bit.ly/2Dg3Rn7.

Many people use the term "fake news" when what they really mean is news they don't agree with.

Certainly, we all have seen our share of poor journalism and biased reporting. There are several levels of less-than-quality information and news being shared across the internet, but it's not all malicious or intentionally inaccurate. Here's a rundown of the various kinds of information online.

Satire/Parody: Use of irony, humor and exaggeration to expose or criticize weaknesses or stupidity, especially in current events and politics. (Example: The satirical news site *The Onion*.)

Shoddy Journalism: Unsourced or inadequately-sourced reporting, with some stories having minimal standards of verification. (Example: *The New York Post*.)

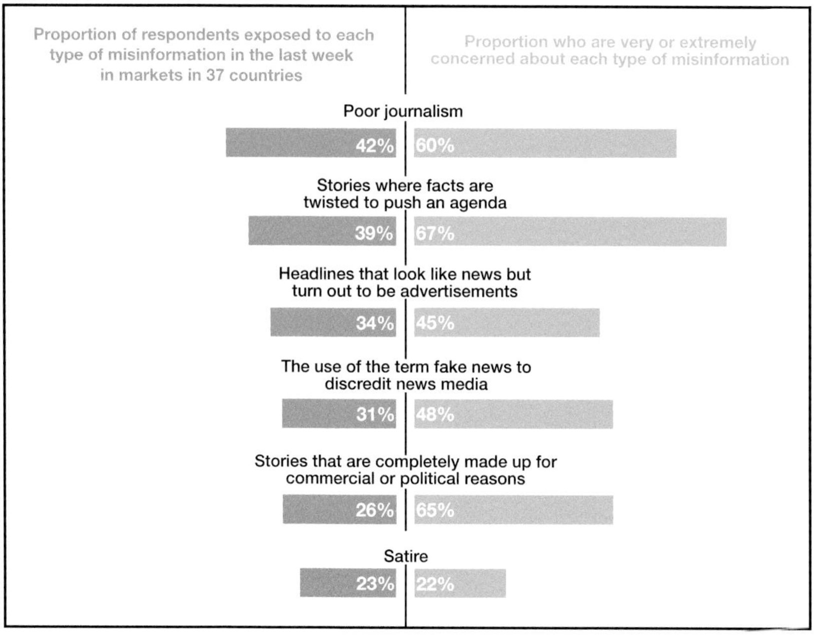

Exposure to Misinformation

Source: Reuters Institute Digital News Report 2018

Biased Journalism: Accounts that favor one perspective over others through story selection, source selection and/or word choice that seeks to elicit emotion or play on stereotypes. Some outlets are untrustworthy but others have a record of factual reporting. [Examples: The Media Bias/Fact Check monitoring site ranks *Mother Jones* as left-center biased with high ratings for factual reporting (Media Bias/Fact Check, 2019) and the *National Review* as right-biased with mixed ratings for factual reporting (Media Bias/Fact Check, 2018).]

Misleading Advertising: These ads often feature **clickbait** headlines designed to entice you to click the link by suggesting provocative information. The links often lead to spam, a sales pitch or shoddy content. (Examples: An ad disguised as a news story, such as a story about "How one man overcame his fear of flying" that turns out to be an advertisement for motion sickness medication. Or, ads for diets that promise amazing results in days and lead to a dumb list of nutrition tips.)

The following three definitions of various kinds of information come from a report for the Council of Europe (Wardle & Derakhshan, 2017, p. 20) aptly entitled "Information Disorder":

Misinformation: "Information that is false, but not created with the intention of causing harm." People who share misinformation often believe the information they are sharing is true. Misinformation often involves breaking news and the rapid-fire release of information before it is checked for accuracy. (Example: *Misinformation* that included hate speech and propaganda contributed to violence against Rohingya Muslims in Myanmar (Do, 2018).)

Disinformation: "Information that is false and deliberately created to harm or mislead a person, social group, organization or country." (Example: "Pizzagate," a debunked conspiracy theory that started with a Facebook post, got picked up on Twitter and went viral with the help of far-right outlets Breitbart and Info-Wars (Robb, 2017).)

Malinformation: "Information that is based on reality, used to inflict harm on a person, organization or country." (Example: A news story that reveals that someone is transgender without their permission and/or without that information being relevant to the public interest.)

WHY WE SHOULD CARE

The spread of misinformation and disinformation affects the whole of a society. For free and independent elections, transparent sourcing of information matters. For a healthy planet, factual information about clean energy solutions matters. For safe and secure neighborhoods, accurate, evidence-based reporting matters.

We should care about credible information because we deserve better than phony news that seeks to play on our ignorance. Also, as creators, if we are unknowingly using inaccurate information to make an argument, then *we* lose credibility. Misinformation is also harmful to people's health, literally; websites that falsely link childhood vaccinations to autism are an example of this. Also, accurate news and information benefits us and helps us in our daily lives, from knowing where to vote to information about new laws such as legalized marijuana.

Because It Hurts Democracy Misinformation in the developing world has caused violence and increased tensions, noted this article from the U.S.-based think tank the Council on Foreign Relations:

> In countries already suffering from ethnic tensions, misinformation can exacerbate tensions and generate violence. In perhaps the most well-known case, Facebook was used in Myanmar to incite violence against the Rohingya. But Myanmar isn't an anomaly: In Sri Lanka, online rumors have led Buddhists to target Muslims; in Nigeria, inflammatory images on Facebook have led young Berom men to pursue Fulani Muslims; in India, fake news on WhatsApp has caused a spate of violent incidents against Hindi speakers. What these examples make clear is how the danger of misinformation has become a societal challenge requiring action not just from technology companies, civil society actors, and internet users, but also governments.
>
> (Sanchez, 2019, para 3)

Yet more examples of efforts to wreak informational chaos: According to U.S. intelligence officials, Russian-led misinformation and disinformation, as well as hacking campaigns, targeted the 2016 U.S. presidential election, and specifically, the campaign of Democratic candidate Hillary Clinton (USA vs. IRA, 2018). It is likely that Russian hackers and trolls who created those imposter news sites and extreme websites helped elect U.S. President Donald Trump over Clinton, said author and Annenberg Public Policy Center Director Kathleen Hall Jamieson (2018).

Also, in the United Kingdom, more than 150,000 Russian-language Twitter accounts posted messages in English that sought to encourage fears about Muslims and immigrants as part of a campaign for Britain to leave the European Union (Kirkpatrick, 2017). The posts were purposely misleading and sensational.

Because We're Part of the Problem Indeed, we should care about verification because studies show that internet users are not very good at evaluating online information, and are actually responsible for spreading misinformation.

Sarah McGrew and colleagues at Stanford University asked students in middle school, high school and college to complete a series of analyses of information online. "Across tasks and grade levels, students struggled to effectively evaluate online claims, sources, and evidence," the researchers concluded (2018, p. 165). "Most students did not consider who created content, did not consider the evidence presented, and did not consult other sources to verify claims" (p. 183).

False information diffused much faster, farther, deeper and broadly than the truth did—in all categories of information, researchers reported in a study published in the journal *Science* (Vosoughi, Roy, & Aral, 2018). The study examined roughly 126,000 rumors spread by approximately 3 million people. The researchers found that the top 1 percent of false news spread to between 1,000 and 100,000 people, likely depending on how novel and emotion-inducing the news was. Truth seldom reached more than 1,000 people. Political news that was false spread the most.

In the event you're thinking that computer robots simply following an **algorithm** (a set of steps used to solve a problem or calculation) drove up that spread of false news, you are mistaken. The *Science* article found that false and true news was spread at equal rates by bots. That means that we humans were doing the work of spreading false news.

Why do people create misinformation? The primary reason is clicks. Creators of false information post material that plays on users' emotions and beliefs. For some creators, simply getting people to view their ideological messaging is enough. But more often, these creators are after cash.

Webpages that include advertisements mean that with each click, the creator makes some money. More clicks, more money.

Because Communication Defines Us While at times the rise of misinformation and disinformation can seem relegated to partisan politics or global power struggles, it is in fact a very personal affront. Why? Information disorder cuts to the essence of humanity because it affects our ability to communicate. Communication is central to who we are. Humans are social beings; we use communication to define ourselves and others.

The scholar James W. Carey (1992) wrote about communication as more than a pragmatic exchange of information—more than texts of "what time?" or "where?" Carey wrote of communication as a *ritual*. Communication is a ritual that is directed "toward the maintenance of society in time; not the act of imparting information but the representation of shared beliefs . . . the sacred ceremony that draws persons together in fellowship and commonality" (p. 18).

Tip: Consider the images.

Dishonest sites take a visual from another time and place and repurpose or misappropriate it to make a fake article look more real and believable. Or, they manipulate the image to prove a point, such as by adding people to make a crowd look bigger to lend support to a person or cause. Look for a credit line for a photographer and/or news agency, as well as a date and time stamp on the story.

Question: Does the picture have telling details? If it says it is in a particular location, does what you're seeing seem like that place?

Tech Tool: Use Google Street View or Yandex Maps to compare an image with the real place.

Question: What about the weather in the image; does it match up with other pictures or the forecast that day?

Tech Tool for Answer: Use Weather Underground for historic forecasts that go back decades. (Click on the "More" button for a dropdown menu.)

Question: Where else has this photo appeared?

Tech Tool for Answer: For still images, do a reverse image search. If you're using Google Chrome as a browser, put the cursor over the photo and right-click (control-click on a Mac). Click "search Google" for image. Bing, Yandex, and TinEye also have reverse image search.

Question: How do I check a video?

Tech Tool: Try Amnesty International's YouTube DataViewer for video verification. Or, take a screen shot of the video and upload that to a reverse image search.

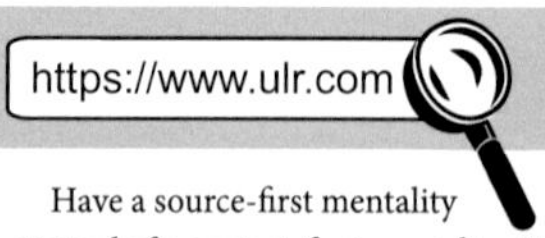

Tip: Look at the URL.

Have a source-first mentality instead of a content-first mentality. When conducting a search online, focus on the domain names attached to each of the search engine results. Some web sites that deal in misinformation will try to fool you with a URL that is very close to a bonafide news source.

Question: How do I know if the article I'm looking at is from an honest source?

Tech Tool: Input the site's URL into a domain lookup such as Whois. Or, in a search listing using the Chrome web browser, select the headline text and right-click your mouse (control-click on a Mac), and choose the option to Search Google for the highlighted phrase. It will help you see what else is being written about this particular event.

Tip: Be skeptical.

If an article, image or post makes you feel a strong emotion, pause; hyper-partisan sites in particular utilize strong language and sensational headlines to hook audiences. Quick hints that a story is valid include: Named sources, quotes and documents with links; accurate grammar and spelling; contact information for the story's author.

Question: How do I check fishy quotes?

Tech Tool: Put the phrase in a search engine to see where else they have been used; if a lot of shady sites turn up, that's a clue. Or if no other sites turn up, that's also a clue. Look to see if the quote is taken out of context to distort its meaning.

Question: What if the whole story seems suspect?

Tech Tool: Look for other news sites mentioning the story. If it is that big, it will show up in other legitimate news outlets.

We need effective and authentic communication for community cohesion. As a society, information and dialogue provides us with tools to make collective decisions. The images above each offer tips to help you quickly test the veracity of images and information online so that you can contribute to the informed communication that is so essential to a healthy society.

ONLINE INFORMATION AND PUBLIC DISTRUST IN NEWS

Harmful and false information has always been around, but the access of so many people to the publishing platform of the internet has meant that bad information has a free and easy passage to a global audience. The ease (no editors or gatekeepers), speed (it can go viral in hours) and public nature (the world at your fingertips) of dissemination on the Web has given a new dimension to the age-old problem of misinformation and its role in society. For a close look at how one fake news story went viral, read this *New York Times* piece: https://nyti.ms/2jnKTTP.

Fewer people are using social media to get their news; in particular, use of Facebook is down in the United States, United Kingdom and France, the Reuters Digital News Report 2018 found. Instead, people are more often using messaging apps to get the day's news, likely because these apps are more private and less confrontational. Apps such as WhatsApp are widely used in Malaysia, Brazil and Turkey, and there is global use of Instagram and Snapchat. While the platforms for accessing online information may be changing, it doesn't mean that the information is any less susceptible to manipulation.

Distrust of News Media People's trust in mass media reporting has been declining for 20 years or so in the United States (Swift, 2016). Globally, people's trust in most of the news they encounter most of the time is at 44 percent, the Reuters report found. Sixty-two percent of respondents in Finland said they trusted most news most of the time, and South Korea was lowest at 25 percent, the report stated.

Not helping matters is that we have long been, and continue to be, partisan creatures. In the United States, the partisan gap on major issues such as racial discrimination, immigration, homosexuality and military strength has grown wider, especially since 2016 (Pew, 2017). Personal values can influence the information that people choose to accept as valid and accurate. Also, many people are lazy thinkers, and if the message of the headline of a news story appeals to them, they believe it and share it.

However, local news is a port in this storm of distrust. A Poynter Media Trust Survey found that 76 percent of Americans across the political spectrum have a "great deal" or a "fair amount" of trust in local television news in their community and 73 percent do so for local newspapers (Guess, Nyhan, & Reifler, 2018, p. 6). Unfortunately, local news outlets, notably in the United States, Canada and the United Kingdom, are failing. In part due to lost advertising revenues, newsrooms are cutting staffs, consolidating or closing (Wardle & Derakhshan, 2017).

COGNITIVE BIASES AND INFORMATION CHAOS

Human cognition is a major reason that misinformation and disinformation are getting such a foothold in the public consciousness. Citizens can self-select their information based on what they believe. Because many of today's news and information sources are highly partisan, people can customize the news options they get through online searching so that the information they agree with rises to the top of the search results.

The contemporary information chaos is created when you add to these mechanics of online news retrieval the natural biases of our thinking. A few cognitive biases of particular note follow:

- We use **motivated reasoning** to draw the conclusions we want to draw from information, regardless of whether or not the information is credible. We do that to avoid cognitive dissonance and to avoid confronting information that contradicts our opinions, especially information that challenges our sense of self or well-being.
- The **confirmation bias** describes our tendency to both *notice* and *value* more highly the information that supports our own beliefs. We do this to the point that we ignore or discount other information that refutes those beliefs.
- The **availability heuristic** describes how oft-repeated information can seem more credible, or at least easier to recall. Easy recall leads us to think it's more important than information we aren't as likely to remember. (A heuristic is like a mental shortcut; it happens due to limited time, knowledge, mental capacity and, sometimes, motivation to focus attention on a topic.) The more a false news story gets commented on and shared, the more people see it. And the more they see it, the more people remember it, which suggests to users that easy recall must signal important information.
- Along these lines, another mental shortcut at work with highly trafficked stories is the **illusory truth effect**, which describes how the repeated exposure to a piece of information leads to belief in its correctness. Research indicates that the *sheer repetition* of information makes it more

believable to people. Familiarity, apparently, leads to believability—even when we know better (Fazio, Brashier, Payne, & Marsh, 2015).
- We use other people's judgments as a basis for our own trust. The **bandwagon effect** causes people to share the item when they see that many others have already shared or liked it. The effect is a psychological phenomenon that describes how people do something because others are doing it, no matter whether the action is in line with their beliefs. The problem is, some of those "people" sharing an item aren't people at all; they're robots, or "bots," meant to artificially inflate the importance of an item. Maybe it should be renamed the botwagon effect. (Oh, and by the way, if you want to check if a Twitter follower is a bot, put the screen name in Indiana University's *Botometer*.)

Truth vs. Belief According to the Merriam-Webster Dictionary, **truth** is the body of real things, events and facts. **Belief** is an *acceptance* that something is true and real. It's this latter definition—belief—that is causing many problems in our digital society. People want *so badly* to believe something is true that they may decide it is real, despite evidence to the contrary (or even no evidence at all). Pause for a moment and think about the sources of news and information that you trust—why do you trust them?

The term "post-truth" gets at this difference between truth and belief. **Post-truth** has been used often since 2016, when Oxford Dictionaries made it its word of the year. The term means that facts are less influential in shaping public opinion than persuasive appeals to our emotions or beliefs. So, for example, appeals to anti-immigrant sentiment may seek to play on people's fears about crime when the data do not support the claim. Research shows that in the United States, there is no link between immigration and crime—except in people's minds (Flagg, 2018).

Opinion Masquerading as News *Opinion* pieces across all media seek to persuade consumers to a particular point of view through argument, word choice and select examples. Opinion pieces should be based on facts and reporting, and shouldn't misrepresent opposing viewpoints.

News stories are not opinion pieces, and shouldn't include a judgment. Journalists can and should write news stories with authority because they understand particular issues so thoroughly, but that does not mean journalists offer a solution or conclusion. It means clearly presenting the parts of a story so that a viewer or listener can understand all the relevant facts. An *opinion* tells you what the author thinks about something; it is a judgment that is not necessarily based on fact or knowledge. An *analysis* is an interpretation or discussion by an expert in the field about a given *news* issue; it may or may not contain the analyst's position on the issue. And a news story tells you about something that happened and includes factual statements, and as much supporting evidence as possible.

The Center for News Literacy at Stony Brook University cautions news literate people to recognize the difference between assertion and verification. Assertion simply claims something is true or right, verification gives proof or support. "Mere assertion is the result of a search for ways to validate a niche audience's political agenda. It tends to emphasize beliefs and emotions over evidence and facts" (Center for News Literacy, 2019).

Assertion simply claims something is true or right, verification gives proof or support.

Suppose a news story quotes a politician unilaterally claiming that a new health care plan will be horrible for all citizens, but she offers no support for her claim. She can't offer a specific instance beyond broad assertions of widespread illness and mayhem. If the assertion is allowed to remain in a news story, the story should also note that the politician could provide no support for her assertion.

The Center also advises users to look out for evidence versus inference, the latter being an *implied* connection but not a proven or perhaps even legitimate one. An example of this would be an article quoting a pseudo-scientist who asserts that childhood vaccines cause autism, which is not true. He may make an implied connection to prove his point: Most infants are routinely immunized right around the time that early signs of autism appear, so therefore the one causes the other. Rather than rightly observing that the signs of autism are coincidentally timed to vaccination, a faulty news story would allow the pseudo-scientist to make the assertion based merely on inference.

Conspiracy Theories The problem with conspiracy theories is that often they are non-falsifiable. The conspiracy claim can't be proven because there's a cover-up going on, or evidence has been hidden or manipulated.

Efforts to argue that there isn't a cover-up just prove how much of a cover-up there is in the eyes of conspiracist. Conspiracy theories cater to our beliefs, not to facts. A helpful recap is provided by this PBS Digital Studios video "Can you win an argument with a conspiracy theorist?" at http://bit.ly/2V9MJWQ.

A review by Andreas Goreis and Martin Voracek, two research psychologists in Austria, of 96 research studies (more than half published between 2015 and 2018) on conspiracies concluded that there are diverse reasons why people believe in conspiracy theories.

> Conspiracies appear to appeal to those who feel disconnected from society, who are unhappy or dissatisfied with their circumstances, who possess a subjective worldview that includes unusual beliefs, experiences and thoughts, and do not feel in control of their life.
>
> (2019, Discussion, para 5)

Two positives from the generally negative views of conspiracy theories is that they may promote more government transparency and serve as a tool to help people challenge social hierarchies, Goreis and Voracek summarized. From a media literacy perspective, expect to keep seeing conspiracy theories in your social media feed and YouTube channels. Why? In part because they satisfy people's need for uniqueness—conspiracy theorists like to think that they know something others don't so that they feel special (Lantian, Muller, Nurra, & Douglas, 2017).

ADDRESSING THE PROBLEM

Who is doing the fact checking before things are published? Who is upholding a standard of ethics and accountability? Who is monitoring for propaganda and hoaxes? The spread and impact of false information was made possible by several factors. Similarly, fixing the problem is the responsibility of many entities, not just one. Technology companies, news outlets, governments, educational efforts and individuals are all doing *some* things to address disinformation. All can, and must, do more.

Technology Companies Three in four respondents in one study said that online publishers have the biggest responsibility to fix problems of made-up and unreliable news, with 71 percent stating that platforms that carry such news are primarily responsible (Newman, 2018). Across all the platforms, a click-based monetary structure means that doing whatever it takes to create an audience is rewarded, no matter the cost to civility and democracy.

In response, lawmakers, interest groups and users have lobbied for more oversight and control of content by tech companies. In turn, the Big Four—Facebook, Twitter, YouTube and Google (which owns YouTube)—are taking steps to address the problem of misinformation and disinformation. Facebook, with more than 2.2 billion active monthly users worldwide, has a major role to play, many lawmakers and experts assert.

The areas targeted for improvements include:

- identifying (either flagging, minimizing or deleting) fake information.
- reducing the financial incentive and profits gleaned from disinformation.
- upping standards for accountability.
- requiring more transparency in who is creating content.
- banning advertising from unethical companies.
- actively addressing hoaxes during elections and breaking news events.

Additionally, social media companies such as YouTube have to combat **data voids**, which are search terms for which there is little legitimate, relevant data. Conspiracies and propaganda can fill this information vacuum, since credible information isn't there to fill the void when a contemptible query is made such as, "Is the Holocaust real?" (Golebiewski & boyd, 2018; boyd, 2018).

Facebook is also developing new products to thwart misinformation and trying to do more to educate users about news literacy. "We cannot become arbiters of truth ourselves—it's not feasible given our scale, and it's not our role," wrote Adam Mosseri, vice president of Facebook's news feed on its website (2017).

However, said Jim Rutenberg in his Mediator column (2016) in the *New York Times*, "Truth doesn't need arbiters. It needs defenders. And it needs them now more than ever as the American democracy staggers into its next uncertain phase," he wrote. "With a mainstream news media that works hard to separate fact from fiction under economic and political threat, Facebook—which has contributed to that economic threat by gobbling up so much of the online advertising market—is going to have a special responsibility to do its part."

What do you think? Does Facebook have "a special responsibility" in regard to false information? At what point, if at all, does Facebook become not

VOX DISCIPULI

The last time I felt tricked by a social media post I saw was a recent picture of the teenage boy with a grin on his face and wearing a MAGA hat staring into the eyes of a Native American man. The picture brought up a bunch of preconceived notions: 'This is your typical white-privileged racist teenager,' and 'This teenager and his friends surrounded this poor Native American and mocked him while he was just minding his own business.' I later watched a video and read an article that went into more detail and showed that the Native American actually approached the teenagers and in a way, taunted them, in my opinion. In the end, my initial notions changed to believing there were two sides to the story. —Scott, 23

Read more about the various perspectives, complexities and confusion caused by this viral story: http://bit.ly/2Ctv1Xj.

merely a publishing platform but an information source that should provide ethical oversight of content?

News Outlets Job no. 1 is to rebuild public trust in the media. Producing high-quality journalism will help build this public trust and attract audiences to credible outlets, according to a Brookings Institute report (West, 2017). Also, strengthening local news coverage in particular, and the connections between communities and their local news providers, is essential to rebuilding trust in journalism.

As of this writing, there are 160 active fact-checking sites around the world, according to the Reporters' Lab at Duke University (2019). PolitiFact and FactCheck.org are examples of U.S.-based fact-checking organizations. The International Fact-Checking Network promotes collaboration among outlets to contribute to accuracy monitoring, particularly around election time. In Europe, "at least 34 permanent sources of political fact-checking are active in 20 different European countries, from Ireland to Turkey," according to a 2016 Reuters Institute for the Study of Journalism report (Graves & Cherubini, 2016, p. 8).

It's important to note that many of these sources are not led by new organizations but by non-profit, non-governmental organizations and alternative media outlets, and sometimes started by activists. For instance, StopFake, in Ukraine, came about after Russia annexed Crimea. It is now professionalized, but it began as journalists, academics and students gathered to form a plan to combat the propaganda campaign from Moscow, the Reuters report noted.

Government In Europe and Asia, roughly 60 and 63 percent of respondents respectively favored government intervention to stop fake news, but in the United States, only 41 percent thought government should intervene more (Newman, 2018). This lower percentage is likely due to the U.S. Constitution's assertion of a free press. Governments worldwide are trying to find the right response to regulating information in a free society. For example, in France, media coverage around presidential and legislative elections is regulated, particularly in the hours before polls close. The government in the United Kingdom is considering independent oversight of the major social media platforms. In the United States, legislators have held many public hearings about regulating social media platforms, but strict regulations seem unlikely. In Germany, new regulations require social media companies to ban hate speech or risk heavy fines (Eddy & Scott, 2017).

Educational Efforts Experts agree that increased media literacy is an essential part of solving the problem of information disorder. What people don't agree on is how far media literacy can take society in the efforts to thwart media manipulation. Journalism schools are teaching data and information verification techniques. Public libraries are offering information-vetting workshops and training to local residents. An international standardized curriculum for media literacy is an option suggested by some experts.

Currently, educational initiatives are partnering with news organizations to help flag honest information and misinformation. For instance, NewsGuard hires experienced journalists to review and ultimately, rate news and information sites by color (green for credible and transparent, red to signal non-credible sites). The Trust Project uses eight Trust Indicators that outlets worldwide, including the United Kingdom's *The Mirror*, are using to communicate sourcing, reporting methods, a reporter's level of expertise and other critical elements of honest journalism. Visit TheTrustProject.org to see a mock-up of what the Trust indicators look like when included in a news story.

Individual Consumers That's us! We can do many things to protect ourselves and our online communities against misinformation and disinformation. Here are some basic rules of engagement with information:

- **First is not best.** Just because something is listed first in the search results doesn't make it best. Google and other search engines rank information based on relevance and usefulness, not reliability or credibility.
- **Disrupt.** We must be the disrupters among our friends, family and followers. Be the person who stops the sharing and calls out the sourcing. Verify the material instead of sending it along mindlessly, including by looking for substantial credible evidence that disproves a statement or position, as opposed to looking for evidence to confirm it.
- **Think.** "Susceptibility to fake news is driven more by lazy thinking than it is by partisan bias per se," wrote Yale University researchers Gordon Pennycook and David G. Rand (2018). They concluded that people who are inclined to be analytical can better spot the lies of fake news, and can better discern fake news from real news—even if the headlines on those news stories align with their individual political ideology.
- **Don't trust your gut.** People's inclination to effortful thinking and their tendency to engage in further reflection as opposed to simply going with their incorrect "gut" response to information were both significant moderators of the confirmation bias (Westerwick, Johnson, & Knobloch-Westerwick,

2017). Unfortunately, too often we trust our instinct. For instance, in a study of 2,500 Singaporeans, the primary way that people judged whether or not news they encountered on social media was valid was "their own wisdom, instinct, and insight" (Tandoc, Jr. et al., 2018, p. 2754).

- **Read.** This sounds so simple as to be insulting, but I'll say it anyway: Read past the headline and the disarming images. Computer scientists led by Maksym Gabielkov of University of Helsinki (2016) found that 59 percent of the 2.8 million online news articles shared in a sample period on Twitter were never even clicked on. Pretty hard to read a story without opening it.
- **Scan for clues.** Look for proper bylines that list a real and full name; reporter contact information; a headline that matches the content; photos that are original; sources that are named; a legitimate URL; typo-free text, if addresses and people are real.

Here's my super-cheesy mnemonic device to help you remember the tips: "First, disrupt. Think with your head, not your gut. You read me, Sherlock?" (Painful, I know, but if it sticks, it's worth the humiliation.)

Technology Challenges Technology will continue to yield innovations—such as lip-synced video and vocal avatars—that can be used in service to society or to create chaos. For example, the University of Washington's "Synthesizing Obama" project took the audio from one speech and used it to animate the former U.S. president's face in a different video (Langston, 2017). A Canadian start-up called Lyrebird is working on audio impersonations, or vocal avatars that create a digital voice based on your real voice recording. In both cases, there are noble uses for the technologies and obvious unethical ones, too.

Verification will continue to be the responsibility of many different players in the media and technology sector, including us as users and creators. We can be aware of our mental shortcuts and natural tendencies to fall for emotional content and agreeable-sounding headlines. We can also act on that awareness and pause to think before believing—and sharing.

CHAPTER REVIEW

- Explain the significance of accurate information.
- Know the difference between biased information and misinformation.

- Understand the various cognitive biases that affect our processing of information.
- Identify what social media platforms are doing to combat misinformation and disinformation.
- Give an example of the availability heuristic.
- Use the fact-checking tools provided to assess the origins and authenticity of news stories in a social media feed such as Facebook.

ACTIVITIES

1. Game time! There are a slew of spot-the-fake-news games. Here are some to try out and compare:
   a. *Newsday* offers an interactive guide to spotting fraudulent news stories. Try it out here: http://bit.ly/2CIy1iK.
   b. Play the Fakeittomakeitgame.com by designer Amanda Warner, who has created an interactive game in which you as the player spread disinformation to gain revenue.
   c. Another game by Warner is Postfactogame.com, which asks you to find the suspicious elements in an online false news story.
   d. Practice sorting false news from real news on Factitious, a site created by the game lab at American University at http://bit.ly/2CsLomS.
   e. Try to spot the deceptive Facebook post in this *New York Times* interactive at https://nyti.ms/2JA3kSm.
2. Visit FlackCheck.org, an Annenberg Public Policy Center website that provides resources to help viewers recognize flaws in arguments in general and political ads in particular. Select a recent statement from a politician and create a slideshow that mimics the format of FlackCheck by first giving the disputed statement, and then providing support or disputation for it, along with complete sourcing.
3. Discover your political biases by taking the various assessments compiled at AllSides.com; once at the website, click on "Media bias" and then "Discover your own bias." Take the quizzes and see your results. Write a one-page paper about your results and if you agree with the results and

why or why not. Also, address how your political bias affects your news and information choices. Identify ways you can provide political balance to your media intake.

4. Librarian Sarah Blakeslee developed the CRAAP test (2004). CRAAP stands for **C**urrency (when was the information published or posted?), **R**elevance (does the information satisfy your needs?), **A**uthority (who are the authors and what are their credentials?), **A**ccuracy (where does the information come from?) and **P**urpose (what is the purpose of the information?) Apply the CRAAP test to the lead article in an online news story of your choice. Share your findings with your peers.

REFERENCES

Blakeslee, S. (2004). The CRAAP test. *LOEX Quarterly, 31*(3). Article 4.

boyd, d. (2018, September 14). Media manipulation, strategic amplification, and responsible journalism. *Medium.*

Carey, J. (1992). A cultural approach to communication. In *Communication as culture: Essays on media and society* (Rev. ed., pp. 13–37). New York, NY: Routledge.

Center for News Literacy. (2019). *Opinion or mere assertion?* Stony Brook, NY: Digital Resource Center. Retrieved from http://bit.ly/2YYAxKy

Do, H. (2018, November 26). Misinformation or disinformation. *Voice of America: Learning English.* website.

Eddy, M., & Scott, M. (2017, June 30). Delete hate speech or pay up, Germany tells social media companies. *New York Times:* Business section, p. 1.

Fazio, L. K., Brashier, N. M., Payne, B. K., & Marsh, E. J. (2015). Knowledge does not protect against illusory truth. *Journal of Experimental Psychology, 144*(5), 993–1002.

Flagg, A. (2018, March 30). The myth of the criminal immigrant. *The Marshall Project.* Retrieved from themarshallproject.org.

Gabielkov, M., Ramachandran, A., Chaintreau, A., & Legout, A. (2016). *Social clicks: What and who gets read on Twitter*? Proceedings of the 2016 ACM SIGMET-

RICS International Conference on Measurement and Modeling on Computer Science, pp. 179–192.

Golebiewski, M., & boyd, d. (2018, May 11). Data voids: Where missing data can easily be exploited. *Data & Society*, 1–6.

Goreis, A., & Voracek, M. (2019, February 11). A systematic review and meta-analysis of psychological research on conspiracy beliefs: Field characteristics, measurement instruments, and associations with personality traits. *Frontiers in Psychology*. https://doi.org/10.3389/fpsyg.2019.00205

Graves, L., & Cherubini, F. (2016). *The rise of fact-checking sites in Europe*. University of Oxford: Reuters Institute for the Study of Journalism. Oxford, England.

Guess, A., Nyhan, B., & Reifler, J. (2018). *All media trust is local? Findings from the 2018 Poynter media trust survey*. St. Petersburg: The Poynter Institute.

Jamieson, K. H. (2018). *Cyberwar: How Russian hackers and trolls helped elect a President what we don't, can't, and do know*. Oxford: Oxford University Press.

Kirkpatrick, D. D. (2017, November 15). Signs of Russian meddling in Brexit referendum. *The New York Times,* Section A, p. 8.

Langston, J. (2017, July 11). *Lip-syncing Obama: New tools turn audio clips into realistic video*. University of Washington news release.

Lantian, A., Muller, D., Nurra, C., & Douglas, K. M. (2017). "I know things they don't know!": The role of need for uniqueness in belief in conspiracy theories. *Social Psychology, 48*(3), 160–173.

Matishak, M. (2018, July 18). What we know about Russia's election hacking. *Politico*. Retrieved from https://politi.co/2XUwNbV

McGrew, S., Breakstone, J., Ortega, T., Smith, M., & Wineburg, S. (2018). Can students evaluate online sources? Learning from assessments of civic online reasoning. *Theory & Research in Social Education*, *46*(2), 165–193. doi:10.1080/00933104.2017.1416320

Media Bias/Fact Check. (2018). *National review*. Retrieved from https://mediabiasfactcheck.com/national-review/

Media Bias/Fact Check. (2019). *Mother Jones*. Retrieved from https://mediabiasfactcheck.com/mother-jones/

Mosseri, A. (2017). Working to stop misinformation and false news. *Facebook Newsroom*. Retrieved from http://bit.ly/2YgnzLm

Newman, N. (2018). Executive summary and key findings. *Reuters Institute digital news report 2018*. Reuters Institute for the Study of Journalism and the University of Oxford.

Pennycook, G., & Rand, D. G. (2018). Lazy, not biased: Susceptibility to partisan fake news is better explained by lack of reasoning than by motivated reasoning. *Cognition*. doi:10.1016/j.cognition.2018.06.011

Pew Research Center. (2017, October 5). *The partisan divide on political values grows even wider*. Washington, D.C.: U.S. Politics and Policy Section.

Reporters' Lab. Duke University. (2019). reporterslab.org/fact-checking/.

Robb, A. (2017, November 16). Anatomy of a fake news scandal. *Rolling Stone*. Retrieved from http://bit.ly/2JAiaX4

Rutenberg, J. (2016, November 21). Mark Zuckerberg and Facebook must defend the truth. *New York Times*, B1.

Sanchez, C. (2019, January 29). Misinformation is a threat to democracy in the developing world. *Council on Foreign Relations*. Net Politics and Digital and Cyberspace Policy Program.

Silverman, C., & Pham, S. (2018, December 28). These are 50 of the biggest fake news hits on Facebook in 2018. *BuzzFeed News*. Retrieved from http://bit.ly/2YXizIu

Swift, A. (2016, September 14). Americans' trust in mass media sinks to new low. *Gallup*. Retrieved from http://bit.ly/2GgLdx1

Tandoc Jr, E. C., Ling, R., Westlund, O., Duffy, A., Goh, D., & Wei, L. Z. (2018). Audiences' acts of authentication in the age of fake news: A conceptual framework. *New Media & Society*, *20*(8), 2745–2763.

United States of America vs. Internet Research Agency, et al. (2018, February 16). U.S. District Court for the District of Columbia. Case 1:18-cr-00032-DLF.

Vosoughi, S., Roy, D., & Aral, S. (2018). The spread of true and false news online. *Science*, *359*(6380), 1146–1151.

Wardle, C., & Derakhshan, H. (2017). *Information disorder: Toward an interdisciplinary framework for research and policymaking*. Strasbourg, France: Council of Europe.

West, D. M. (2017). *How to combat fake news and disinformation*. Washington, D.C.: Brookings Institution.

Westerwick, A., Johnson, B. K., & Knobloch-Westerwick, S. (2017). Confirmation biases in selective exposure to political online information: Source bias vs. content bias. *Communication Monographs, 84*(3), 343–364.

4 Analyzing

How Media Messages Deliver Meaning through Content and Creativity

You know how there are some people you hate to go to the movies with, because they take it apart and analyze all the fun and fantasy out of it? On the way out of the theatre, your companion is busy finishing her Dots candy while decoding the complicated subtext of the dialogue. And you're thinking: "*I liked it until you started talking. I thought the car chase was cool.*" Often, we automatically conduct our own analyses inside our heads, deciding what we think of a product, candidate, storyline or song based on factors of which we are both aware *and* unaware.

This chapter is devoted to the basics of how to analyze a media message. It is no small task, and often seen as a real killjoy kind of exercise. Yet, evaluating media enhances appreciation of the media you like, sharpens your abilities to make critical choices about all media, and

LEARNING OBJECTIVES

Terms: Deconstructing, text, manifest text, latent text, critical autonomy, genre, convention, code, context, point of view, gaze, male gaze, semiotics.

- Understand how the media constructs reality.
- Recognize the genre of a text by identifying its codes and conventions.
- Apply the media analysis tools of context, format, point of view and gaze.
- Utilize visual, aural and compositional analysis to deconstruct a media message.
- Identify the signs and symbols of a media message.
- Define various propaganda techniques.

Talk with one another about how you take a selfie. Do you construct the image? Move yourself or things in the frame of the image so the background is as you'd like it? Fix your hair? Take multiple images? Use a filter? Is the final image the "real you"?

it helps protect you from manipulation and lies. You really can both *enjoy* media and be a critical consumer at the same time. Examining how a piece of media is constructed helps us both appreciate it and understand its potential power over us.

CONSTRUCTING REALITY

Media messages all want to sell us *something*—that might be a product, a service, a way of life, an ideology.

Media messages are constructions, and each message has an end goal—to influence perceptions, behavior and attitudes. Media messages all want to sell us something; that might be a product, a service, a way of life, an ideology. Isn't that often true of the selfies you pose for and then post? You want to sell viewers an idea of yourself as fun, attractive, friendly, or strong. When it comes to commercial media, here are some common end-goals of messages:

Acquisition; buy the ticket to *the* action movie of the summer
Conversion; don't buy that detergent, buy *ours*, it smells better
Loyalty; keep watching this program, and the one after it, *and* the one after that. . .
Competition; slay four more enemies to get to the video game's *elite* level
Advocacy; give blood, vote for *this* candidate, save the whales
Adoption; *this* is the sport/diet/entertainment for you
Persuasion; candidate X has the *same* values as you do

Media messages from a Western point of view often want to convince us to adopt a set of values (materialism, capitalism), and a lifestyle (affluent, independent), and through these values and lifestyle, we are—ta-da!—fulfilled (attractive, fit, happy)! As we all know, media messages make it look easy to achieve it all, when in reality, well, it's *reality*.

One of the strongest attractions to media is that we see idealized portrayals of people and situations. It's also one of the dangers of it, as overconsumption of media can result in distorted views of how real life actually works.

When we encounter messages, from music videos to magazine fashion spreads, we know someone paid for that content to be created. So, while advertising agencies and production companies, for example, do the actual creating, they are creating on behalf of a person or company that has an end goal in mind.

How aware are you of the *manipulation* of images of models in advertising? At what point do you consider altered images that have been airbrushed and Photoshopped no longer an actual person?

Whatever the purpose of a media message, it is utilizing creative techniques to convey meaning. The elements of a message combine to set a tone and convey an idea to a specific audience. There are trade-offs when creating a message; the message creator is picking and choosing from a variety of creative techniques. We need to become savvy at **deconstructing**, or identifying and analyzing, the creative elements of media messages (Center for Media Literacy, 2019). When we deconstruct a message, we understand how the message seeks to create meaning and influence our beliefs and actions.

READING A MEDIA TEXT

A **media text** is more than words on a page. "Reading a text" in this context means a media message that is being evaluated. Reading a media text means to take apart and evaluate the various elements of a message to understand how it communicates meaning. A text may consist of any number of creative elements, such as graphics, visuals, sounds and words.

There are two basic differentiations in this analysis. A **manifest text** is the clearly-intended, obvious meaning of a message—the one intended by the creator. Such as the straightforward story of the movie *Black Panther*: A son returns home after the death of his father to take his place as king of Wakanda, but a powerful enemy threatens his rule and his country.

The **latent text** is the individual interpretation of the message by each audience member. For example, New York City pastor Richard Hayes' reaction to *Black Panther* was personal (Hall & Tyler, 2018):

> I think in many instances we've overlooked the immense contributions that have come from the African continent: contributions to math, contributions to engineering, contributions to science. And I think this story, seeing how advanced Wakanda is being portrayed as, almost kind of tells us about the ability that we were able to build pyramids when other folks were struggling in caves.
>
> (para 9)

When we as media consumers read a text in a way that is other than the preferred, or anticipated, reading of a text, we are practicing **critical autonomy**. Critical autonomy uses text deconstruction to understand the various elements within a message and how they work together to create an intended reading. For example, in the remake of the movie *Ghostbusters,* audiences were excited about the all-female cast, but less so about the only black actor, Leslie Jones, being a transportation worker and not a scientist, wrote Maryann Erigha in her 2019 book *The Hollywood Jim Crow: The Racial Politics of the Movie Industry.* The interpretation by some viewers, unintended by the creators, was that Jones' character kept "Black women circumscribed into their narrow box of roles in mainstream cinema" (p. 35).

Message Content This is where most of us start when analyzing a message. Simply, our focus is on what the message is telling us. So, start asking any and all of the following types of questions when you first encounter a media message:

- What is this message about?
- It is clear? Is it intentionally vague?
- What is happening in the message?
- What is the action and the setting (if any)?
- What ideas or concepts are communicated in the image? How do I know this?
- What is my emotional response to the image?
- What sort of mood does this message create?
- What am I learning from this message? How am I learning it? Who is communicating it?

Many elements work to create the final message content. We will explore the parts that make up the whole next.

Codes and Conventions The "language" of media messages involves a conscious series of choices by a message maker. **Genres** are categories of media messages that follow socially agreed upon forms and styles called **conventions**. Media messages use conventions to create meaning. Conventions are built by using **codes**, sort of like pieces of a puzzle that form a final image.

Conventions happen because certain codes are used together often. It's as if the same puzzle pieces are used again and again to make a familiar final image that we know of as a convention. There are four main areas of codes (remember them by SWAT):

- **S**ymbolic codes such as setting, acting, color and *mise en scene*, which is French for "everything within the frame" and in media terms references props, set design, costumes and staging.
- **W**ritten codes that include anything in text or print in the message, such as statements, captions or titles and the ways they are designed (font, size, style).
- **A**udio codes that include dialogue, sound effects, background music, voice over, and background noise.
- **T**echnical codes, such as lighting, editing, and camera work.

The conventions of a horror movie, for example, include the technical code of low lighting, the symbolic code of an abandoned mansion, and written code such as dialogue from the lead character that is purposely ambiguous and hints at dangers to come: "Let's go up that dark staircase to see what's making that slurping noise, Johnny." The first pieces of the puzzle that cue this convention are the dark and stormy night, a camera pan over the forsaken stone edifice and a shadowy figure in an upper window. Take this short interactive quiz on film conventions on the website The Film Space: http://bit.ly/2WkEibB.

Similarly, fashion magazines follow a set of conventions, as do all mediums, including popular music, comic books, TV sitcoms, and news shows. A convention of TV news programs is that major events may be distilled to a 30-second report, and less if it is not a strong visual story. Another broadcast news convention is iconography that labels a story (such as "Countdown to the Election" or "Tragedy on Main Street") and a running update of news across the bottom or side of the screen.

Genres Using codes and conventions, a genre immediately sets expectations for us as audience members about what we might expect. Likewise, different genres are combined or a convention is broken in order to create new meaning or enhanced impact; an example would be to film a horror scene in daylight, like the lakeside picnic scene in director David Fincher's eerie flick *Zodiac* (it's easy to find a clip of it online). Another example of a broken convention is *The Office* sitcom, as it uses the conventions of a documentary (such a single camera and no laugh track) to showcase the absurd situations that occur within the setting of a bland suburban office.

Team up with a peer and visit The Film Space website and practice identifying movie genres from its collection of movie trailers. Have your partner pick a trailer from a particular genre without telling you which it is; you watch the trailer and identify its genre and the codes and conventions that cued your answers. Go to: http://bit.ly/2TvGtXQ.

MEDIA LITERACY SELFIE

I'd like to interrupt our regularly scheduled chapter to turn the lens for a moment on media literacy itself. In this chapter, we are solidly in skill acquisition territory. A common complaint about media literacy is that it teaches skills such as spot-the-stereotype, or tag-the-message-parts. And it's true that part of media literacy is skill acquisition such as this chapter discusses; these are the tools of analysis. Media literacy requires these tools and skills in order to understand how messages are built, but media literacy certainly does not end here. Repeat: does not.

Media literacy also requires knowledge about the world; it requires knowledge about societies, current events and cultures so that we as consumers and creators are able to consider the context of messages. Finally, media literacy is an attitude. This attitude is one that expects to both enjoy media *and* engage in critical thinking about media; those two things can co-exist, and when they do, we are the richer for it.

VOX DISCIPULI

Especially when you see stuff on Twitter or Facebook or Instagram, you should never take it at face value. You'll see videos saying stuff like, 'Look at this racist situation!' But you don't get the full story. Even if what you see is part of it, it's not the full story because someone is trying to make you mad without giving you all the information. One way or the other they are trying to get your attention. You have options, you can Google what is happening in the video and someone, somewhere, will have done a piece on it. Whether it's a reputable news source or not, someone has more information that you do. Or you can just ignore it. Because if it's so important, it will pop up again with more detail if it is in fact actually something to get mad about. —Christian, 18

TECHNICAL CHOICES

When creators make a media message, they have several important building blocks with which to shape their message. Context, format, point of view and gaze are among the major elements of media creation, though hardly the only elements. Our job as consumers is to use this knowledge of decisions made in creating messages to analyze why they were used. When we analyze messages, we can better grasp the decisions made to shape meaning, message purpose and manipulate audience reactions.

When we analyze messages, we can better grasp the decisions made to shape meaning, message purpose and manipulate audience reactions.

Context Context refers to the circumstances and conditions—both internal and external—of a media message. The *internal* context of a media message invites us to think about what the message itself is telling us, such as the story told by lyrics of a song. Context influences the meaning of the message. The meaning of a simple kiss onscreen changes depending on whether it's between romantic partners, is a farewell to a dying parent or is a signal of betrayal.

Additionally, the *external* world into which a message is sent—the social, political and cultural context—influences the meaning of a message. After Colin Kaepernick of the professional football team the San Francisco 49ers knelt on one knee during the national anthem to protest racial injustice, his fame for the controversial stance led Nike to feature him and other African-American athletes in a television ad as part of the "Just Do It" campaign. The media message of the ad campaign was a direct outgrowth of external events.

Format The way in which something is presented is its format. How will a message be told? In what medium? In what form does the information *want* to be told? Media content often lends itself to a particular format, and indeed, the content *should* influence the format. As audience members on the receiving end of the message, we need to be aware of how the format influences our understanding as well as our emotional and cognitive reactions to the message content. We might dismiss data presented in the format of a table as boring but when it is put into a colorful infographic, we take note.

Changing Contexts, Changing Meanings

Credit: Ryan Lewis

A new format for news organizations is immersive video, also called *360-degree video*, that puts a viewer on the scene of a place or event. It's an effective tool to convey immediacy and support user-directed consumption of a message, since users can manipulate the view to see all angles. Immersive videos have focused on any number of situations, from the earthquake-ravaged Kathmandu to swimming with sharks in the ocean to a marijuana harvest in California. The medium offers a new way to communicate with audiences. See examples of immersive video in news reporting at the BBC: https://bbc.in/2Ft7nvU. What do you see as the pros and cons of this format for news reports?

We might dismiss data presented in the format of a table as boring but when it is put into a colorful infographic, we take note.

Point of View Part of reading media texts is noticing and evaluating the **point of view**, which describes the perspective and viewpoint (literally and conceptually) of the creator. That means that the creator of a message adopts a camera view, or a narrator's view—it's the perspective from which we as the audience consume the message.

The creator also adopts a point of view in terms of who or what is driving the message: Who is highlighted in the show? Who is invisible? Who gets favorable treatment—what are their demographics? Which characters' perspectives are included? Which characters' viewpoints are diminished or omitted? What is the creator trying to communicate with point of view?

Gaze While point of view describes a vantage point and perspective, often of a main character or narrator, the term "**gaze**" refers *to a way of looking at* an object. Gaze describes the relationship between the subject(s) of the message and the viewer.

Gaze is about a viewer's identity and how their perspective is different from the subjects in the image, the creator's gaze and even another audience member's gaze. There are many iterations of the gaze, but all have to do with who is doing the looking/gazing, as it were. So even if you are a female audience member, you may be in the position of viewership from the distinct point of view of a male appraising a female subject's sexuality and attractiveness.

Indeed, the term "male gaze" was coined by Laura Mulvey in her original 1975 essay on cinematography titled "Visual Pleasure and Narrative Cinema." The **male gaze** addresses the limited point of view in which female characters are portrayed in service to male eyes and interests. "Women are simultaneously looked at and displayed, with their appearance coded for strong visual and erotic impact so that they can be said to connote to-be-looked-at-ness" (1999, p. 837).

The male gaze is dominant in cinema and advertisements. A female gaze has been discussed in more recent years; the definition is less distinct but can include a female perspective, and characters and stories with a distinctly female emotional center (Cohen, 2017). Practice looking at advertisements online or in a nearby magazine and identify the gaze in each.

CREATIVE CHOICES

Among the many creative choices that creators have in message-making, some of the most important are audio, composition, camera work, editing, colors and lighting and signs and symbols. Each of these elements are creative tools that help shape a message.

Audio Sound communicates important elements of a media message. For example, street noise sets an authentic tone for on-the-scene news reports as well as urban scenes in movies. Sound effects are critical to sci-fi and action movies in particular.

Dialogue is part of the audio code, and an element to note when analyzing a message is who is doing the speaking. Generally, women have fewer speaking parts than men, studies show. For example, male characters spoke two times as often as female characters (28.4 percent compared to 15.4 percent) in the top 2015 box office movies (Geena Davis Institute on Gender in Media, 2015).

Lend Me Your Ears

Credit: Ryan Lewis

Television dramas would be hollow without music to cue our emotions. Researchers Karen Collins of the University of Waterloo and Bill Kapralos of the University of Ontario Institute of Technology emphasize the importance of sound to media messages:

> Done well, sound can help to communicate important information to an audience, serve as a symbol or leitmotif, help to situate the audience in a specific location in time or place, create or strengthen a brand's attributes, and create a sense of realism. (Done poorly, sound can have the opposite effect.) In particular, sound plays a role by helping to immerse the audience in media, to stimulate emotional investment, anthropomorphize objects and create attachments.
>
> (2018, para 1)

By the way, the word "leitmotif" used in the previous quote means a recurring phrase of music associated with a character, situation or idea. An example would be the two-note theme of the approaching shark attack in the movie *Jaws*.

> To appreciate the power of those two notes, listen to this redub of the classic scene in *Jaws* with comically alternate music: https://bit.ly/2ScXtkY. Collins and Kapralos also suggest watching this clip of the final scene from *Star Wars: A New Hope* without the soaring score from award-winning composer John Williams. It is awkwardly quiet. Go to: http://bit.ly/1XNr8AE.

Composition **Composition** describes the assemblage of various "ingredients" of a message; it's the way the whole is made up of various parts. Questions to consider when analyzing the composition of a message include:

- Who is relating to whom?
- Where are the key subjects placed?
- Who or what is in the background?
- Who or what is prominent?
- Who or what is isolated?
- How are items in the image juxtaposed for a certain effect?

- What items have been appropriated, meaning that they have significance due to a prior association or cultural history (such as the use of a Native American headdress)?

The British website called Magforum.com is a handy site from which to sample a wide range of magazine types. Pick a few aimed at specific demographics and consider the text, images and composition of the cover.

An example of composition creating a real problem for a company is a magazine ad for the Intel computer processor (Modine, 2007). In the ad, a satisfied-looking white man stands with his arms folded. He's wearing casual business attire and is in an office setting. He is flanked on either side by six African-American men in sprinter's gear, crouching as if ready to take off from the starting blocks. The text reads: "Multiply computing performance and maximize the power of your employees." Soon after its release, consumers balked at the message of the culturally-insensitive imagery, including the dominance of the business man and the submissive position of the others. Intel apologized for being "insensitive and insulting" and pulled the ad.

Camera Work Camera shots and camera movement are used to direct our attention to specific elements in a scene, and to draw us into a film or show. Camera shots of particular note that are used in both still and video camera work include:

- **Point-of-view shots** to show the action from a particular character's vantage point
- **High-angle shots** that serve to make the subject (animate or inanimate) seem small and inconsequential or vulnerable
- **Low-angle shots** that make a subject (animate or inanimate) seem intimidating, foreboding and/or powerful

Editing Editing is about preparing raw material for publication through any number of processes: arranging, revising, condensing, selecting, modifying and correcting. Editing can occur with words on a page or screen, still photos or video and sound. The Best Film Editing awards at the Oscars are studies in how abrupt or nuanced edits contribute to the entirety of a media message; the edits tell us as viewers what to linger on, what to pay attention to. Editing is highly subjective, and the purpose of the message dictates much of the editing.

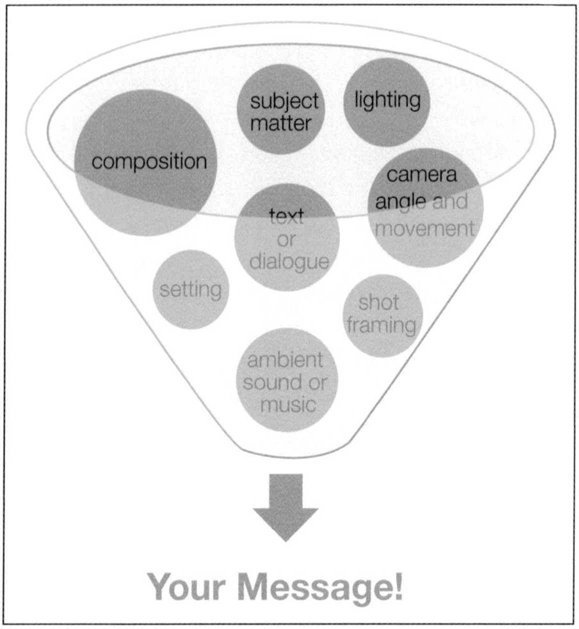

Media Message Components

Questions to ask when considering a message's editing include: What has been edited into or out of the image? How does the creator frame our view of the action or image? What elements are missing from the scene? To practice applying these questions about editing, see the Bronx Documentary Center's website (alteredimagesbdc.org) for a collection of posed and manipulated documentary photography. Select images to examine for modification and effect.

Colors and Lighting These areas of creative choice are often overlooked when done well, and glaringly evident when done poorly. For instance, if a movie scene is poorly lit and overly dark, audience members cannot discern the action and that detracts from their understanding of the message. Lighting is used for dramatic effect. It's also used to direct your attention to something or away from something else (think spotlights, fake sunlight and moonlight, silhouettes). Natural lighting conveys normality and the everyday. Notice how live music concerts utilize lighting to create atmosphere.

Colors are used to get your attention and suggest a mood. Notice the colors used in movie title graphics; they cue us as to the genre or style of the film.

Marketers talk about "exciting red" and "sincere blue." Green is seen as competent and purple as sophisticated. With the advent of prenatal testing, the already color-coded dressing of girls in pink and boys in blue that was earlier decided by clothing manufacturers and retailers was simply strengthened (Maglaty, 2011). Those gendered colors remain strong in advertising for infant and children's clothing, furniture and toys. For a startling depiction of just how gendered advertisements are, go to www.genderremixer.com/lego/ and have a try at mashing-up gendered ads. Note especially the use of colors, voice overs and sound effects that immediately cue a gendered message for these children's toys.

Signs and Symbols A third key concept of media literacy is that different people experience the same media message differently. This is particularly evident in the symbols and signs of a message, which are so culturally dependent.

Semiotics is the study of symbols and meanings. Semiotics can aid in our understanding of media texts. Different cultures assign different meanings to objects. We *ascribe*, or attribute, meaning to objects because of their societal significance.

Semiotics are dependent on cultural interpretations. For instance, a cowboy hat on a Hollywood movie poster is a cue for a Western movie with all the trappings—horses, guns, masculinity, danger. A marigold is linked to the Mexican cultural remembrance of the dead in the rich visual art of *Dia de Muertos*; hence, it is on Disney·Pixar's marketing for *Coco*. A rainbow flag is the symbol of LGBTQ pride. A rose is never just a rose, as far as I can tell, signifying as it does romance or passion in so many cultures.

If you're interested in more on semiotics, here's a link to a short instructional video about semiotics on James Hayes' Film in the Making website. This snippet briefly examines two major film releases, *Eyes Wide Shut* and *Aliens*: http://bit.ly/2YghMCl.

PROPAGANDA

Propaganda is strategic communication intended to manipulate thinking and influence a large group of people through emotional, ideological and psychological appeals. There are numerous propaganda techniques. Propaganda can be positive, as in public service announcements to discourage texting and driving, or negative, as in character attacks on a political opponent.

Part of message analysis is the ability to recognize propaganda techniques. Some of the common approaches include:

- **Oversimplification:** Reducing a complex idea or topic to a rudimentary explanation so as to distort or misrepresent it. An example is that the reason that more school children are scoring poorly in assessment tests is because there are more working mothers now.
- **Euphemisms:** A kinder, gentler word for a harsher, crueler reality. For example, "collateral damage" instead of civilian deaths during armed conflicts.
- **Bandwagon:** Everyone else is doing it, so you should too. As in, "Pepsi is the choice of a generation."
- **Transfer:** To try to carry over the prestige and respect people feel for one thing to something else, such as when political candidates pose with their countries' flag to transfer feelings of patriotism to him- or herself.
- **Emotional appeal:** Emotion-packed images, words and scenes to evoke a feeling that is connected with a person, product or experience. For example, a scene of a ridiculously happy family running on a pristine sandy beach that is oddly vacant of other people; this kind of fun only happens in Michigan!
- **Fear:** The disaster that will result if we don't follow the suggested course of action. Such as a weeping couple in front of their burned-down house, followed by the pitch that tears wouldn't be needed if they only had homeowners' insurance.
- **Plain folks:** Appealing to people as if one is just like them. Presidential candidates love to do this, posing as down-to-earth folks who always wear jeans and eat at coffee shops, like the regulars.
- **Testimonial:** An often-famous person endorses or supports a product or idea; they may or may not have any credible standing to do so. Examples include athletes on cereal boxes and movie stars campaigning for political candidates.
- **Assertion:** Stating a debatable idea as a fact, such as "female citizens don't trust the governing body because women aren't equally represented in it."

- **Glittering generalities:** Vague, positive-sounding words and phrases that don't say anything specific. Such as, "This is a hopeful time in our country."
- **False choice:** Reducing a complex situation to but a few solutions, with one being the clear winner. For example, "the only choice for our city going forward is to vote for the water tax."

Propaganda techniques are so common as to be unnoticed. It takes knowledge of the types of propaganda as well as practice in identifying propaganda. Select some common advertisements popping up on your social media or playing during time-outs in whatever sports you're watching on TV. Or, select a campaign commercial at livingroomcandidate.org (these are by U.S. presidential candidates from 1952 to 2016). Identify the influencing techniques used from the list.

As you become more familiar with the tools of analysis, you will find you are able to critically note specific elements of a message construction while also enjoying the creativity in the production. It is possible, and desirable, to hold both simultaneously in your everyday engagement with media.

CHAPTER REVIEW

- Explain how media construct reality.
- Differentiate between manifest and latent readings of a text.
- Identify the codes and conventions in a media message.
- Describe how gaze functions in advertising.
- Evaluate the effect of one of the following elements in a message: camera work, composition, colors and lighting, editing.
- Identify the use of various propaganda techniques in a political campaign.

ACTIVITIES

1. Go to the British-based Imperial War Museum's website that features collections of photos, art and videos, among other artifacts. Pair up with someone and ask some questions about any of these images: What's important

about the information? What's relevant? What opinions and viewpoints are embedded in the message? What is the style and tone of the message? Whose viewpoint is showcased? Who is the intended audience?

2. Visit MediaWatch.com and click on "Gallery" in the upper navigation bar. There is a gallery for "Odious Images" and one for "Inspirational Images." Spend time with both, and use the skills learned in this chapter to analyze the messages. Write a brief analysis on what is noteworthy about the images in the Inspirational gallery, and whether or not you agree all should be there. Explain your answer.

3. Go to the U.S. Library of Congress and search the massive archive of images *from around the world* at www.loc.gov/pictures. Demonstrate your understanding of signs and symbols by creating a short tutorial on semiotics using one of the posters. You may create a short video or a slideshow. Post it to YouTube.

4. Watch a popular artist's music video. Analyze both the lyrics and the video itself, noting the many creative and technical choices made. Consider the composition in particular, and how the video's meaning would change if the male and female characters in the video changed roles, or if different races or ethnicities were used. Also, consider any social messages that inform the context of the video.

   Write your responses to these questions:

   a. Does the video present the beliefs of one particular group?

   b. Describe the representations of men and women in the video. Are any stereotypes used? If so, to what effect?

   c. Who is in a position of power? Who is not? Who benefits as a result?

   d. Does the video exclude any groups of people or their beliefs?

   e. What definitions of happiness, success, or morality are implied?

   This activity is from Media Information Literacy for Teachers (2019), a project of the United Nations Alliance of Civilizations and the United Nations Educational, Scientific and Cultural Organization. See http://bit.ly/2JQqg0b.

5. Watch any TV show for ten minutes *without* sound and write down what you notice. Then, only *listen* to the show and don't watch it, and note

your observations by comparing and contrasting visual and audio messaging techniques (Collins & Kapralos, 2018).

6. Analyze an advertisement using the skills learned in this chapter. It may be helpful to review examples of the analyzation process and things to consider. Frank Baker's Deconstructing a TV Commercial (2009) on the Media Literacy Clearinghouse is an excellent guide. See http://bit.ly/2upBkqe. Another helpful site is The LAMPlatoon, which features broadcast ads and analyses. See http://lamplatoon.thelamp.org.

REFERENCES

Baker, F. (2009). *Deconstructing a TV commercial.* Media Literacy Clearinghouse. Retrieved from http://bit.ly/2XSdjJC

Center for Media Literacy. (2019). *Five key questions form foundation for media inquiry.* Center for Media Literacy. Retrieved from www.medialit.org

Cohen, A. (2017, September 18). Not safe for work. *The Nation.* Retrieved from http://bit.ly/2M47X7b

Collins, K., & Kapralos, B. (2018). Sound design for media: Introducing students to sound. *Journal of Sonic Studies, 6.* Retrieved from http://bit.ly/2Ti0HGl

Erigha, M. (2019). *The Hollywood Jim Crow: The racial politics of the movie industry.* New York, NY: NYU Press.

Geena Davis Institute on Gender in Media. (2015). *The reel truth: Women aren't seen or heard.* Retrieved from https://seejane.org/research-informs-empowers/data/

Hall, C., & Tyler, M. (2018, February 20). "I'm rooting for everybody black": Black people on Black Panther. *Elle.* Retrieved from http://bit.ly/2Gi72we

Maglaty, J. (2011). When did girls start wearing pink? *Smithsonian Magazine.* Retrieved from http://bit.ly/2JTE7PZ

Modine, A. (2007, August 2). Intel revolted by its own 'insensitive and insulting' ad. *The Register.* Retrieved from http://bit.ly/2Ocywtc

Mulvey, L. (1999). Visual pleasure and narrative cinema. In L. Braudy & M. Cohen (Eds.), *Film theory and criticism: Introductory readings* (pp. 833–844). New York, NY: Oxford University Press.

5 Creating

How to Create Messages with Purpose, Expression and Ethics

LEARNING OBJECTIVES

Terms: 360-degree media literacy, positionality, media appropriation, fair use, copyright law, SEO.

- Appreciate how creating content informs your consumption of content.
- Apply each of the five media literacy concepts to content creation.
- Recognize that identity formation is facilitated by and through new media.
- Explain how speaker, author and content affects context.
- Know basics of copyright law and fair use.
- Understand techniques to attract an online audience.

We create for an audience, even if it's an audience of one—a best friend or partner or parent. Researchers have looked at the qualities of the most-shared social media posts, and there are similarities in their findings. For example, positive news is popular. So are lists; 10-item lists in particular. So, in that spirit, here is my list.

HOW TO CREATE MEMORABLE SOCIAL MEDIA POSTS

1. Share your best stuff on a Tuesday to get the most shares (Kagan, 2017).
2. Use images to draw attention to your posts.
3. Add color to key words.
4. Add a video or meme to your text.
5. Add filters to your images.

Talk with a peer about your approach to creating content. What do you most often post about and why? Who is your real or imagined audience? How does your content change based on audience? What standards do you have when creating content?

6. Animate your text.
7. Write a great headline ("How to" and "What is" are good starts).
8. Be amusing or awe-inspiring.
9. Share credible material.
10. Make lists of 10.

Users of media are also creators of media. Creating messages in the digital age offers constantly changing options to share your personality and ideas. The list of tips is a hat-tip to the formulaic ways that social media messages are created to gain attention and develop an audience. Want to be an #influencer? Then those tips are made for *you*.

In this chapter, you have the opportunity to challenge yourself by applying media literacy's critical thinking to what *you* create. You'll learn to consider decisions about design, style and ownership, about interpretation and perspective and about purpose. Acquiring media literacy skills means you are able to think critically about and evaluate more fully the media you make or modify. This chapter is about the exciting possibilities and the everyday ethics of creating your own media messages.

MEDIA LITERACY AND CONTENT CREATION

My term, **360-degree media literacy**, references the intentional consumption *and* creation of digital content, as the first informs the second, and vice versa, resulting in a holistic set of skills, knowledge and understanding of media messages.

Across the world, people are making digital content daily. In China, for example, more than 89 million people have written their own blog (Wee, 2009). Worldwide, nearly two-thirds of internet users ages 16 to 24 had recently uploaded or shared a video online (Global Web Index, 2017) and in the United States well over half of teenagers ages 12 to 17 make their own content to post online (Lenhart, Madden, Smith, & MacGill, 2007).

Creating content allows users to understand the decisions made in producing the material they in turn *consume* online. Content creation begets consumer knowledge; by navigating maker spaces, we better know the choices made and motivations for those choices when acting as consumers of media.

From remixing music to creating videos to sharing analog artwork online to posting blogs and creating webpages, users worldwide are creating and publishing daily. Even the simple act of constructing your social media profile is an act of digital creation: Curating the images you select. Uploading your personal quote. Fashioning your bio tag and listing your likes and dislikes. Inherent in the process are choices about presentation, tone and style. Your profile is a carefully curated message featuring you.

The term "media user" melds together those who create media and those who consume media, as if both were done equally by all. Many digital media users would likely not characterize themselves as media creators. They pop online to update social media to their friends; that's not being a *media producer*. Or is it?

Mizuko Ito (2007), a cultural anthropologist of technology use at the University of California-Irvine, described what many of you likely do daily, and it sounds downright revolutionary. She speaks of "the undisciplined practices of teenage music sharing, game hacking, and personal journal blogs" and what they signal:

> These emergent digital culture forms signal the active participation of previously marginal and invisible groups in what we must now recognize as cultural production, not simply as derivative acts of active consumption or ephemeral personal communication. What does it mean when those previously constructed as "consumers"—non-generative, passive audiences for professionally produced culture—are handed the means not only to distribute media through alternative peer-to-peer networks, but to remix, repackage, revalue, and produce media through amateur cultural production?
>
> (p. 89)

Navigation and Sharing as Authorship "What will the author look like in the future?" wondered Northwestern University professor Nicholas Diakopoulos (2005, p. 10). One reality, he noted, is that increasingly the reader of messages will gain creative power due to the impermanence

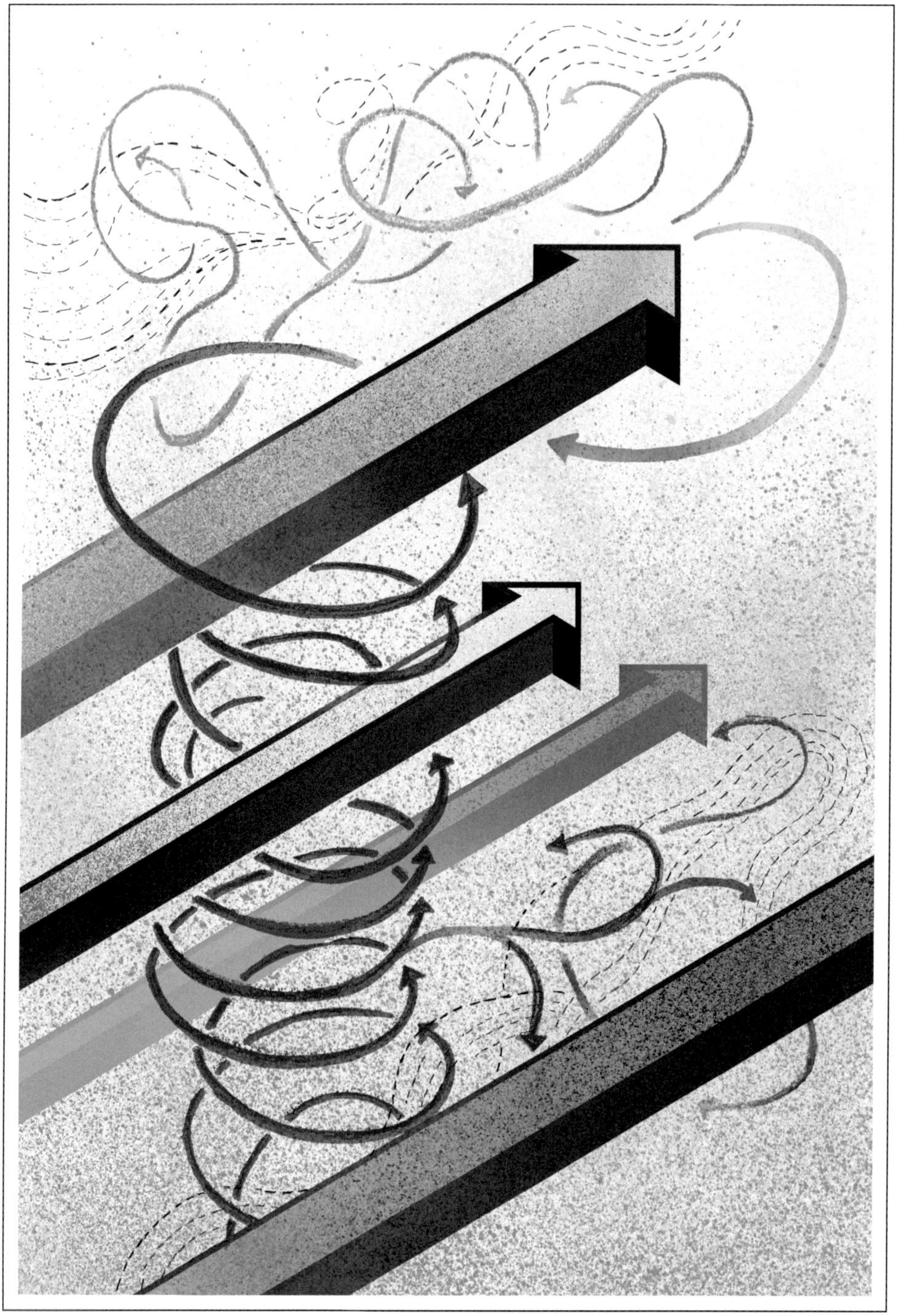

Navigation as Authorship

Credit: Ryan Lewis

of digital media. Something as simple as whether the reader of an article chooses to click on some hyperlinks and consume the material, and in turn follow *those* links, is a form of authorship via navigation.

"Interactivity allows the reader of a hypertext to choose a path through the network of interconnected media elements," Diakopoulos wrote, "thus generating a personalized work simply through the trajectory of links chosen" (p. 5). So even if you are not actively blogging or posting video to YouTube, in these digital times, you, too, are a creator.

As Henry Jenkins, Sam Ford and Joshua Green note in their book *Spreadable Media: Creating Value and Meaning in a Networked Culture* (2013), the contemporary media environment affords many modes of creation, if one is willing to understand the word "media" in an expansive way:

> We all now play a vital role in the sharing of media texts. The everyday, often mundane decisions each of us makes about what to pass along, who to share it with, and the context under which we share that material is fundamentally altering the processes of how media is circulated. In some cases, participants are remixing this content as it spreads; in others, they are recontextualizing. But in every case, these participants are expanding the potential meaning the content had and, in some cases, enhancing its value.
>
> (p. 304)

APPLYING MEDIA LITERACY TO YOUR CONTENT

In the following section, I apply the Center for Media Literacy's five media literacy questions (2019) to the content that you create, since media literate consumers will assess your work using this type of criteria.

Why Should *I* Create This Message? Author identity matters when making media; it speaks to the purpose and credibility of the message. Obviously, lived experience often makes you the best person to author a message. Additionally, you are also the legitimate spokesperson to represent your work products, or to build cohesion with your professional, school or social groups through information sharing. If you're an expert at something that is the focus of your message, then that's another good reason for you to be an author. Offering your unique perspective on a trending topic because of your demographics or background are also compelling reasons.

The content you post says something about you—your own personal "brand" and the things you value.

Here's an example of the relevance of author identity: When it comes to the media literacy question of authorship, Naif Al-Mutawa, the author of a comic book series called *The 99*, has credibility on many fronts. As a Kuwaiti clinical psychologist with an MBA who is also a Muslim, Al-Mutawa is uniquely positioned to create this comic about superheroes inspired by Islam. The characters fight stereotypes and combat extremism. The series features superheroes with the 99 attributes of God.

> We live in a world in which the most culturally innocuous symbols, like the falafel, can be misunderstood because of baggage, and where religion can be twisted and purposefully made what it's not supposed to be by others. In a world like that, they'll always be a job for Superman—and *The 99*.
>
> (At 17:08 of Al-Mutawa's TED Talk, "Superheroes inspired by Islam")

The 99 comic books are in at least eight languages. A licensed theme park based on the series opened in Kuwait. Al-Mutawa said he hopes that by linking "enough positive things to the Koran," that he can help move people away from harmful stereotypes of Muslims as terrorists (15:48 of TED Talk, "Superheroes inspired by Islam").

What Creative Techniques Am I Using? The medium selected to deliver the message is a key first choice in creative language. Digital media in particular abounds with possibilities for creative communication. If you spend a lot of time on a particular social media platform, it's worth taking time to learn about the different tools each site offers. Check out the platform's tips and support page for current tutorials on everything from new filters to fresh categories.

When we have a clear idea of *what* we want to communicate, we can select the best medium to do that. The graphic offers a brief synopsis of the

	Text	Video	Still Photos	Audio	Graphics
Effective	• For complex explanations, efficiency, conciseness.	• Showcase action, dialogue, debate and "aha" moments.	• Chronicle and capture moments and events, to demonstrate.	• Convey a mood and tone, put the listener in a place.	• Data and numbers, to portray change, make comparisons, add energy.
Suggested Uses	• How-to posts, checklists, quizzes, surveys, case studies, reviews, best practices, expert Q-and-A.	• GIFS, to give instructions or demonstrate, interviews, bloopers.	• Slideshows with music, with captions to narrate an event, as memes.	• Musical or live performances, speeches, interviews, dialogues, ambient sounds.	• Timelines, infographics, process charts, explainers, animated motion.

Let Your Content Be Your Guide

communicative power of five different media and the types of content they serve best. As creators, we also begin to develop a sense of where to post different content, and which platforms best suit our purposes.

Once you have decided what you want to say, and the medium through which you are going to say it, then other creative factors come into play, depending on the medium. For example:

- A Twitter post may require more wordsmithing and a strong image to get your point across.
- A Snapchat or Instagram story makes it easy to share experiences among friends.
- LinkedIn is geared toward career networking, so a professional photo and a detailed bio (up to 2,000 characters) are essentials.
- Personal blogs are often the best vehicles to share your opinions, anecdotes, tips and personality.
- YouTube showcases your particular talent or interest, and don't forget to cross-post your work.
- SoundCloud is just one among several music and podcast streaming platforms for aspiring musicians or storytellers.

Sometimes, the culture we are creating for has a strong say in how we shape a message. Educator and philosopher Marshall McLuhan noted the cultural bias in the United States to text and type. This cultural bias disregards "the ear man and the tactile man," McLuhan noted (1964, p. 8). In other places, a tradition of oral storytelling may dictate that an audio story is the way to tell a tale.

How Might Other People Understand This Message Differently from Me? Another way to think about this media literacy question is to ask, "Who is the audience for the message, and how might they interpret my meaning differently than I intend?"

Often, a message's meaning changes depending on the intended recipients. Our individual knowledge of the world is dependent in part on our lifestyle and values, and those shape our messaging. So too, our audience has different lifestyles and values that will shape their understanding of our messages. Don't assume others read life like you do. Others will interpret events and ideas differently than you will because of who *they* are. Consider closely the perspective of others unlike yourself when you are creating content of a sensitive nature.

Consider closely the perspective of others unlike yourself when you are creating content of a sensitive nature.

Creators often misstep in this area of media literacy. We are so sure that what we think is funny is humorous to everyone else. Or that others will see the inanity of that politician! Or agree with our opinion because, well, we're *right*. In fact, fully 84 percent of social media users in a 2016 Pew poll felt that the statement, "People say things when discussing politics on social media that they would never say in person" describes social media behavior well or very well (Duggan & Smith, 2016). Whatever you create, consider audience, timing and platform before you post.

Be aware of unintended audiences as well as the diversity of your potential audience. Consider possible interpretations by others unlike yourself. Avoid assuming everyone is like you are or can obviously tell "where you're coming from." If you're concerned about something you've authored, ask a few people to look it over and get their input and reactions before going public with your work.

Justine Sacco, a communications executive for a company called IAC, thought her Twitter followers would obviously know she was kidding when she posted just before launching on a long flight to South Africa: "Going to Africa. Hope I don't get AIDS. Just kidding. I'm white!" While she was onboard the long flight, the post went viral, causing a trend of anger-filled posts using #HasJustineLandedYet. People did not understand the message as Sacco intended. She lost her job. She told author Jon Ronson that she never thought anyone would take her sarcasm literally, and that she was making fun of the bubble that living in America can give one when it comes to conditions in the developing world (Ronson, 2015).

What Lifestyles, Values and Points of View Are Represented In or Omitted from This Message? You create content that is unique to you. Your content often comes from your personal history—your culture, ethnicity or race, sexual identity and orientation, generation, income level, education, religion or spirituality, political leanings and family background.

At the heart of this key concept is positionality. **Positionality** in social science terms describes how your identity influences your understanding of the world. Positionality references the social and political conditions that have in part created your identity with reference to issues of race, class, gender, sexuality and ability. "Positionality also describes how your identity influences, and potentially biases, your understanding of and outlook on the world" (Dictionary.com, 2019).

Positionality necessarily shapes our knowledge of the world. "We come to know the world more fully by knowing how we know the world," states author and educator David Takacs (2003, p. 29).

Another example of positionality is the work of then-15-year-old Rayouf Alhumedhi, a teenager who worked with key partners to submit a proposal for a hijab emoji to Unicode, the keeper of global emojis. The "person with a headscarf" emoji was approved in 2017. The Hijab Emoji Project website (2016) describes how it came about:

> When Rayouf Alhumedhi, 15 at the time, was creating a new WhatsApp group chat with her friends last year, the group wanted to make the title of the group a series of emojis: one to represent each girl. But Rayouf

> had a problem—none of the emojis really looked like her, because she's a Muslim, she wears a hijab. Given the millions of women in the world who wear a headscarf every day, this seemed like a gross oversight. So she set out on a mission to fix that.

In other words, who we are influences our knowledge of the world and how we move through it. Being within a culture, or being of a specific ethnicity, or being of a particular sexual orientation, or geography, or family unit—each of these realities defines the boundaries of our perspectives. "When we develop the skill of understanding how we know what we know, we acquire a key to lifelong learning," Takacs said (2003, p. 28).

VOX DISCIPULI

On all platforms except for Instagram, I share mostly text. I'm a reader and a writer, so text is definitely the medium that I'm most comfortable with. On Instagram, I post all photos, since that's what the app is focused on, for my friends or followers. I post things about my travels, my achievements, and fun adventures with my friends. Usually my caption is something punny or some kind of play on words. On my professional Twitter I post text and photos from news events for the public, on my private account I mostly share posts by others. On something like Reddit or Tumblr, my posts aren't necessarily private, but these are definitely spaces where your public persona takes a major backseat. Many people on Reddit maintain anonymity because they are on the app seeking help and assistance with everything from weight loss, social anxiety or coming out. Tumblr is big on fandom culture, where groups of people gather around shared interests such as particular movies or books. It's more about establishing yourself within these communities rather than sharing a lot of information about yourself. —Zoe, 20

Why Am I Sending This Message? Go back to basics: What is your goal or purpose in posting? Why does this message need to be sent? To inform? Persuade? Entertain? Interact? Express? As we learned in Chapter 1, these are the five purposes of communication.

In short, know *why* you are about to publish something. Content that is entertaining, relevant, helpful—these characteristics are always welcome online. Knowing why you are creating a message helps you to craft it wisely and with the greatest impact, because message purpose influences tone, style, audience and interactivity.

A study (Brandtzæg & Heim, 2009) of 1,200 social networking site users in Norway found that the top reasons for participation were to get in contact with new people (31 percent), to keep in touch with friends (21 percent) and general socializing (14 percent). In another study, Nardi and colleagues (2004) found that people blog to chronicle their lives, express their opinions, as a cathartic outlet for emotions, as a testing place for ideas and as a community forum.

CONTEXT AND AUTHORSHIP

Context influences the meaning of a message. As we learned in Chapter 4 on Analyzing, context refers to the circumstances and conditions—both internal and external—of a media message. Many factors are important in context: Who is speaking to whom about what? What's the timing of the message? Through what medium? On what digital or analog platform?

Part of context is understanding that your identity as a creator influences the way you craft your message and the way it is understood by any given audience. **Speaker + Content + Audience = Context** is a valuable equation to describe how meaning is made. It is a reminder that who is talking, and about what, and to whom, influences how that content is understood. The sum total of those ingredients gives us the context to understand the whole of the message.

To better grasp this concept, find a political speech online and play around with the elements of speaker, content and audience to change the context, and hence the meaning, of a message.

Context Collapse Social media platforms tend to "flatten" audiences into one generalized group, a phenomenon called "context collapse" (Marwick & boyd, 2010, p. 123). **Context collapse** references the smashing of diverse audiences into one massive social media audience that is not at all homogenous, and for which different voice, language, norms and assumptions are essential for nuanced and effective communication.

The audiences for our various social media accounts are different, right? Often they represent an awkward conglomeration of acquaintances and intimate friends, family members and co-workers. In face-to-face communication, we constantly adjust our dialogue to a listener's reactions and responses; our presentation of ourselves is collaborative. That's difficult to do online, as we must navigate "imagined audiences" (Marwick & boyd, p. 114).

"Social media collapse diverse social contexts into one, making it difficult for people to engage in the complex negotiations needed to vary identity presentation, manage impressions, and save face," wrote Marwick and boyd (p. 123).

For example, they note that on the social media platform of Twitter, "the tension between revealing and concealing usually errs on the side of concealing on Twitter, but even users who do not post anything scandalous must formulate tweets and choose discussion topics based on imagined audience judgment" (p. 124). From personal experience, I would agree with that observation. Unless you choose to protect your tweets and only make them visible to your followers, all tweets are public. It's impossible to predict audience reaction to a potentiality of hundreds of people or more.

Offending Online What happens when we do post something scandalous and then decide we need to apologize? Or, when we *unintentionally* offend online followers, in particular those who are in-real-life (IRL) friends? First, it's a good habit to pause before sending to review your post: Double-check for correct spellings, typos, accurate names, titles, dates, facts and double-meanings of words or unintended implications.

If you do post material that is offensive or taken as such, unfortunately, social media is pretty unforgiving. It has a ridiculously long memory. Even if you delete a comment or tweet, screen grabs can capture it before it's gone, and bots also save posts. Erasing a post might help you forget it, but it won't mean it is forgotten from archives.

So, some things to consider if you do publish something stupid and step in it:

- Don't make it worse with snarky replies.
- Don't reply to every snarky reaction you receive.

- If your message has an error or offends when you didn't intend it to, pause and think about your response before acting. You don't want to compound the problem with an equally bad response.
- Talk about it with others who may have also been offended by your message to better understand others' viewpoints. Acknowledge your effort in your response.
- If you choose to apologize, apologize fully, with "I am sorry that I did this." Resist the urge to offer excuses. No fauxpology or non-apology apology, as in, "I'm sorry if you felt offended." Politicians and public relations firms especially use these. Own your error, and move on, hopefully wiser.

Not surprisingly, there is an entire blog site dedicated to evaluating the fine art of apologies, including those involving social media. See Social Media Apologies at www.sorrywatch.com/ for examples.

APPROPRIATION AND AUTHORSHIP

Creative production in digital spaces often includes repurposing and reusing material from others, and the subsequent sharing of that reworked material. Digital media offers the opportunity to share, reframe and reuse material.

Media appropriation references the taking, copying or altering of existing work for one's own creative process. Digital media has brought appropriation to a whole new level of fluidity: The promulgation of open source materials, Creative Commons, software development kits, wiki-type collaborations with multiple authors—these "are all examples of a liquid modern interpretation of originality" (Deuze, 2006, p. 70). Effective media appropriation recasts the context of the original content so it's given new meaning. Remixing is all about taking original material (yours or someone else's) and changing it to make something new.

Effective media appropriation recasts the context of the original content so it's given new meaning.

"The best examples of this kind of creative work are often marked by a reframing of the original narrative, and so produce a fresh perspective on both the source material and the context in which it first existed," wrote Ben Murray, a former BBC digital editor and current digital art director. "The news report, the cult TV show, the summer blockbuster, the chart hit or iconic photograph—all are open to endless reinterpretation by anyone with the right software" (2015).

Copyright Law However, when we create using others' works, we run the risk of copyright infringement in most countries, including the United States, where so much commercial media content originates. **U.S. copyright law** protects unauthorized use of an authored work, either published or unpublished. Creative works, whether those works be video games, news articles, movies or recorded music, are protected under copyright law.

So, you cannot republish, reproduce or redistribute copyrighted work without the author/owner's permission. The chief exception to copyright infringement is what is called "fair use." **Fair use** allows small excerpts of a work to be used without permission from the original creator or copyright owner. U.S. copyright law typically allows brief excerpts of copyright material to be quoted verbatim for purposes such as *criticism, news reporting, teaching* and *research.* So, for instance, you could quote excerpts from movie dialogue for purposes of a movie review, or use quotes from a lawmaker's speech in a news story.

If you are dealing with works produced in foreign countries, or if you're not in the United States, most countries have their own versions of copyright laws. Also, most countries have entered into agreements for use of foreign works under international copyright treaties and conventions. Before reusing another person's work, always check the law depending on where you are and where the works you want to use originated.

FAIR USE

What if you are creating your own song, and want to use a beat from a popular rap song in a few measures? Fair use is often a defense against copyright infringement. Four factors are used by U.S. courts to decide if you infringed on the original copyrighted work (Stim, 2019):

- The **purpose and character** of the use. (Does it fall into one of the specific situations noted earlier—*criticism, news reporting, teaching* and *research*? If so, you're probably on solid ground. But if it's not fair use, then simply giving the original author credit doesn't protect you from a lawsuit.)
- The **nature** of the copyrighted work. (Is it a Grammy-winning hit this year or an obscure and older work? Material created before 1963 may be in the public domain.)
- The **amount** of the original work that is used, and how essential it is to the original. (There is no set limit of what is allowed; it depends on how large the original work is. Also a factor is whether you took the essence of the work, such as a distinctive bass guitar line.)
- The **effect** of the use on the market or value of the original. (Oftentimes, infringement isn't discovered until the secondary work starts to attract attention and the prospect that market value or profits are being diverted becomes an issue.)

In short, you can certainly draw inspiration from copyrighted works. You can use limited portions of copyrighted works in your own media under the fair use doctrine. But your focus should be on making your work original and unique. There is no international fair use law, but the concept of fair use has influenced copyright law in other countries, including South Korea and Canada.

Transformative In 1994, the U.S. Supreme Court made an important decision that involved, of all fun things, the rap group 2 Live Crew and singer-songwriter Roy Orbison.

The court unanimously ruled as fair use 2 Live Crew's use of the opening line of Orbison's song "Pretty Woman." (Take a quick listen to both songs to see what you think!) 2 Live Crew's song was a parody that depended on the "the original's first line of lyrics and characteristic opening bass riff" to establish it as parody, stated Justice David Souter, writing for the court (Campbell v. Acuff Rose, 1994, e.). The rap group didn't use any other part of the "Pretty Woman" lyrics or music. Souter wrote that:

> The enquiry focuses on whether the new work merely supersedes the objects of the original creation, or whether and to what extent it is "transformative," altering the original with new expression, meaning, or mes-

> sage. The more transformative the new work, the less will be the significance of other factors, like commercialism, that may weigh against a finding of fair use.
>
> (b)

This is not an unambiguous area. In fact, copyright was intended to preserve free speech, not detract from the open exchange of ideas and innovations. Edward T. Wang wrote (2011) about how the vagueness of copyright law may in fact further free speech interests:

> As the Supreme Court put it: "the Framers intended copyright itself to be the engine of free expression. By establishing a marketable right to the use of one's expression, copyright supplies the economic incentive to create and disseminate ideas." Copyright is therefore, at its theoretical core, largely compatible with the First Amendment's protection of free speech: copyright ensures that there is speech being created for the First Amendment to protect.
>
> (p. 1472)

Courts ultimately rule on copyright infringement, and the fair use categories are subject to interpretation by judges. Copyright protection extends longer and longer, and permissions for use of copyrighted material are pricey and sometimes impossible to acquire. It's important to keep actively using material within fair use parameters instead of succumbing to the chilling effect of better-safe-than-sorry non-use.

Fair use supports the concept of free speech. To help you remember the high points of copyright law and fair use, take a listen to these energetic music videos: copyright (http://bit.ly/2TzngEF) and fair use (http://bit.ly/2Tu-7iMf). They are compliments of Michael RobbGrieco and colleagues at the Media Education Lab at Temple University.

Fair use supports the concept of free speech.

Creative Commons Creative Commons is a U.S.-based non-profit that has affiliates around the world. The heart of the Creative Commons mission is that ideas and innovations happen through collaboration and sharing, so the organization has developed a variety of free copyright licenses that anyone can use to share their work with stated conditions, such as attribution. The Creative Commons' vision "is nothing less than realizing the full potential of the Internet—universal access to research and education, full participation in culture—to drive a new era of development, growth, and productivity" (2019).

There are currently more than 1 billion Creative Commons (CC) licensed works. For people like you and me, it allows us to legally use CC-copyrighted work easily as long as we follow the conditions, and for us to permit others to legally use our work through remix, repurpose and reuse. Look for the CC icon with a circle around it to signify a Creative Commons license.

MEDIA LITERACY SELFIE

So if Creative Commons is so great, what am I doing writing a for-profit book through a publisher? Interesting question. This is a commercial textbook, written for the publisher based on a contract that gives me an unpretentious percentage of every book sold. The reason an author elects to publish with a major publishing house is because of marketing and reach. It's hard to get noticed in the wilderness of the internet.

If a tree falls in the forest and no one is around to hear it, did it really fall? If an author writes a book in a fairly obscure Midwestern city and no one is around to notice, will anyone read the book? Media involves author *and* audience, and I'm an author in search of an audience.

By signing a contract with a commercial publisher, I moved my work on media literacy from the classroom and educational sphere to the marketplace. That has implications for my book's findability, usability and reach. Per my contract, I cannot reuse substantive portions of my own book without getting permission from the publisher, even though I wrote it.

ATTRACTING AN AUDIENCE

A message is only as good as the audience that finds it. So much of the focus of successful media creators is on attracting the audiences that further their goals.

Everyone is looking for a connection. Professionals are looking for networking opportunities. Family and friends are looking to share memories and moments. Retailers are looking for sales and loyalty. What do *you* want to get out of the media messages that you create? Job leads? Feedback? Social connection?

The digital age offers a virtual makerspace for message making. The process of creation is collaborative and reactionary. Whether we are conscious of it or not, we all create with an audience in mind. Videos we make, games we build, articles we write, photographs we take, presentations we construct from data and music we remix or make: All of these forms are made for the message to be consumed by others. We believe we will be watched and listened to, noticed.

We seek input and reactions from others and we respond accordingly. Done well, creating messages and sharing them on the right platforms will get reactions. Audience reactions can create a useful feedback loop that contributes to your creativity and helps you hone your message approach.

Search Engines Getting your creative output noticed means getting it discovered in the vast digital marketplace. Tailor your messages to specific audiences via specific platforms, and make sure you are using the right digital tools to tell your story (see the previous figure "Let your content be your guide"); these both improve your chances of getting your media noticed. Packaging of your content is hugely important to getting it promoted, and that starts with **search engine optimization (SEO)**, an art unto itself. SEO means that people can easily find your work online in a search engine because it is listed high in results. By using key words in your headline and summary blurb, you help boost the odds that your content will appear high in a search results list. To practice writing SEO-friendly headlines, try rewriting news story headlines.

Honestly, many people don't read beyond the headline. This is why catchy online headlines that promise to shock/surprise/anger the reader, as in "You'll never believe the double-life this college student was leading!" get traffic. However, if you employ clickbait headlines that don't match the nature of your content, you will eventually lose your audience. A headline head-fake won't earn you sustained traffic.

Use Social Media No matter the format you use to create your media content, use social media to market that content.

The most adept self-promotion happens on social media platforms when you have developed a social media presence separate from your promotion. That is, build a social media presence through exchange of ideas, by retweeting or sharing posts, offering interesting articles or timely observations. You won't attract new followers or keep current followers by merely touting your media products on social media. Instead, provide a link to your blog that features your photography, or to your new video on YouTube when you can tie your original content to a reason for posting. It may be an event, a news article, a response to another's post, a commemoration of a significant person or a commentary on a trending topic.

Blogger and entrepreneur Jason Calicanis says that younger media creators need to know that the power of social media is in developing an audience (Childress, 2014).

> I have young people come up to me and go, "I'm interested in breaking into this specific arena." I say: "Where's your social media presence? Show me your blog about that topic. So you really care about aviation? Where's your blog about aviation? OK, where's your Twitter handle? What is your brand? What does your personal brand mean, and how have you curated it? Let me see your LinkedIn page. Let me see your Twitter. Does your Twitter have a background that says that you're a pilot? . . . How do we know through your online presence that you're passionate about the topic you're passionate about?" . . . This is the new resume. Coming to your next company or opportunity with an audience means you're valuable. Coming without an audience, coming without the ability to amplify whatever your employer or project you're working on, that means you're going to be weak and not needed.

I don't want to end a chapter on creation with the singular concept that you're weak and not needed if you don't have an online following. Creation of media has many, many purposes, and one of them is audience development. But as we learned previously, equally prevalent and useful reasons for message creation are for self-reflection, to communicate your identity, to connect with others on current topics and as a creative outlet. Participation in political and civic issues is another significant reason for creating media.

We'll address that issue in our last chapter of the book. For now, I leave you with my personal guideposts to media creation:

- Be **authentic.**
- Focus on post **quality**, not quantity.
- **Segment audiences** by platform to allow message customization.
- **Tell a story**. Use the power of personal narrative.
- Demonstrate **respect** for other viewpoints.
- **Review** content before posting.

CHAPTER REVIEW

- Demonstrate what navigation as authorship is.
- Describe how positionality affects message creation.
- Know the factors that influence message context.
- Understand what appropriation is.
- Apply fair use to remixing a song or repurposing a poem.
- Identify various approaches to building an online audience.
- Memorize the author's media creation guideposts.

ACTIVITIES

1. Create a magazine cover that you'd like to see for your age group and sexual orientation or identity. Magazine cover makers such as Canva or Adobe Spark are available free of charge online. Think about the media literacy concepts from a makers' point of view as you design a cover that seeks to engage with a specific audience but respectfully so. How to attract attention without objectifying bodies? Share it with a group for feedback and assessment.
2. Check out "Becoming a Web Celeb" at Common Sense Media: http://bit.ly/2IEuZzu. The entire site is loaded with great content, but this one fits well with creating and the implications of feedback, both solicited and unsolicited, supportive and nasty. Another of note for the topic of

creating is called "Copy-Paste Culture" and it is available on the organization's archived site at http://digitalbytes.commonsensemedia.org; click on "Innovation" to find the module.

3. Watch this public service announcement: www.unodc.org/listenfirst/. It's from the World Drug Campaign of the United Nations Office on Drugs and Crime. Using the concept that listening to children is an investment in their drug-free future, team up with others to create a storyboard of another 50-second video on the same message. Free and downloadable storyboards are available online. Be specific about your video design and detail the message elements of content, point-of-view, camera work, lighting and other choices. Repurpose or reuse of commercial content in limited ways per fair use guidelines is encouraged.

REFERENCES

Al-Mutawa, N. (2010, July). Superheroes inspired by Islam. *TEDGlobal 2010*. Retrieved from http://bit.ly/2Y18vge

Brandtzæg, P. B., & Heim, J. (2009). Why people use social networking sites. In A. A. Ozok & P. Zaphiris (Eds.), *Online communities* (pp. 143–152). Berlin & Heidelberg, Germany: Springer-Verlag.

Campbell, aka Skyywalker, et al. v. Acuff Rose Music, Inc. Certiorari to the United States Court of Appeals for the Sixth Circuit. No. 92–1292. Argued Nov. 9, 1993. Decided March 7, 1994.

Center for Media Literacy. (2019). *Five key questions form foundation for media inquiry*. Center for Media Literacy. Retrieved from www.medialit.org

Childress, S. (2014, February 18). Jason Calicanis: You are your own media company. *Frontline*. PBS: Public Broadcasting Service.

Deuze, M. (2006). Participation, remediation, bricolage: Considering principal components of a digital culture. *The Information Society*, *22*(2), 70. doi:10.1080/01972240600567170

Diakopoulos, N. (2005). *Remix culture: Mixing up authorship* (pp. 1–11). Retrieved from www.nickdiakopoulos.com/publications

Dictionary.com. (2019). *Positionality*. Retrieved from www.dictionary.com/e/gender-sexuality/positionality/

Duggan, M., & Smith, A. (2016, October 25). The tone of social media discussions around politics. In *The political environment on social media.* Washington, D.C.: Pew Research Center: Internet and Technology.

Global Web Index. (2017). Share of internet users worldwide who uploaded or shared a video online in the last month as of 3rd quarter 2017, by age group. In: *Statista—The Statistics Portal.* Retrieved from https://blog.globalwebindex.com/chart-of-the-day/online-videos/

The Hijab Emoji Project website. (2016). Retrieved from www.hijabemoji.org/

Ito, M. (2007). Technologies of the childhood imagination: Yu-Gi-Oh! media mixes, and everyday cultural production. In J. Karaganis (Ed.), *Structures of participation in digital culture* (pp. 88–110). New York, NY: Social Science Research Council. Retrieved from http://bit.ly/2JGfEyF

Jenkins, H., Ford, S., & Green, J. (2013). *Spreadable media: Creating value and meaning in a networked culture.* New York, NY: New York University Press.

Kagan, N. (2017, November 27). How to create viral content: 10 insights from 100 million articles. *BuzzSumo.*

Lenhart, A., Madden, M. Smith, A., & MacGill, A. (2007, December 19). *Teens and Social Media.* Pew Research Center: Internet & Technology.

Marwick, A. E., & boyd, d. (2010). I tweet honestly, I tweet passionately: Twitter users, context collapse, and the imagined audience. *New Media & Society, 13*(1), 114–133. https://doi.org/10.1177/1461444810365313

McLuhan, M. (1964). The medium is the message. From: *Understanding media: The extensions of man* (pp. 1–18). Retrieved February 19, 2019, from http://bit.ly/2LTVdQm

Murray, B. (2015, March 22). Remixing culture and why the art of the mash-up matters. *TechCrunch.* Retrieved from TechCrunch.com.

Nardi, B. A., Schiano, D. J., Gumbrecht, M., & Swartz, L. (2004). Why we blog. *Communications of the ACM, 47*(12), 41–46.

Ronson, J. (2015, February 12). How one stupid tweet blew up Justine Sacco's life. *New York Times Magazine.* Retrieved from https://nyti.ms/30HDDD4

Stim, R. (2019). Fair use: The four factors courts consider in a copyright infringement case. Retrieved form NOLO.com.

Takacs, D. (2003). How does your positionality bias your epistemology? *Thought & Action: The NEA Higher Education Journal*, 27–38.

Wang, E. T. (2011). The line between copyright and the first amendment and why its vagueness may further free speech interests. *Journal of Constitutional Law, 13*(5), 1471–1498.

Wee, W. (2009, December 29). STATS: User generated content in U.S., Japan, China. *Tech in Asia*. Retrieved form Techinasia.com.

6 Spending

How the Big, Big Business of Media Affects You, and Where You Can Profit

What do the *Black Panther* comic series, a Detroit Tigers baseball game, the *Mean Girls 2* movie and a *Desperate Housewives* episode all have in common?

Each of them is brought to you by the U.S.-based Walt Disney Company. The company owns Marvel Entertainment, ESPN, the Freeform pay TV channel and ABC Studios.

Oh, and with the March 2018 purchase of 21st Century Fox for $71.3 billion, Disney now has access to the Fantastic Four and the X-Men characters. The merger buys Disney a controlling stake in the streaming service Hulu, and the thousands of 21st Century Fox movie titles to stream on Hulu . . . plus, it got the FX television network and the National Geographic Channel, another animation studio, and on it goes (VanDerWerff, 2019).

LEARNING OBJECTIVES

Terms: Conglomerate, media consolidation, oligopoly, capitalism, vertical integration, cross promotion, media convergence, hegemony, audience segmentation, algorithm, parity, active and passive audiences.

- Understand the evolution of mass media ownership and control.
- Know the arguments for and against media regulation.
- Evaluate the pros and cons of media consolidation.
- Explain various approaches to audience segmentation.
- Define advertising's role in commercial media.
- Recognize how algorithms impact daily life.

- Identify the role of diverse hires in media content.
- Differentiate between active and passive audience characteristics.

What questions do you have about media ownership? Do you think it matters who owns the media companies that you use? How do you think you as a consumer are viewed by media companies? What is your attitude toward advertisements on your social media or streaming music site?

Mega-mergers and consolidation of media companies keep happening, and overall, it's not healthy for the wee consumer. We're facing down a future of just three or four mass media giants, all based in the United States, that provide an *overwhelming* majority of the world's media content (VanDerWerff, 2019; Rapp & Jenkins, 2018).

This chapter explores the evolution of media ownership and its implications worldwide as well as in our own lives. Hang in there, as the subject matter may seem abstract, with talk of profits in the billions of dollars and updating regulations on media ownership (a snoozer, so I keep it brief), but keep your focus on what it means *for you* as a consumer and a creator, and how the commerce of mass media affects social, political and financial economies trickles down to actually having tangible influence on your daily life.

MASS MEDIA INDUSTRIES

The largest media companies in the world include Comcast, AT&T, Walt Disney and Thomson Reuters. The majority of the world's massive media enterprises are based in the United States (Seth, 2019).

Of these, many are telecommunications or tech companies that have merged with or acquired media companies. The joining of media companies with companies in telecommunication and technology has led to massive communications companies getting yet bigger.

Media History It wasn't always like this. To fully appreciate the human innovation that got you to where you are today, with a tiny TV and filmmaking capabilities in the phone that fits in your hand, we need to go back. Waaay back. To 1453.

Cue the rewind music for the flashback to Johannes Gensfleisch zur Laden zum Gutenberg, a blacksmith and goldsmith with a very funky name and equally funky beard who was embroiled in lawsuits over funds to support his work on the world's first printing press. His story of financing and preserving his right to his invention sounds shockingly familiar today. Soon after the printing press came books. Then, newspapers arrived in Europe in the early 1600s and in colonial America in 1690, followed by magazines in 1741, thanks to Benjamin Franklin.

A century or so later came the telegraph and photographs, broadcast radio in the early 1900s, movies in the early 1930s followed by television in 1940s; cable television and personal computers arrived in the 1970s. The internet was developed in 1989 (Technological advances, 2012).

"Our use of the Net will only grow, and its impact on us will only strengthen, as it becomes ever more present in our lives," Nicholas Carr stated in his book *The Shallows* (2010, p. 92). "As the Net expands, other media contract." Specifically, Carr notes, digital production and distribution are contracting the sales of physical media such as music CDs, DVDs, snail mail and textbooks.

Media Consolidation In the United States, commercial media has been part of an economic system based on capitalism, in which trade and industry are privately controlled for profits rather than controlled by the state or government. **Media consolidation** is the concentration of the ownership of media outlets. Media consolidation creates an **oligopoly**, which is a state of limited competition. Today's mass media is driven by profits, and advertising remains the primary fuel of that engine. In Europe and other parts of the world, media is more often owned and controlled by the government or follows a public model that is taxpayer- and user-funded. But, because of the *vast concentration of global media in the United States,* this chapter will focus on U.S. policies and issues.

In the 1950s, scores of media companies existed in the United States. By the early 1980s, writes author Ben H. Bagdikian in *The Media Monopoly* (2000), 50 corporations dominated the mass media. By 1990, he continues, there were just 23 media companies, and they dominated the media landscape *worldwide*. In 1996, Congress passed the Telecommunications Act that opened the door for companies to own even more media outlets. Since that loosening of ownership restrictions, the number of mergers and acquisitions has skyrocketed.

AT&T merged with Time Warner in 2018. Disney and 21st Century Fox merged in 2019, as did CBS and Viacom. A handful of major media conglomerates produce most of the world's media products. **Conglomerates** are a widely diversified corporation with smaller companies that operate separately but are controlled by a single owner.

Think about it: A few major conglomerates control most of the world's media offerings. What are the implications for us media consumers? Does it expand the choices we get or narrow the selection? Can you think of any other non-media industries with similar centralized power?

Also contributing to mega-mergers is the success of the tech industry giants such as Apple, Google and Facebook. These tech companies have propelled traditional media companies such as News Corporation or Time Warner to further consolidate, to become, in industry parlance, "too big to fail." The mergers of already huge companies are happening particularly since Silicon Valley companies are no longer mere platforms for content, but venturing into content *development*; Apple TV, as just one example, is launching an original TV series.

Why Consolidate? (And Why Do We Care?) Media consolidation allows for vertical integration *and* cross-promotion, also called cross-marketing.

First, **vertical integration** means that a company owns more than one aspect of a product's production; for example, a company might own the studio *and* the television channel on which the shows are aired, or, it might own the studio and the cinemas that the movies are shown in, or the cable TV channel on which the movies rerun. For us as consumers, it means that our eyes, ears and money may well be going to the same massive media company, even if we aren't always aware of how our dollars are distributed.

Cross-promotion is a form of marketing in which customers of one product are marketed with a related product. Disney's 2013 hit movie *Frozen*, which grossed $1.3 billion at the box office (Robehmed, 2015), spawned

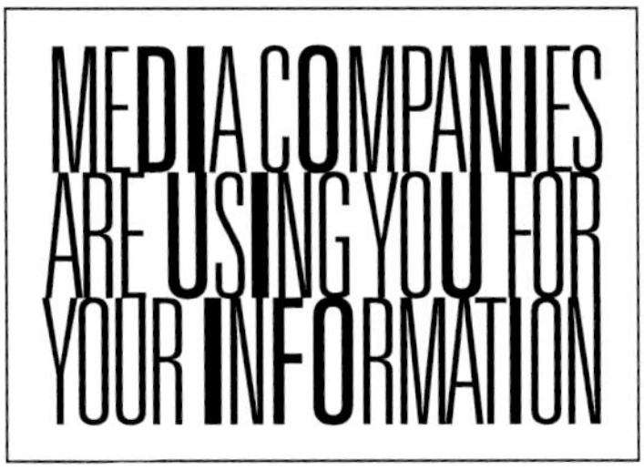

Credit: Ryan Lewis

legions of related products. The cross-promotion of *Frozen* resulted in toy figurines, clothing, linens, lunch boxes, ice shows, theme park rides, a TV show called *Once Upon a Time* and more. The result is that *Frozen* brought Disney $1 billion in *retail* revenue alone in 2013 (Appelbaum, 2014). For us as consumers, it means we are flooded with merch, and it can seem there is little new or unique in the world.

Tech Mergers If they aren't competing with them, many mass media companies are partnering with technology firms, as you can see from the AT&T and Time Warner merger. Media convergence is the joining of media content producers with computer and software companies and telephony—a comical word that basically means sending voice signals using electronic equipment, such as a videoconference. The result of these mergers are hybrids that not only produce the media, but distribute, track and market the media in formats from the big screen to a computer screen to a smartphone screen, across the globe.

PROS AND CONS OF MERGERS

Media convergence has positive and negative implications for media consumers. On the one hand is the threat of cultural dominance of one country over others. On the other hand are opportunities to share content produced locally, and for regional content to get a broader audience. Unlike broadcast licenses that are controlled by a limited number of companies, the shift from broadcast to digital "may in the process loosen the grip of corporate control over many types of content, resulting in the active circulation of a greater diversity of perspectives," assert Henry Jenkins and his co-authors of the book *Spreadable Media* (2013, p. 162).

As discussed in Chapter 1 on Using, media messages have embedded values and points of view. Today's transnational companies focus on entertainment programming that often champions Western ideas and values. The result is a cultural sameness across the globe, and the dominance of Western culture over regional and national culture. Or, as Japanese sociologist Koichi Iwabuchi put it, the media products lack "cultural odor" (2002, p. 28). Global media conglomerates have the effect of homogenizing media content. We might have more TV channels than ever, but do we have more variety? Streaming services that are creating original content are finding large audience followings in part because they are taking risks in storylines and character types.

The social, cultural, ideological and/or economic influence exerted by a dominant group upon less-dominant groups or societies is called **hegemony** (*heh-**gem**-in-ey*). In particular, the mass media creates a cultural hegemony through its broad reach and emotional appeals. Media consolidation can lead to less diversity in both the types of content and in the types of people producing content. "Media concentration and economic power can shape what media is produced and how this media effects processes of socialization and acculturation," write Michael Hoeschmann and Stuart Poyntz in their book *Media Literacies* (2012, p. 72).

For example, the phenomenal rise of the Pokemon media franchise put a Japanese product into homes worldwide. But, the product was not imbued with a cultural presence of Japan, noted authors Erin Smith and gamer Eve Deitsch (2007). Quoting Iwabuchi, they write, "There is a profound contradiction, then, in the way Japanese popular culture manifests Japanese culture in that it 'simultaneously articulates the universal appeal of Japanese cultural products and the disappearance of any perceptible Japaneseness'" (Smith and Deitsch, 2007, p. 61).

Global to Local Media conglomerates have the resources and reach to distribute entertainment programming. The conglomerate plucks a good idea from one country, tests it in others, and, if the audience response is positive enough (meaning profitable), then launches it in the United States, Japan and other major markets.

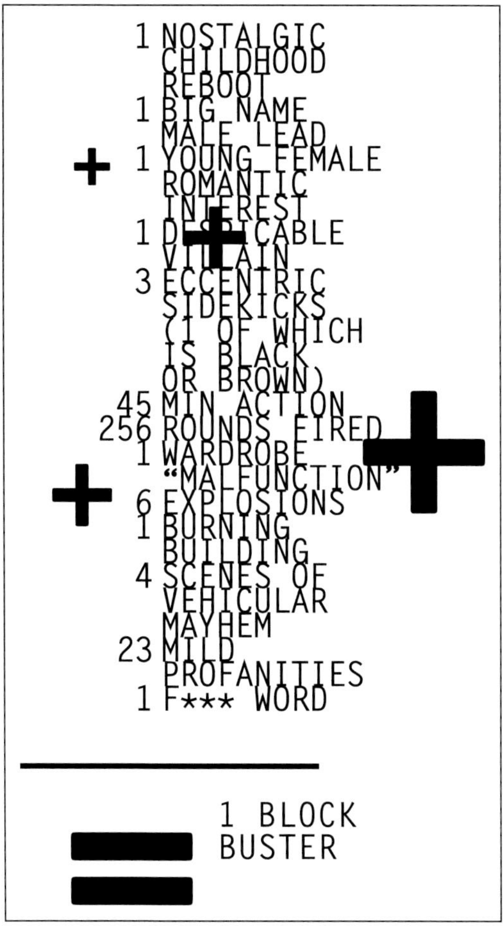

Blockbuster Movie Formula

Credit: Ryan Lewis

When global content is localized, a common narrative or genre is extended worldwide.

"Shows such as *Pop Idol, Survivor, America's Next Top Model,* and *Who Wants to Be a Millionaire* have been franchised to countries around the world," noted Amelia H. Arsenault and Manuel Castells in their article on the structure of global multimedia business networks (2015). Another example the authors give of localizing global content is Viacom, which owns MTV (Music Television). MTV customizes content in order to service 140 countries. It has Asian,

Middle Eastern, Latin American, African and European channels, and they each use *local* talent. Viacom's motto? "Think globally, act locally."

Local to Global Media conglomerates also work the other way, and globalize local content, Arsenault and Castells noted. Here's an example: The show that American audiences know as *Ugly Betty*, which debuted in the United States on ABC in 2006, began as a Columbia telenovela called *Betty La Fea* in 1999 (McCabe & Akass, 2013). A canned version circulated in 21 countries was repackaged in new markets such as Spain and Germany, and eventually arrived in the United States. The Disney conglomerate signed broadcasting deals with 130 territories worldwide. The original Columbian star, named Beatriz, became Jassi in India, Wudi in China, Esti in Israel, Bea in Spain, Maria in Greece and Lotte in the Netherlands (Miller, 2010).

The Bottom Line The bottom line in a capitalist economy such as the United States **is** the bottom line, meaning revenues.

The motivation of publicly-traded media corporations (remember, all the big media conglomerates are based in the United States but function globally) is to serve shareholders. This is a capitalist idea that puts first the goal of commerce before community, and looks to avoid government regulation as much as possible.

Mass media conglomerates are not focused on serving the public's right to know, and this reality has serious implications for democratic societies worldwide, said Edward Herman and Robert McChesney, authors of *The Global Media: The New Missionaries of Corporate Capitalism* (2004). Instead, today's transnational companies focus on entertainment programming, programming which champions Western ideas and values.

What "Western ideals and ideas" are promoted through your favorite TV show, movie or video game?

GOVERNMENT REGULATION

Now *here's* a subject you're eager to read about! The United States has intentionally separated the communication industries to avoid one company owning all the various kinds of communication and media outlets in a given geographic region. A central concept in regulating media ownership (which the United States does through its Federal Communications Commission) is to safeguard against a monopoly so that diversity—of viewpoints, of programs and formats and of ownership, particularly in the same geographic market—is ensured.

WAKE UP!!

I know, this stuff seems so boring. Because it is. And that is what keeps the public from understanding the government decisions that *directly affect your daily life*, such as whether there are competing news outlets in your town, or how fast your movie streams over your laptop at home. Stuff you would likely care about if you knew about it. So here is your chance, you lucky reader.

Net Neutrality A 2018 ruling from the Trump administration put the power to regulate the internet back in the hands of the FCC. The idea that internet service providers should treat all internet communications equally and not discriminate against or privilege any entity over another is called **net neutrality**.

Net neutrality says this: All internet service providers treat all data and users equally. No matter the user, the content, the platform, application or website, the type of equipment used or the method of communication (streaming video vs. email, for example), under net neutrality, internet service providers treat it all the same. Internet service providers couldn't charge more money for some content (such as the content it owns) over other online content (such as their competitors' content). It couldn't block or purposely slow down service. The state of net neutrality is still an open question in the United States. The European Union currently has a form of net neutrality.

Pros and Cons of Regulation Those *advocating* for improved government regulation of media ownership argue that concentrated media ownership quashes diversity of programming, ideas, the watchdog role of journalists and the ability for individual communities to receive relevant local content.

"Among media that produce the largest audiences, commercial pressures dominate content decisions. This has occurred concurrently with media being subject to fewer and fewer regulatory requirements and less oversight. Consequently, media firms are generally free to behave in ways designed to generate large audiences, with little regard to social or cultural effects" (Picard, 2005, p. 343).

Media scholar Robert W. McChesney notes that in areas of the internet that can be profitable, private companies have taken a firm hold. Google, for example, owns 90 percent of the desktop search engine market (Stat-Counter, 2019).

Corporate political power has triumphed over any meaningful government regulation, says McChesney in his book *Digital Disconnect* (2013). Too often, he says, government regulation is about guaranteeing the existence of profitable industries, not fighting for the public interest.

In your experience as a media consumer, is diversity of viewpoints and programming evident in the radio, television and newspaper coverage in your community? Can you access a variety of news programs, television shows and radio shows that reflect different perspectives and different content?

Those *critical* of government regulation of media ownership argue that limits on media ownership would not only result in content control of media but would also be unnecessary, as there is diversity of media voices now (Compaine, 1979). With the World Wide Web, it is much easier to get various opinions and information online; we aren't as dependent as we once were on a local newspaper or local TV station to provide information and news.

The dynamism of technology will continue to bring about new competition, regulatory detractors assert. Also, concentration of ownership improves the range of programming options offered, say some. PayPal founder Peter Thiel argued that monopolies are the new normal, and a preferable one, as they allow for unfettered creativity by well-resourced companies that can benefit society (2014). Do you think the government should continue to regulate ownership in the media and technology industry? If so, in what ways? If not, what are the likely outcomes of deregulation?

THE BUSINESS OF AUDIENCE

One way to think about audiences is to think about their *utility*. That is, what are they *used* for? Media companies use audiences for profit. In this way, audiences are a commodity. Audiences are sorted into market segments depending on the media product being offered. Programming is specifically designed to fit their particular interests or needs.

Media companies gauge the success of creating profitable audience segments through measures such as sales, subscriptions, online traffic, page views, click throughs, ratings and advertising. When media companies produce a product, it is designed with a primary or target audience in mind. To better market a product, potential audiences for it are sorted into homogenous clusters, or segments, based on criteria ranging from age to lifestyle that are described in the next section. The advertising then also follows suit, targeting groups of people most likely to buy or use a product.

When media companies produce a product, it is designed with a primary or target audience in mind.

Segmentation is a major change from 1950s-era networks that provided free programming in exchange for attention to ads between shows. Everyone watched the same thing! Everyone got the same ads! Imagine that. That was back when audiences were seen as an undefined mass, a blob of people who could be herded around by a media company. Today, you know things are different. You are a highly studied creature. Media companies are continually seeking new ways to get your attention, and your money. Messages are customized to appeal to you. In many ways, it is an *individual* experience.

Segmentation Criteria Common criteria for segmentation are geography (country, region, even Census tracts and blocks) and demographics, which include age, gender, income, education, ethnicity and income. Also used are less concrete measures: Psychographics model group consumers based on their lifestyle, values, social class and personality; and behavioral segmentation models group consumers by way of purchasing characteristics and patterns, such as loyalty to a brand or product knowledge.

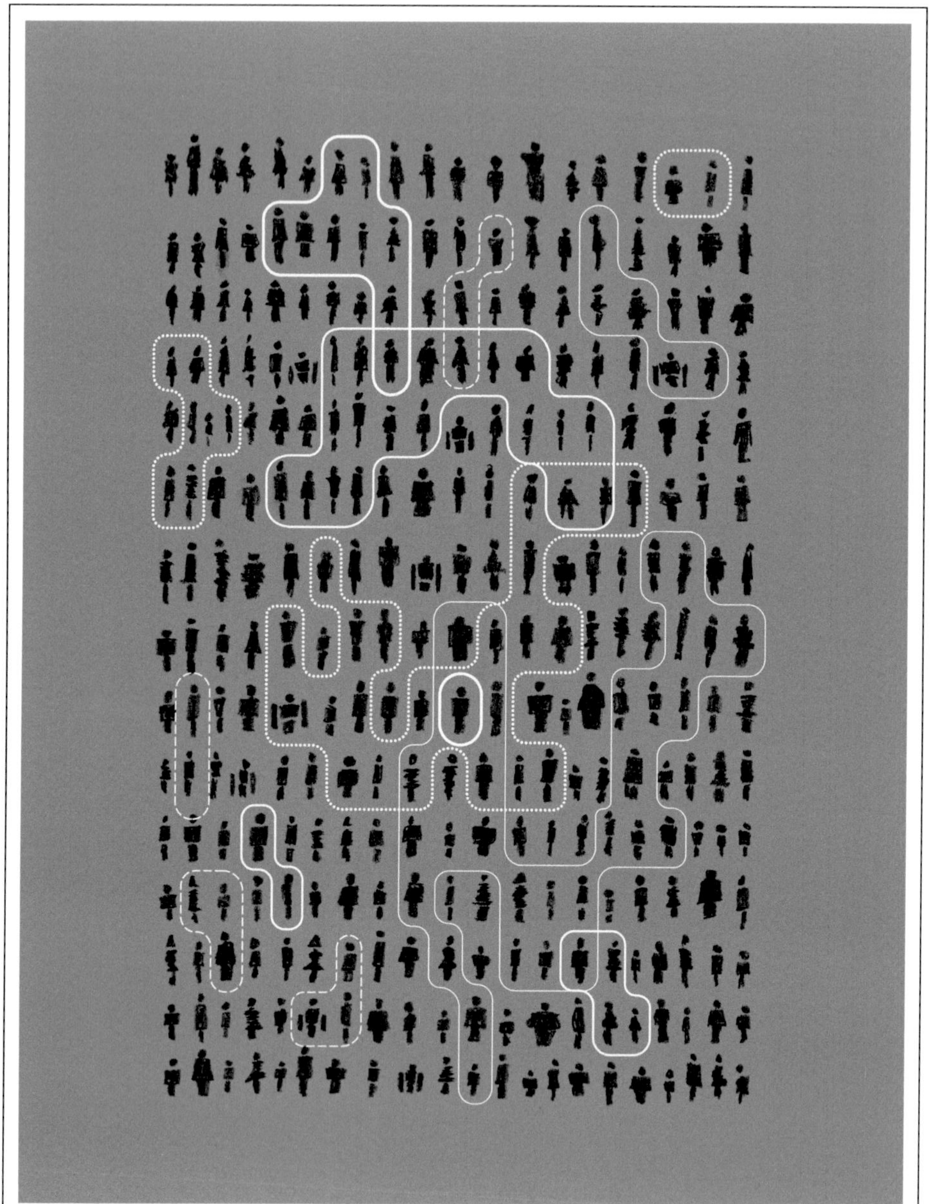

Market Segments

Credit: Ryan Lewis

An example of such niches is found in the categories for the VALS (an acronym for Values and Lifestyles model) for psychographic segmentation. We have all likely noticed that we receive different advertisements online based on our past search history or purchasing patterns, our gender, age and style choices, as well as lifestyle. This is an example of target marketing, and with computer cookies that track our online habits, it has become much easier to sort consumers. An HTTP cookie is a small piece of data sent from a website and stored on your computer's browser. Cookies track your movements on a given website. What audience segment(s) are you in? Take a quiz to find out: http://bit.ly/2Wstvfz.

VOX DISCIPULI

I do post to Instagram most frequently because photos are the main thing I share across any platform. I share a variety of subject matter including photos of myself, from my personal life (i.e., friends, family, trips) and some of the work I do on the side as a freelance makeup artist. My Instagram account is public so anyone that either follows me or just views my profile can see what I post. Personally, it's a great way to reach clients and potential clients so they can see my work ahead of time and save the trouble of sending photos. —Madison, 25

Homemade Audiences Celebrity endorsements to gain audience and consumer attention have been around since before Babe Ruth endorsed Red Rock Cola in the 1930s. In more contemporary times, Spain's tennis star Rafael Nadal has endorsed everything from Tommy Hilfiger underwear to KIA cars (Antonovica & Curiel, 2016). But with social media, everyday media users get a shot at celebrity fame and salary. And it starts with an audience.

Musicians, visual artists, budding filmmakers, writers, cooks, crafters—you name it—all sorts of people with a talent or passion are seeking an online following. Developing an audience following takes work, but people have done it and quite successfully, using social media as the entry point. (YouTube videos of young Justin Bieber got him discovered, like it or not.) Consistent posting of engaging content is essential to amassing enough followers that, in turn, corporate advertisers and sponsors want a part of your audience, too.

Here's an example of how two musicians gained fame from their very own living room and ended up on a world tour. The folk-pop singing duet called "Us the Duo" in 2014 debuted a self-released album of original songs that didn't get much attention. The pair, Michael and Carissa Rae Alvarado, posted some six-second videos (and in a unique move, showed just the bottom half of their faces—a framing that has since become their trademark) to the now-defunct social media video site Vine.

One of the videos caught the attention of a major Vine user, who then re-Vined it to his 4.9 million followers (Hampp, 2014). This caught the attention of news outlets: *Good Morning America* had the pair on the show soon after. A record contract with Republic Records then followed. The duo has since released several albums, their music has been streamed over 100 million times and counting, they have more than 7 million followers on social media and one way they have paid their way is by partnering with Amazon, AT&T and Burt's Bees on national campaigns, according to the couple's website (ustheduo.com).

Influencers People with extreme passions have found they can make a living telling the world about it on social media. Marketers call them "influencers." Influencers are people seen as having enough clout to influence others to follow their opinions, advice and actions. Influencers garner lucrative contracts by having a million or so followers; corporations pay them in exchange for mentions in videos, photos, tweets and blogs. (By the way, micro-influencers have maybe a fifth of that following and get paid less. There are even nano-influencers, who have as few as 1,000 followers and are usually paid in free products (Maheshwari, November 2018).)

The Influencer Marketing Hub (2019) said the size of the influencer marketing industry in 2018 was $4.6 billion and it's projected to grow in 2019; though, admittedly, this source is hardly unbiased. The survey found that nano-influencers with fewer than 1,000 followers had an engagement rate of 7.2 percent on Instagram, compared with 1.4 percent on Twitter. Generally, the more followers the lower the engagement rate. Do you follow an influencer on social media? How did you find that person? Do you trust the endorsements? If so, why?

By posting themselves talking about, opining, experiencing, critiquing and doing their passions, social media users gain followers. The more followers a person has, the more others on social media figure they must know about a specific topic. Oh, and it's also hugely helpful to be attractive, relatable and authentic (Fastenau, 2018).

For every action, there is a reaction, however. In this case, the rise of paid influencers has led to fraud through fake followers that are really just bots masquerading as people; some even take personal details from real people to seem authentic (Maheshwari, March 2018). So now fraud detection of fake followers is a thing. Because companies paying hundreds of thousands of dollars for social media mentions want to ensure there are real people on the other end of those endorsements.

ALGORITHM AUDIENCES

Increasingly, the internet has facilitated the sorting of people into audience segments through **algorithms**, which are computer "recipes" or procedures developed to solve a specific problem. Put simply, algorithms are formulas into which data—in this case, our past purchases, lifestyle choices, what we like to do and what causes we care about—place us into various marketing niches.

Media companies use sophisticated sequences of algorithms to determine what to produce next for consumers (Mager, 2012). The concept of "the social power of algorithms" helps us to imagine these equations as more than objective and impersonal; the outcomes of algorithms shape society, wrote scholar David Beer (2017, p. 2). For example, Beer notes, algorithms are self-feeding; the results of one outcome are fed back into the algorithm design, and compound any effects, including discriminatory ones.

Algorithms have no shortage of data to crunch, *ProPublica* reporters Julia Angwin, Terry Parris Jr. and Surya Mattu found (September, 2016). For example, "Facebook offers advertisers more than 1,300 categories for ad targeting—everything from people whose property size is less than .26 acres to households with exactly seven credit cards." The reporters' *ProPublica* story has a link to find out what Facebook knows about you; for me, Facebook has *52,235 separate data items* for marketers to target ads at me, all based on my "likes" and page views and such. And I'm not on FB much. *Yikes.*

The "black box" of algorithms implies how little media users know about the way these codes are built and the decisions made in fine-tuning them. Algorithms can result in inadvertent bias. Angwin, Parris Jr and Mattu found, for example, that the cost of an SAT review course from the *Princeton Review* differed based on where people lived—same product, different price—because of their demographics. Asians were nearly twice as likely to get charged more than non-Asians for the service. This is an example of *unintentional* discrimination, and while it is not illegal, it is something that is happening, and, "as we enter a world of mass customization, we need to be on the lookout for this kind of discrimination" (October, 2016).

What may appear as neutral formulas are not neutral at all; algorithms filter, channel and rank data. The results are manifold; they affect what you see first in search results, whether you get invited to a retail sale or how much you pay for your product.

Algorithm and Outcome "Algorithms are inevitably modelled on visions of the social world, and with outcomes in mind, outcomes influenced by commercial or other interests and agendas," observed Beer (2017, p. 4). "As well as being produced from a social context, the algorithms are lived with, they are an integral part of that social world; they are woven into practices and outcomes."

> Digital technology has fragmented audiences like never before.

Technology—via algorithms that do all manner of tracking, filtering and sorting of audiences and content—affects the media we receive. It affects the programs *and* advertisements we get served because of the audiences that are generated and that we are placed in. Digital technology has fragmented audiences like never before. We can each customize our media experiences. For example, you might stream *The Office* on Netflix on your laptop while your roommate plays *Fortnite* on his smartphone.

Media convergence is changing advertising pricing and approach. That is, advertising has traditionally been based on the *potential exposure* to ads. With the fragmentation of media products across so many mediums and channels, and lowered confidence that consumers will actually *see and hear* their ads, advertisers aren't paying the rates that they used to. An emerging model of ad rates is "cost-per-action" pricing, which basically measures whether users are clicking through the ad or better yet, buying something (Napoli, 2003, pp. 171–172). This type of pricing is dependent on audience trackability on the internet. Detailed customer data is something that traditional media such as a TV ad couldn't deliver.

These fragments of audience can result in diminished advertising profits for media production companies, since advertisers are looking for the biggest return on their ad dollar. Reduced profits mean less money to pour into media products and new content production, which in turn affects the quality and amount of media content we as audiences get. Audiences might have more ways than ever to access media, but the content might not always be all that great—or new.

"As the quality of the audience product declines, the pressure to reuse, recycle, and repackage media content will become more intense," predicts media scholar Phillip Napoli. It's why cable channels play old movies and rerun shows. It's cheap.

Targeted Advertising Advertisers, which are the engine of all private media, assign different worth to different audience members. Consumers with financial means experience an entirely different world of media than consumers without means. You are either a "target" of advertising dollars or a "waste" of advertising dollars, to use author Joseph Turow's characterizations in his book *The Daily You* (2011, p. 190).

To sell the advertising that funds their engines, media companies need to have content that attracts the customers who are highly valued by marketers. The most valued customers are those who spend money and buy things and services. Because of this, they are sought by advertisers. So, it's likely not surprising that media companies produce content to attract customers with high value to advertisers.

Ethnic minority status is linked with lower incomes, data shows, so audiences consisting primarily of people of color are less valued by media companies, notes scholar Phillip Napoli (2003, p. 123). This is in keeping with Turow's point about audiences sorted as "target" or "waste." The implications are that people who are seen as less profitable for advertisers will

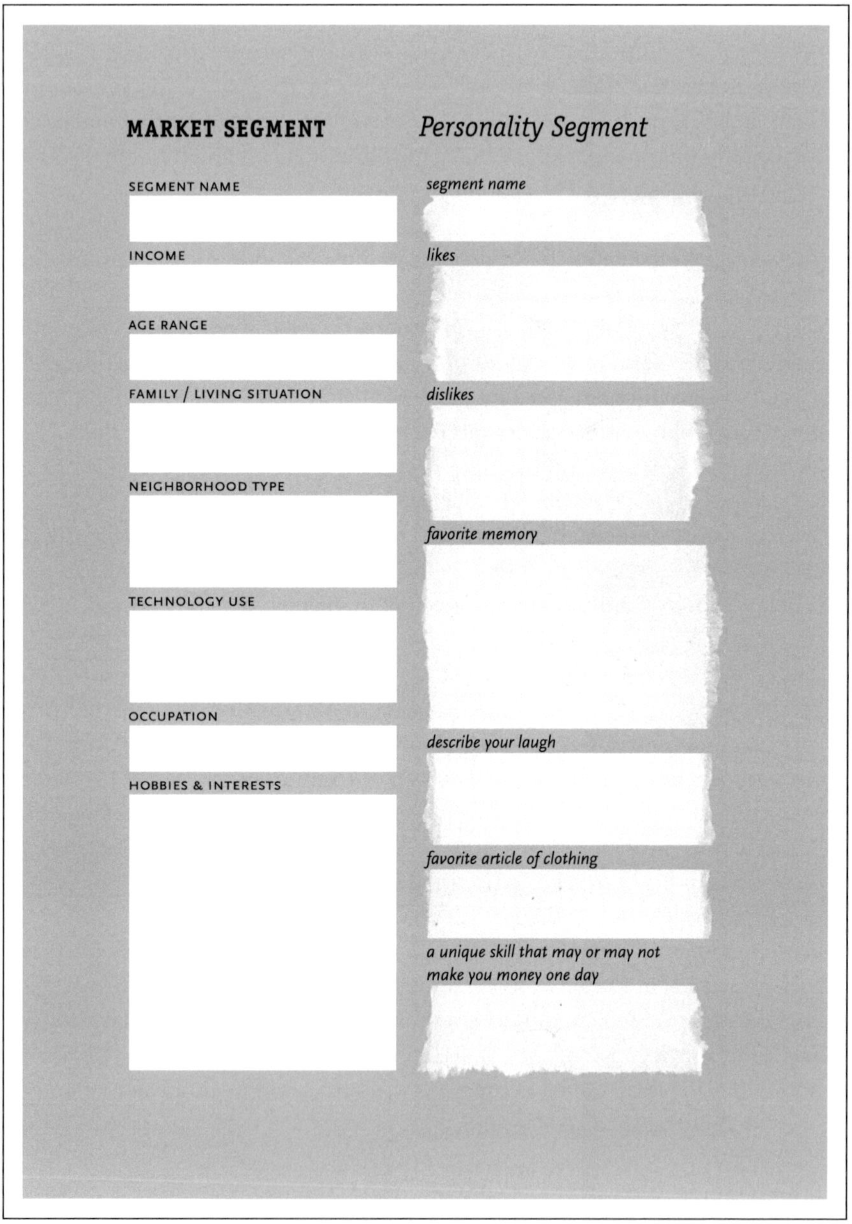

MARKET SEGMENT

SEGMENT NAME

INCOME

AGE RANGE

FAMILY / LIVING SITUATION

NEIGHBORHOOD TYPE

TECHNOLOGY USE

OCCUPATION

HOBBIES & INTERESTS

Personality Segment

segment name

likes

dislikes

favorite memory

describe your laugh

favorite article of clothing

a unique skill that may or may not make you money one day

Market Segment—Personality Segment

Fill out the boxes in both columns. Compare marketers' specific and monetizable categories for you with your unique attributes that can't be quantified, such as your amazing ability to sleep while sitting up.

Credit: Ryan Lewis

receive poorer-quality options in ads for everything from mortgages loans to car insurance.

The U.S. government filed a lawsuit in 2019 against Facebook for what it said is discriminatory advertising. Facebook allegedly allowed advertisers to pick and choose to whom they sent ads, excluding people in certain neighborhoods or zip codes from seeing ads, for example, and picking from criteria that allowed them to exclude parents, those who are non-American-born, non-Christians and others, according to the civil charges filed by the Department of Housing and Urban Development.

DIVERSITY AND THE MEDIA INDUSTRY

Media ownership patterns have an impact on our media choices, quality and content.

Media messages are created by a largely male and white workforce and leadership. Media organizations, from movie casts to comic book publishers, are dominated by men. "Straight white men dominate comic books, both on and off the page," said comic book critic Oliver Sava (2014). "They write and illustrate the majority of titles, and those books tend to star straight white male protagonists, especially in the superhero genre."

At news outlets globally, males occupy 73 percent of top management jobs and nearly two-thirds of reporting positions, according to the Global Report on the Status Women in the News Media that examined more than 500 companies in nearly 60 countries (Byerly, 2011). Women are nearing parity in the senior professional positions, at 41 percent of the newsgathering, editing and writing jobs. **Parity** describes the condition of equal representation; in this case, of women in these jobs with the number of women in the overall population.

Off-Screen Affects On-Screen Diversity When it comes to the movie industry, women made up only 31.8 percent of the speaking characters across the 1,100 popular films from 2007 to 2017 analyzed by the USC Annenberg Inclusion Initiative (Smith, Choueiti, & Pieper, 2018; Smith, Choueiti, Pieper, Case, & Choi, 2018). Also, according to the initiative's website, "Across the 100 top-grossing films of 2016, 47 did not feature a single Black woman or girl speaking on screen, 66 movies were devoid of

Asian female characters, and a full 72 erased Latinas" (Annenberg Inclusion Initiative, 2019, para 1).

But those numbers change when women are behind the scenes of moviemaking.

Hiring women and people of color makes a difference in how films are made. Data indicate a *positive* relationship between the number of females behind the scenes and the number of females on screen.

For example: There were only 53 female directors compared to 1,223 male directors in the 1,100 popular films from 2007 to 2017. But when a woman was directing, those stories had 5.4 percent more girls/women on screen than those stories without female direction, the study found. Stories with female writers and creators attached had 10.7 percent and 12.6 percent more girls/women on screen than those without female writers or creators.

Also, in their analysis, Annenberg researchers found that the number of films that had a Latino character with a speaking part was just 6.2 percent. The U.S. population is 17.8 percent Latino, so that means the difference between the actual population and the characters on screen was an 11.6 percent deficit. This statistic is based on the concept of parity; in this case, that the demographics of characters on screens should correspond with real-life demographics.

The United States is the basis for this survey because the major media companies are based in America. Think about how parity would change if done on the basis of populations in African or Asian countries. But since so much media is produced in the United States, these populations will likely never see full parity in all of their media entertainment options. What do you think of the concept of parity as applied to media representation? Is it a valid measure? Should there be some other measure of inclusion?

Diversity Pays Things are changing, albeit slowly. The U.S. racial/ethnic composition will be fundamentally changed by 2045, when population projections are that people of color will outnumber people who are white and non-Latino. And, observed UCLA's Hollywood Diversity Report, "America's increasingly diverse audiences prefer diverse film and television content" (Hunt, Ramón, Tran, Sargent, & Roychoudhury, 2018, p. 3).

As proof of that statement, the report found that: "Films with casts that were from 21 percent to 30 percent minority enjoyed the highest median global box office receipts and the highest median return on investment, while films with the most racially and ethnically homogenous casts were the poorest performers. Minorities accounted for the majority of ticket sales for five of the top 10 films in 2016 as ranked by global box office receipts" (p. 4).

Noting the Hollywood "myth" that films dominated by people of color won't sell well overseas, the report stated that, indeed, "2016 films with the most diverse casts tended to be released in fewer international markets than those with overwhelmingly White casts" (p. 76). Perhaps that's how the myth got started?

Also in the United States, predominately black casts or storylines were garnering substantial non-black viewership, according to Nielsen (2017):

> ABC's hit sitcom *Black-ish* follows a father and husband (Anthony Anderson) who's trying to create a sense of black cultural identity for his affluent family of four and has 79% non-black viewership. Tracee Ellis Ross, who plays his wife, won the best actress in a comedy series Golden Globe for her role.
>
> (para 4)

In 2017, female musical artists such as Nicki Minaj and Rihanna were outnumbered nearly five to one by men, according to an Annenberg analysis of inclusion in the recording industry (Smith, Choueiti, & Pieper, 2018). This, even though women made up 53 percent of digital music purchasers in 2014.

MEDIA LITERACY SELFIE

What is the assumption in noting the figure in the previous paragraph on women purchasing digital music? That female music consumers will want to listen to more female than male artists? That female artists will produce music that female consumers will like and purchase? Is this a legitimate connection to make? Is it relevant? If so, how is it relevant?

AUDIENCES ARE US

Two dominant ways to think about media audiences are either passive, and *acted upon* by media products, or as active, and engaged with media, whether by producing it, analyzing it or responding to it. Let's look at both ways.

Audience as Acted Upon This view has a lot to do with technological determinism. This is the idea that technology is the driver of human progress throughout history, and humans are along for the ride. Though humans create the technologies, they are not in control of them (Carr, 2010, p. 46, citing Marshall McLuhan in "Understanding Media," the Gadget Lover chapter).

Among the most obvious passive audience members are youth. Children are sometimes described as "victims" of mass media. Advertisers are keen to market to children in particular, as they are not critical buyers. Also, by hooking a child on a product or brand, advertisers hope to have a client for life.

The participatory, personal, persuasive and spontaneous nature of modern ad campaigns directed at youth is particularly engaging, notes David Buckingham, a leader in the media literacy education movement (2013). "So are young consumers just being duped and exploited—or are they being empowered and liberated? Personally, I do not regard young people as passive victims; but on the other hand, I don't think any of us is really in control, or completely savvy, about this. And that, of course, is one reason why we need more media education," Buckingham concludes in his essay on marketing and youth culture (para 25).

Audience as Actor The instrumental view of media audiences is that media tools are neutral, and we as users decide their use for good or evil. As *The Shallows* author Nicholas Carr stated, "Instrumentalism is the most widely held view of technology, not the least because it's the view we would prefer to be true" (p. 46).

We do want to believe we decide the use of media tools. Because if it isn't true, it means we are pawns and unthinkingly programmed to take whatever media gives us. If there is a third way, it hasn't emerged forcefully as yet. Media literacy encourages us as users/consumers/creators to take control of our media use and our critical consumption of media. By interpreting media messages, creating our own messages, and intentionally seeking the media we want, we as audience members can be very active in the media process.

"To measure your needs by that which is projected via mass media is a mistake that has no mercy," said Haki R. Madhubuti, an author, educator and poet, as well as a publisher (Howard University, 2019). "The average person views a minimum of one thousand advertisements a day. To say 'no' to the most outrageous commercials is an act of responsibility that needs to be taught early and often."

Want to have a laugh after a long day? You binge-watch *The Office* or maybe watch your favorite YouTuber; either way, you are deciding how you will use media and what you want out of it. The question of this chapter is whether you'll be able to find it—either because media companies aren't making it anymore due to profit concerns, or because the content isn't available in your market due to monopolistic ownership or because the internet provider you have has decided you're low priority when it comes to streaming video.

Where is media convergence taking us? Where are *we* taking it? Stay tuned.

CHAPTER REVIEW

- Trace the development of media through time.
- Describe media convergence.
- Argue the pros and cons of government regulation of media.
- Explain net neutrality and why it matters.
- Give an example of globalized media programming.
- Show how advertising supports mass media.
- Define the role of algorithms in shaping modern societies.
- Explain the relationship between a diverse staff/creators and diverse media content.
- Sort various audiences into active and passive categories.

ACTIVITIES

1. Make a traditional origami box called a Masu Box. Here are simple directions: https://origami.me/box/. This box becomes a hypothetical box of medicine. You decide what the medicine is called, what it does and for whom. On that latter point, select a market segment (from factors such as age, gender, geography, income, occupation or lifestyle) that will be the audience you are targeting for this fantastical box of medicine. Work in groups of three to develop your ad. One caveat: You cannot target your age group.

   Create a PointPower slide of a mock print advertisement using a photo of the box and perhaps, but not essentially, with a model depicting the desired user group. Or, you can choose to do a 30-second video spot. Either should be designed to speak directly to the interests and needs of your particular market segment. But, here's the key: Market to this segment without using stereotypes or assumptions about the people in that marketing segment.

   Once you've got your packaging and advertisement done, pitch your product to a group of people—a class, your family, your friends. Ask them to guess your target audience; what specific cues were there in your media messaging? Most importantly, ask your group if they saw any stereotypes within your messaging, and discuss those elements and the influence of implicit biases (which are stereotypes or attitudes that affect our behavior and judgment without our conscious knowledge) on your content creation.

   Note: I derived this exercise from the very fun and very useful white towel exercise in *The Teacher's Guide to Media Literacy: Critical Thinking in a Multimedia World*, by Cyndy Scheibe and Faith Rogow (Corwin, 2012).

2. Watch this PBS video: https://to.pbs.org/2yY63wT. It's from 2001 but many of the same themes of marketing exclusively to youth and of the implications of ownership consolidation apply. Write a one-page reaction paper to the video and its themes.

3. The following two activities are from or inspired by the United Nations Educational, Scientific and Cultural Organization (2019):

   a. "Create an ad outline for a product or service that is indigenous to a particular community or region. Identify and explain the technical and creative strategies that would be most effective for reaching that audience. Explain how your ideas are different from those developed by North American or European ad agencies targeting the same market" (fourth bullet under "Pedagogical approaches and activities). See http://bit.ly/2HX02WT.

b. Select an advertisement by a transnational corporation (Coca-Cola, Nike, Revlon, McDonald's, Rolex, Volkswagen) to examine closely. Identify the elements of the ad that make it appealing and universal, even for people who don't understand the language used in it. Analyze the ways in which a culture or lifestyle is sold. Identify the messages and values being conveyed. Share your observations in whatever format you choose.

4. Go to the library or bookstore and select a magazine you typically don't read. Analyze the contents, including images and ads, to determine at which audience(s) this periodical is aimed. Share your conclusions with others in your preferred medium.

REFERENCES

Angwin, J., Parris, T. Jr., Mattu, S. (2016, September 28). Breaking the black box: What Facebook knows about you. *ProPublica.* Retrieved from http://bit.ly/2y2lbc1

Angwin, J., Parris, T. Jr., Mattu, S. (2016, October 5). Breaking the black box: When algorithms decide what you pay. *ProPublica.* Retrieved from http://bit.ly/32DFJGb

Annenberg Inclusion Initiative. (2019). *The inclusion rider: Legal language for ending Hollywood's epidemic of invisibility.* Retrieved from https://annenberg.usc.edu/research/aii

Antonovica, A., & Curiel, J. E. (2016). Sports celebrities multiple use in marketing messages: Example of the Spanish tennis player Rafael Nadal. *Marketing and Branding Research, 3,* 179–193.

Appelbaum, B. (2014, November 18). How Disney turned '*Frozen*' into a cash cow. *New York Times Magazine.* Retrieved from https://nyti.ms/30Ir4Yw

Arsenault, A. H., & Castells, M. (2015). The structure and dynamics of global multimedia business networks. *International Journal of Communication, 2,* 707–748.

Bagdikian, B. H. (2000). *The media monopoly* (6th ed.). Boston, MA: Beacon Press.

Beer, D. (2017). The social power of algorithms. *Information, Communication & Society, 20*(1), 1–13. doi:10.1080/1369118X.2016.1216147

Buckingham, D. (2013). *Selling youth? Marketing and youth culture.* Retrieved from http://bit.ly/2Dl5LD6

Byerly, C. M. (2011). *Global report on the status of women in the news media.* Washington, D.C.: International Women's Media Foundation.

Carr, N. (2010). *The shallows: What the internet is doing to our brains.* New York, NY: W. W. Norton & Co.

Compaine, B. M. (1979). *Who owns the media? Concentration of ownership in the mass communications industry.* White Plains, NY: Knowledge Industry Publications.

Fastenau, J. (2018, March 6). Under the influence: The power of social media influencers. *Medium* and *Crobox.*

Hampp, A. (2014, March 24). Folk-pop duo Us becomes Vine's first major label signing (exclusive). *Billboard.* Retrieved from http://bit.ly/2XPRY3v

Herman, E., & McChesney, R. W. (2004). *The global media: The new missionaries of corporate capitalism.* New York, NY: Continuum.

Hoeschmann, M., & Poyntz, S. (2012). *Media literacies: A critical introduction.* Hoboken, NJ: Wiley-Blackwell.

Howard University. (2019). *Library guide: Haki R. Madhubuti—Poet, essayist,* editor, publisher. Retrieved from www.howard.edu/library/reference/guides/madhubuti/

Hunt, D., Ramón, A. C., Tran, M., Sargent, A., & Roychoudhury, D. (2018). *Hollywood diversity report 2018.* UCLA College of Social Sciences.

Influencer Marketing Hub. (2019). The state of influencer marketing 2019: Benchmark report. Retrieved from http://bit.ly/2KyBW5Q.

Iwabuchi, K. (2002). *Recentering globalization: Popular culture and Japanese transnationalism.* Durham, NC: Duke University Press.

Jenkins, H., Green, J., & Ford, S. (2013). *Spreadable media: Creating value and meaning in a networked culture.* New York, NY: NYU Press.

Mager, A. (2012). Algorithmic ideology. *Information, Communication & Society, 15*(5), 269–787. doi:10.1080/1369118X.2012.676056

Maheshwari, S. (2018, March 12). Uncovering Instagram bots with a new kind of detective work. *The New York Times.* Retrieved from https://nyti.ms/2GlP0Jj

Maheshwari, S. (2018, November 11) Are you ready for the nanoinfluencers? *The New York Times.* Retrieved from https://nyti.ms/2SoUEiA

McCabe, J., & Akass, K. (Eds.). (2013). *TV's Betty goes global: From telenovela to international brand.* Reading contemporary television series. London: I.B. Tauris.

McChesney, R. W. (2013). *Digital disconnect: How capitalism is turning the internet against democracy.* New York, NY: The New Press.

Miller, J. (2010). *Ugly Betty* goes global: Global networks of localized content in the telenovela industry. *Global Media and Communication,* 6(2), 198–217.

Napoli, P. (2003). *Audience economics: Media institutions and the audience marketplace.* New York, NY: Columbia University Press.

Nielsen. (2017, February 8). *For us by us? The mainstream appeal of black content.* Retrieved form Nielsen.com. Insights.

Picard, R. (2005). Money, media, and the public interest. In G. Overholser & K. H. Jamieson (Eds.), *The Press: Institutions of American democracy* (pp. 337–350). Oxford and New York, NY: Oxford University Press.

Rapp, N., & Jenkins, A. (2018, July 24). Chart: These 6 companies control much of U.S. Media. *Fortune.* Retrieved from http://bit.ly/2Lu51kI

Robehmed, N. (2015, July 28). The '*Frozen*' effect: When Disney's movie merchandising is too much. *Forbes.* Retrieved from http://bit.ly/2JP9jQg

Sava, O. (2014). Strides and backslides: How to tackle diversity in comics: Comics roundtable. *AV/AUX.* Retrieved from http://bit.ly/2U0z8og

Scheibe, C., & Rogow, F. (2012). *The teacher's guide to media literacy: Critical thinking in a multimedia world.* Thousand Oaks, CA: Corwin.

Seth, S. (2019, August 3). The world's top ten media companies. *Investopedia.* Retrieved from http://bit.ly/2TykGAv.

Smith, E., & Deitsch, E. (2007). Lost (and found) in translation: Game localization, cultural models, and critical literacy. In G. E. Hawisher & C. L. Selfe (Eds.), *Gaming lives in the twenty-first century: Literate connections* (pp. 53–70). New York, NY: Palgrave Macmillan.

Smith, S. L., Choueiti, M., & Pieper, K. (2018). Inclusion in the recording studio? Gender and race/ethnicity of artists, songwriters & producers across 600 popular songs from 2012–2017. USC Annenberg Inclusion Initiative.

Smith, S. L., Choueiti, M., Pieper, K., Case, A., & Choi, A. (2018). Inequality in 1,100 popular films: Examining portrayals of gender, race/ethnicity, LGBT & Disability from 2007 to 2017. USC Annenberg Inclusion Initiative.

StatCounter. (2019). Worldwide desktop market share of leading search engines from January 2010 to January 2019. *Statista—The Statistics Portal.* Retrieved from http://gs.statcounter.com/search-engine-market-share

Technological advances: From the printing press to the iPhone. (2012). In: *A primer on communication studies* (v. 10). Section 15.1. Creative Commons 3.0 license.

Thiel, P. (2014, September 12). The Saturday essay: Competition is for losers. *Wall Street Journal.* Retrieved from https://on.wsj.com/2Y3xIGO

Turow, J. (2011). *The daily you: How the new advertising industry is defining your identity and your worth.* New Haven: Yale University Press.

United Nations Educational, Scientific and Cultural Organization. (2019). *Unit 5: Transnational advertising and 'superbrands.' Information literacy for teachers.* Retrieved from http://bit.ly/2HX02WTVanDerWerff, T. (2019, March 20). Here's what Disney owns after the massive Disney/Fox merger. *Vox.* Retrieved from http://bit.ly/32DyUUL

Winkler, E. (2018, May 15). Can super-voting stocks survive the CBS challenge? *The Wall Street Journal.* Retrieved from https://on.wsj.com/2Y7Ppcw

7 Connecting

How Media Communicates Culture, and How Cultures Respond

Here's a nano-quiz to kick off this chapter. This one is a 20-second round of just true or false answers off the top of your head. No research allowed and no lifeline, either. Here we go:

1. True or False: Murder/homicide is the most prevalent type of crime in the United States.
2. True or False: Black males are responsible for most of the crime in the United States.
3. True or False: Gay men molest children at far higher rates than heterosexuals.
4. True or False: Africa is a country.
5. True or False: In Africa, people speak African.

To ensure there's no cheating, share your answers with someone, anyone—the person next to you, your friends on Snapchat, or the café barista.

LEARNING OBJECTIVES

Terms: Media representation, stereotypes, accessibility, cultivation theory, correlation, causation, margin of error, identification, public media.

- Identify prevalent media representations of various ethnicities and sexual orientations.
- Explain how media representations lead to stereotyping.
- Understand the associations between media depictions and real-life attitudes.
- Know some specific approaches to challenging negative media stereotypes.
- Explain the role of public media in providing cultural programming.

After the Learning Objectives, I'll be right back with your answers. In the meantime, know that this chapter will look at how mass media and public media communicate various cultures, which are the beliefs, traits and behaviors of various racial, religious or social groups. The chapter will in turn explore how audience members and members of those cultures *respond* to these representations.

MEDIA REPRESENTATIONS

Welcome back! OK, for the grand prize of 10,000 new followers on the social media platform of your choice, go to the answers in the text box below.

NANO-QUIZ ANSWERS

1. False! Property crime is the most common crime in the United States—7.7 million cases were reported in 2017 (FBI, 2018).
2. False! Of all people arrested in the United States, 73 percent are male and 68 percent were white. About 27 percent were black or African American. (FBI, 2018). Note: Media literacy encourages users to think critically about language, and here's a good example: Not all of the 73 percent of the males arrested were *white*, and not all 68 percent of white persons arrested were male. So the statements must be separate.
3. False again! This is a myth. "According to the American Psychological Association, children are not more likely to be molested by LGBT parents or their LGBT friends or acquaintances. Gregory Herek, a professor at the University of California, Davis, who is one of the nation's leading researchers on prejudice against sexual minorities, reviewed a series of studies and found no evidence that gay men molest children at higher rates than heterosexual men" (Schlatter & Steinback, 2011).
4. Again, false! Africa is a continent made up of 54 countries. Each country has its own political, social and economic structures.
5. You guessed it: False! There is no "African" language. It is estimated that there are more than 2,000 languages spoken in Africa; some languages are spoken across many countries, such as Swahili in East Africa and Zulu in Southern Africa (Oniang'o, 2017).

If you got any wrong answers, don't feel bad. Your answers may have been strongly influenced by depictions in news, entertainment and social media.

Mass media has immense persuasive power. It establishes cultural norms through casting, characters and characterization. It communicates values through storylines and news headlines. When television shows, news websites and other media outlets portray a version of the world that is not based in reality, it is not surprising that we, especially if we take in a lot of media, believe the faulty portrayals.

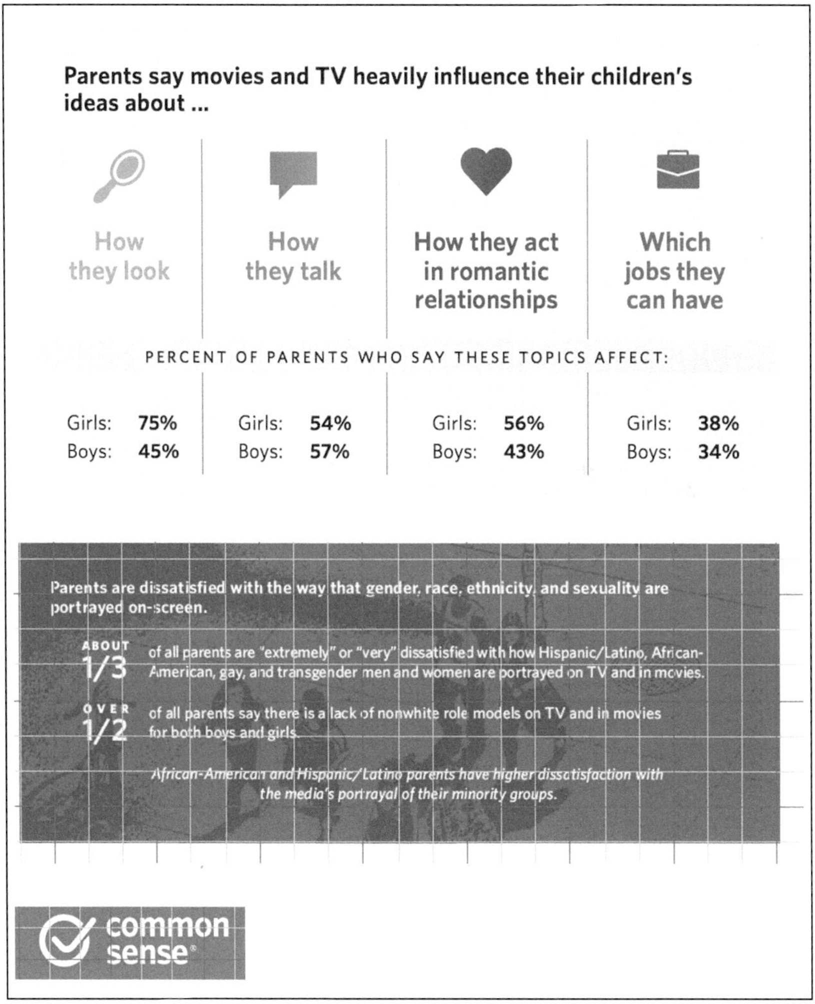

Media Portrayals in Movies and TV Heavily Influence Youth, and Parents Are Dissatisfied with That

Source: Common Sense Media, based on a survey of 933 parents of children ages 2–17 living in the United States, 2017

For example, entertainment media often depicts black males as criminals. Popular video games feature black males in sports games, but their representation in other games is diminished to mostly gangsters and street people, researchers found (Williams, Martins, Consalvo, & Ivory, 2009). TV news coverage *overrepresents* black men as perpetrators and *underrepresents* them as victims; while 37 percent of all perpetrators portrayed on television news were black, only 21 percent of actual arrestees were black, a 2000 study by Dixon and Linz stated. "These representations may have a powerful impact on viewers," wrote the authors (p. 151). What do you think? Do these representations have a powerful effect on you?

Media representations are not neutral; they communicate values and beliefs.

In addition, positive representations aren't prevalent in the media to counter these skewed portrayals; in news program commentary and analysis, black speakers accounted for less than 3 percent of statements made by invited experts on shows (Entman & Rojecki, 2000, p. 69).

Media representations are the ways in which media messages, rooted in a particular ideological and value-based perspective, portray individuals and groups of people. All media representations convey values and ideologies. But we in turn interpret media messages based on *our* values and belief systems. Most media messaging isn't content to mirror reality. It re-creates it, usually with a distinct value or ideological perspective. Media representations are not neutral; they communicate values and beliefs.

The profit-driven choices by big media have often limited the representation of people marginalized in societies due to race/ethnicity, religion, sexual orientation, age or physical or mental disabilities. For example, the representation of gay men on TV makes a statement about the cultural traditions of public society in the United States in the 1950s and 1960s; that is, gay men weren't represented at all. They were invisible, in the closet. It wasn't until 1977 that the first openly gay character was featured in a popular sitcom: ABC's *Soap* starred actor Billy Crystal as Jodie Dallas, a gay man having an affair with a famous quarterback.

Stereotypes In order to efficiently depict various groups of people, media representations can easily fall into stereotypes. **Stereotypes** are overly-simplified generalizations that convey a set of values, judgments and assumptions about a group of people, and often comment on their behavior, characteristics and/or history.

Stereotypes can be positive or negative, or both. Their essence is to rob social groups of individualization, and thus, they are often distorting and usually destructive. What makes stereotypes such an efficient way to communicate meaning is their *repetition*. Media consumers quickly pick up on the cues of a character type because we've seen them before: the jock, the joker, the handsome professional, the bumbling dad, and so forth.

These portrayals have been seen and heard so often, in so many kinds of messages—from maple syrup bottles to children's animated movies—that audiences *automatically and uncritically accept them*.

As evidence: In a U.S.-based study that included 1,200 children ages 10 to 17, researchers found that children notice the stereotypes being communicated to them through television shows, movies and music videos. Over one-third of children said that they never see males performing domestic chores such as cooking and cleaning, but the majority see them as leaders, problem solvers, athletic and confident (Heintz-Knowles et al., 1999).

Accessibility When people don't have significant in-person contact with people who aren't like themselves in significant ways, such as gender, sexual orientation, income, race or ethnicity, generational age and geographic location, they often rely on media representations for their knowledge. Stereotypes are often **accessible** information that is easily retrieved from memory. People who use media heavily are at risk for conflating media portrayals with real life. "Because of their pervasiveness, media stereotypes are frequently and easily accessible as cognitive shortcuts for influencing subsequent evaluations" (Ramasubramanian, 2011, p. 499).

Our minds are inclined to accept easy-to-reach media stereotypes in part because of the *repetition and vividness* of media portrayals, which serve to improve media consumers' recall of them (Busselle & Schrum, 2003; Srull & Wyer, 1989).

Walter Lippmann, an American newspaper commentator and author, used the term "stereotype" to describe what he described as the "pictures in our head" that oversimplify people, places and ideas (1922, p. 25).

Lippmann, in his book *Public Opinion*, wrote that "the picture inside so often misleads men in their dealings with the world outside." He noted many factors that contributed to the distortions of media simplification, including the "difficulty of making a small vocabulary express a complicated world."

CULTIVATION THEORY

Media representations' impact on real life is described by **cultivation theory**. This theory asserts that media is a socializing agent, and by giving audience members repeated exposure to the same conceptualizations of society—for instance, that Arab males are violent and untrustworthy, or that Asians are all smart and over-achieving—heavy media users in particular adopt such interpretations as truth.

Research studies have confirmed experimentally that exposure to stereotypical African-American characters and behaviors in entertainment programs has negative impacts on people's beliefs and attitudes about African Americans, as well as towards affirmative action policies (Ramasubramanian, 2011). Other media representation research has found that the more television white viewers consumed, the more their evaluations of Latinos reflected TV characterizations of criminality, intelligence and work ethic—"markedly so when viewers' real world contact with Latinos was not close, resulting in a greater reliance on televised images in decision making" (Mastro, Behm-Morawitz, & Ortiz, 2007, p. 362).

Portrayals Affect Perceptions Widespread negative media portrayals are associated with people's real-life negative perceptions. This means the media's negative stereotypes may influence the way people think about Muslims, people of Arab descent, gays and lesbians, transgender individuals, people with mental illness and other marginalized communities.

For example, there was "a disturbing under-representation of Native Americans, Asian Americans and Latinos on primetime television," concluded an analysis of the 345 most-viewed U.S. television shows within 12 separate television seasons spanning the years 1987 to 2009 (Tukachinsky, Mastro, & Yarchi, 2015, p. 20). Women of color were often presented as hyper-sexual and not very professional.

Missing Minorities

Speaking or named characters in **414 stories** (109 motion pictures and 305 broadcast, cable, and digital series) released in 2014 or 2015:

Of those characters with enough cues to ascertain race/ethnicity (n=10,444) –

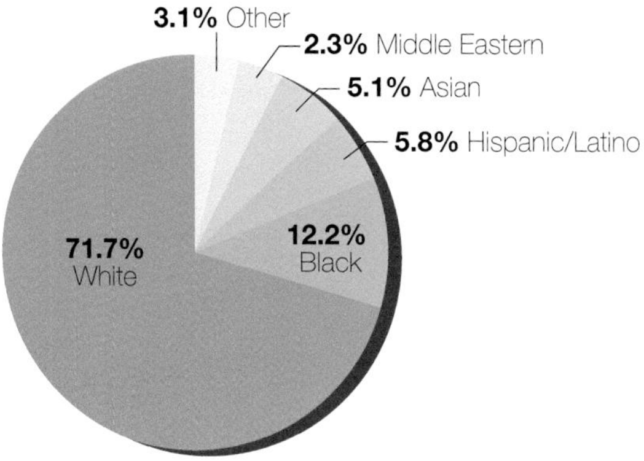

Thus, 28.3% of all speaking characters were from underrepresented racial/ethnic groups, which is below (-9.6%) the proportion in the U.S. population (37.9%)

SOURCE: Inclusion or invisibility? Comprehensive Annenberg Report on Diversity in Entertainment. Stacy L. Smith, Marc Choueiti and Katherine Pieper. February 2016. Institute for Diversity and Empowerment at Annenberg.

The researchers juxtaposed their analysis with U.S. public opinion surveys. Sure enough, media representations influenced real-life attitudes:

> The prevalence of hyper-sexualized Black and Latino characters was associated with more negative attitudes towards Blacks and Latinos in the U.S. Conversely, as more Blacks and Latinos on television occupied high social and professional status, White Americans tended to hold more favorable views of these social groups. These results illuminate the importance of improving the quality of representations of ethnic minorities.
>
> (p. 21)

While the study was limited to the United States, the researchers noted research showing negative depictions and underrepresentation of non-whites in Canada, Muslims in the United Kingdom, Turkish immigrants in Germany and Arabs in Israel. They conclude that because depictions of ethnicity and race cannot be regulated in the media, media literacy education of audiences around racial and ethnic stereotypes becomes essential.

In a final example of media's negative stereotyping of a nation's racial minority, consider a study on the attitudes of Han Chinese, the ethnic majority in China, toward one of the nation's minority groups, the Uyghurs. Media can prime negative information about this minority group, which then activates negative stereotypes toward people from the group, the researchers found. Brain scans of subjects after media priming showed that "the media can influence people's judgments toward other groups in subtle, subconscious ways" (Jin, Pei, & Ma, 2017).

VOX DISCIPULI

The media has historically perpetuated stereotypical notions about Black women and has depicted us as one-dimensional beings. The caretaker who carries everyone's burdens and pain, even those who aren't directly a part of her family or community. The oversexualized temptress. The angry loud embittered woman. These are some of the narratives that the media has circulated for generations.

We're seeing and hearing more stories that capture Black women leading full complex lives. I'm 29 years old, so I've had the opportunity to witness an era, the 1990s, in which Black entertainers and influencers were thriving and generating an array of work. I saw women that I identified with or represented the Black women I grew up around, and I saw women whose experiences were drastically different from the world around me. I've also witnessed that trend or type of storytelling taper off into the 2000s. I went through a period of yearning for the same level of programming that I saw in my early childhood. Diverse imagery is now making a resurgence. While I recognize the strides that have and are being made, there's still so much more work that needs to be done. There needs to be more representation of Black womanhood. The negative depictions and stereotypes of African American women are still circulating and are deeply rooted in America's consciousness. —Kendra, 29

Real-World Effects Of course, no study can *strictly isolate* the effects of negative media depictions on real-world behavior. It is difficult to prove that media stereotypes directly lead to real-world behaviors. For example, it's simply not known whether violence in the media leads to violent behavior in the real world. But there is substantial evidence that violence in the media causes short-term effects of aggressive thoughts, emotions and reactions (Bushman & Huesmann, 2001; Browne & Hamilton-Giachritsis, 2005).

Given the amount of media consumption in Western societies in particular, and the consistency of stereotypes in mass media presentations, a great deal of scholarly research provides correlative or associative evidence of media representations affecting peoples' attitudes and beliefs, which social science indicates then affect behaviors. **Correlation** means there is a relationship or connection between two or more elements. However, correlation is not **causation**, meaning something caused an effect, and we can't say for sure whether stereotypes of certain groups lead directly to negative behavior toward those groups.

How well do you understand this idea of "correlation is not causation"? How does it influence your attitude toward media's potential effects on cultural awareness and understanding?

READING RESEARCH CRITICALLY

This chapter contains a lot of references to research studies. How do you as a reader who is short on time and patience determine if a "new study" or a "surprising finding" should be taken seriously? Here are a few things to think and ask about when "research" and "experts" are cited:

- In which journal is it published? A quick check of a journal's "impact factor" (just Google it) is one indication of how credible it is within its discipline. (A higher number, such as 6 or more, indicates more citations of articles from that journal, which is a sign that other academic researchers trust it.)
- Check the lead author's name; is this person an expert in the subject? Look for other articles in the same area of study by this author. If several authors are listed, often the final author is the supervisor or principal researcher, so search that name first.
- Is the journal peer-reviewed? This means that the findings were reviewed by other experts in the same field before it was published.
- How many participants were in the study? (That is the "n" in the data.) Findings from a survey of 7, 17 or even 70 people don't say much about a

general population, but may be highly relevant in cases with specific populations.

- Was the study replicated by other researchers? Good research doesn't come out of the blue; it is part of a scaffolding of work done by many experts in a field who work from one another's findings to verify them or fill in gaps in knowledge. Be cautious about completely new work that is without precedent.
- When was the study done; how current is it? Has anything significant in that field happened since the research was done?
- Are the findings clearly stated? By the way, words such as "suggest" or "may" or "could" are often used, and correctly so, by conservative researchers careful to not overstate their findings.
- Was the study paid for by a third party and if so, who? Is the funding source disclosed and are there any potential conflicts of interest? (For example, a drug company paying for a study of its drug is likely to hire a researcher who is favorably disposed to its product.)
- What is the margin of error? This is typically seen with polls or surveys. The **margin of error**, or MOE, is the potential miscalculation or uncertainty of the sampling results. An MOE of +/-5 means the results could be 5 values above or 5 below the actual survey results. A lower MOE means you can have more confidence in the results. So a finding of 8 points difference with a MOE of +/-5 is actually as little difference as 3 points or as much as 13 points.

MEDIA AS CONNECTOR

MediaSmarts, Canada's Centre for Digital and Media Literacy, noted that,

> We rely as much on the media as on anything else to tell us about the world. For instance, research has shown persuasively that media consumption can affect how we see others and how we see ourselves, even if we don't realize it—a condition known as *implicit* or *unconscious* bias—and the presence or absence of different groups in media has been shown to affect how people feel about those groups.
>
> (2019, "Tips")

Media messages can offer compelling depictions of cultures that may facilitate real-life understanding and empathy.

Media messages can offer compelling depictions of cultures that may facilitate real-life understanding and empathy.

Some examples of culturally diverse programming include the Aboriginal Peoples Television Network in Canada, the world's first national indigenous TV network, begun in 1999. Another example of inclusion in the media is the U.S.-based public television show *Sesame Street*, which now has a character named Julia, who is autistic. "The most impressive evidence of Julia's power came from people with autism, who saw something they'd never seen before: a reflection of themselves. Letters and emails flooded into Sesame from across America and around the world," said a 2017 *Smithsonian* article written several months after Julia's debut (Suskind, 2017).

Singer Beyoncé's "Lemonade" music video in 2017 made a statement based on events at the time, in part by including three mothers holding photos of their black sons—Trayvon Martin, Michael Brown and Eric Garner—killed in interactions with police. In showcasing these mothers in her video, Beyoncé was making a social commentary in a year when women were challenging cultural narratives in vocal ways, including the use of the #MeToo hashtag by those who had been sexually harassed or assaulted.

The founder of a nonprofit that aides sexual violence survivors, activist Tarana Burke created the Me Too initiative in 2006 as a way for women to show support for one another. The solidarity tag #MeToo went viral in 2017, after actor Alyssa Milano used it in a tweet. This is an example of the silencing or disregard of black women's voices, some said, because Burke, who is black, had not previously had the support of white feminists (Garcia, 2017).

Another example: Marvel comics created a character called Kamala Khan (AKA Ms. Marvel), a Pakistani-American teenager who combats crime and also the assumptions of Americans about Muslim immigrants. When the extremist group American Freedom Defense Initiative bought ad space on San Francisco buses to champion its anti-Muslim messages, street artists and activists made over the hateful ads with their own messages featuring Ms. Marvel and statements such as "Calling All Bigotry Busters" (NBC News, 2015).

Positive media depictions, it is hoped, expand audiences' views of people with whom they may not have much actual interaction.

NEGATIVE MEDIA REPRESENTATIONS

Media literacy, critical thinking about content, moderation in media use and interpersonal relationships with diverse people—these are antidotes to damaging media representations. What follows are research-based practices we can employ today and every day to counter the stereotype-laden media we consume:

- A conscious effort to *be aware of one's biases* and active concern about prejudice are key elements in changing one's discriminatory attitudes (Devine, Forscher, Austin, & Cox, 2012).
- Practice replacing a negative stereotype with a more neutral or positive one (Devine et al., 2012).
- Prejudice is reduced when people are repeatedly exposed to diverse representatives of minority groups through *direct interpersonal contact* (Pettigrew, 1998; Simon, 1998). Real-life relationships allow for a broader understanding of minority group members as opposed to a one-dimensional media representation.
- Consuming media with *counter-stereotypical depictions* of minority groups repeatedly over time may reduce stereotype dependence in attitudes and behaviors (Schiappa, Gregg, & Hewes, 2005). A series of studies found that when people watch media with gay and transgender characters, they report feeling more positive attitudes toward gay men and transgender people in actual life.

Identification Audience members can identify with fictional characters and adopt their perspective (Livingstone, 1998). **Identification** means to feel affinity toward a character so powerfully that as media consumers, we feel empathy for their situation and their motives and goals, wrote Haifa University communication professor Jonathan Cohen (2006). "Identification has both affective (empathy) and cognitive (understanding goals and motives, perspective-taking) components" (pp. 184–185).

For example, when you find yourself so involved with what is happening to the main character of your favorite TV drama that you're emotionally upset when things don't go their way in an episode, you're in identification mode with that character. Identification with media characters and narratives allows audience members to lose themselves in the narrative, transporting them out of their daily routines and into engaging mediated worlds.

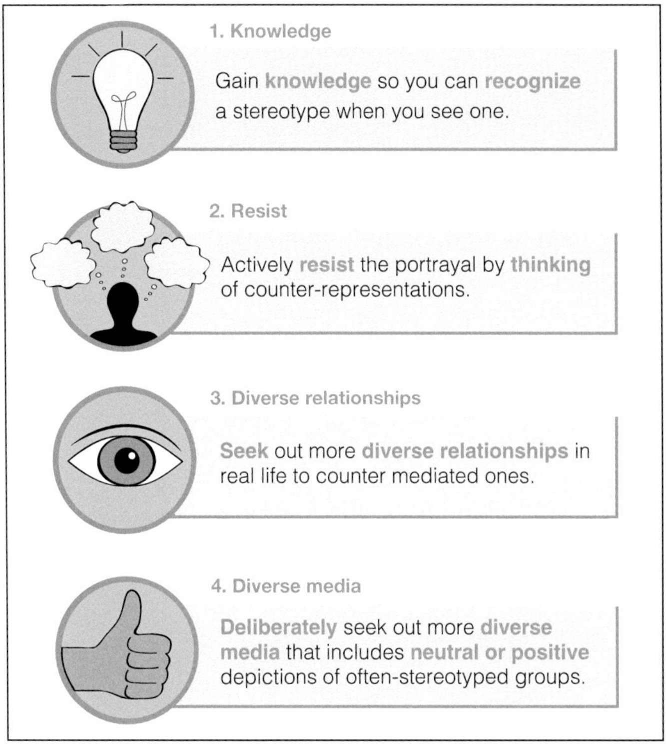

Combatting Negative Media Representations

However, Cohen summarized, this identification can mean audience members don't critically appraise media programs. Have *you* ever experienced identification with a media character?

Preserving and Promoting Diversity In countries in which there are many cultures together, media can combat ignorance by showcasing differences, and thus increase understanding and tolerance (Hargrave, 2007).

In other words, people who are underrepresented or misrepresented in a country need a voice that informs them in their own language about essential civic activities; how to vote, who is running for election, etc. Further, there is the need to educate and inform the majority in a country about their neighbors.

Inclusive media programming focuses on media messages *for* an underrepresented group of people; media that is not focused on diversity will create programming that is *about* an underrepresented group of people. The former serves that group by providing programming that takes their perspective, the latter objectifies them. One form of media that often supplies that form of inclusive programming is publicly owned media.

Watch this real-time analysis by The LAMPlatoon of the contents of an ad for a low-calorie meal replacement shake. See http://bit.ly/2U4UaBw. The ad does many things well, such as inclusivity. What values are communicated?

PUBLIC MEDIA

In the United States, most media outlets are for-profit, with owners who sell advertising as a way of paying for their programming. But in many other countries, **public media**, which is largely funded by governments, donations and subscriptions, is a dominant force. The United States has public media too—think radio pledge drives and *Sesame Street*—and it has the ability to educate the public about issues of importance through innovative programming such as news stories, music, radio programs, TV shows and documentaries. Media that don't rely on turning a profit are often in a better position to combat ignorance by showcasing differences, and thus increase understanding and tolerance (UNESCO's Convention for the Protection and Promotion of the Diversity of Cultural Expressions, 2005).

Hallmarks of healthy public media are:

- Universal accessibility
- Freedom from vested interests
- Commitment to quality programming as opposed to high ratings
- Attention to underrepresented groups and minorities
- Contributions to a sense of community

Here's an interesting thought: Do you even *know* when you are tuned into to public media? What are the signs you're tuned in to something noncommercial? Is it the choice of topics covered? The delivery? Another way to think about it: When you're in a new city and turn on the radio or television, what clues do you use to determine whether or not a news outlet is public media?

Showcasing Diversity Australia's Special Broadcasting Service is funded by the government. It has the smallest budget of any broadcaster in the country but manages to offer 18 hours of programming a day in any one of 70 languages. Some 4.2 million Australians tune in weekly. Its content uses subtitles and not dubbing in order to preserve the integrity of the original program. Programs are in Spanish, Cantonese, Yiddish and more.

Public media can be an important conduit for communicating national values and providing citizens with information as well as expanding the diversity of programming in a region. However, many critics of citizen-funded public media (especially in the United States) argue that it is overwhelmingly liberal in its viewpoint. This raises interesting questions about whether the quest to reflect a country's diversity can be separated from a political perspective and seen as a good thing on its own, or whether some people always see diversity through an ideological lens.

Attracting Audiences One challenge of public media broadcasting is to be engaging enough that people want to watch it and listen to it, but not be so good that commercial media complain they are taxpayer-funded competition.

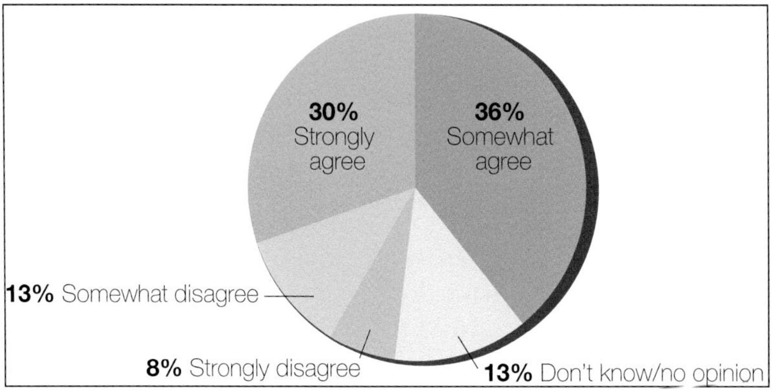

Shares of Consumers Who Believe That Public TV Has Interesting Programs
Source: Morning Consult, Statista, 2018

Long perceived by audiences as a lecture or sermon on what one should think, public broadcasting in the 21st century is struggling to appeal to younger generations. As a Dutch public broadcaster stated, "Public broadcasting is associated with effort, commercial broadcasting with relaxation" (NOS, 1999, p. 2). *Ouch.*

The fragmentation of audiences due to near-infinite channel choice is hurting public media too.

Sue Gardner has many titles, but of late, she is a special advisor to the Wikimedia Foundation, the non-profit that operates Wikipedia, where she used to be its executive director. Gardner, writing on public broadcasting's uncertain future (2017), stated:

> The challenge for public broadcasters is to figure out how to artfully, strategically insert themselves into a crowded, competitive, private sector-dominant global media landscape in a way that understands that people have many options, and that the purpose of public media is to provide value where markets can't or won't. What might that look like?
>
> (p. 13)

You heard her: What might that look like? Discuss!

Dis-Connect Digital media has the potential to both help and hurt audience exposure to cultural representations. For example, audience members looking for more positive cultural representations can now find alternatives more easily. Comic book critic Oliver Sava said, "The Internet has made it possible for creators and fans to have their voices heard, and those voices demand better representation for people who don't fit the traditional mold" (2014, para 2).

However, the endless programming options also mean people can quite easily *avoid* expanding their knowledge of unfamiliar cultures. A theme of this chapter on connecting is that the fragmented audiences have myriad media choices for programming. So it's up to you to choose wisely when it comes to diverse programming that represents you and others in full and complex portrayals.

CHAPTER REVIEW

- Analyze the media representation of an underrepresented group in your country's media.
- Provide definitions for correlation, cultivation theory, identification.
- Identify the margin of error in a scholarly article that uses data.
- Find an example of public media programming that preserves a nation's cultural diversity.
- List four ways to combat negative media representations.
- Describe three positive media representations and why they are counter-stereotypical.

ACTIVITIES

1. Check out Alphadesigner.com for global maps of stereotypes about various cultures and peoples. Are these stereotypes the same as those you hold? Download a world map. Fill it in with your personal stereotypes—which may in some cases be blank nothingness for some countries and regions, because we don't see or access much media about those places. That tells you something too, doesn't it? Share your map with a peer.
2. Test the criticism that public media outlets are overly liberal in their ideological stance. Watch or listen to an informational program on your local public television or radio station. Do you think it is ideologically biased as conservative, liberal or some other political viewpoint? Identify specific ways the bias is evident in the program. Suggest ways to provide more balance to the program, or providing more balance to the overall station programing.
3. Search Google Scholar to find a scholarly article that showcases findings from research on the influence of media representations of media consumers—refer to the tips in "Reading Research Critically" given earlier in the chapter to help you. Read the abstract and ask questions about the findings as a group discussion or in a short paper.
4. Select a single episode of a sitcom to watch as a group. Identify the stereotypical behaviors, characteristics and attitudes portrayed by the char-

acters. Be as specific as possible, noting word choices of characters, attire and mannerisms. Determine whether or not you know anyone in real life that is similar to the characters. Compare your conclusions with others.

REFERENCES

Browne, K. D., & Hamilton-Giachritsis, C. (2005). The influence of violent media on children and adolescents: A public-health approach. *The Lancet, 365*(9460), 702–710. https://doi.org/10.1016/S0140-6736(05)17952-5

Bushman, B. J., & Huesmann, L. R. (2001). Effects of televised violence on aggression. In D. Singer & J. Singer (Eds.), *Handbook of children and the media* (pp. 223–254). Thousand Oaks, CA: Sage.

Busselle, R. W., & and Schrum, L. J. (2003). Media exposure and exemplar accessibility. *Media Psychology, 5*(3), 255–282.

Cohen, J. (2006). Audience identification with media characters. In J. Bryant & P. Vorderer (Eds.), *Psychology of entertainment* (p. 183–197). Mahwah, NJ: Lawrence Erlbaum Associates Publishers.

Devine, P. G., Forscher, P. S., Austin, A. J., & Cox, W. T. L. (2012). Long-term reduction in implicit race bias: A prejudice habit-breaking intervention. *Journal of Experimental Social Psychology, 48*(6), 1267–1278.

Dixon, T. L., & Linz, D. (2000). Overrepresentation and underrepresentation of African Americans and Latinos as lawbreakers on television news. *Journal of Communication,* 131–154.

Entman, R. M., & Rojecki, A. (2000). *The black image in the white mind.* Chicago, IL: University of Chicago Press.

FBI. (2018). 2017 crime statistics released. FBI.gov.

Gardner, S. (2017). *Public broadcasting: Its past and its future: 2017 Public media white papers.* Miami: Knight Foundation.

Garcia, S. (2017, October 20). The woman who created #MeToo long before hashtags. *The New York Times.* Retrieved from https://nyti.ms/2Gm9KR4

Hargrave, A. M. (2007). *Cultural diversity practices among broadcasting regulators.* Report for the Broadcasting Regulation and Cultural Diversity Network. Retrieved from http://bit.ly/2V1iNMy.

Heintz-Knowles, K., Li-Vollmer, M., Chen, P., Harris, T., Haufler, A., Lapp, J., & Miller, P. (1999). *Boys to men: Entertainment media. Messages about masculinity: A national poll of children, focus groups, and content analysis of entertainment media*. Oakland, CA: Children Now.

Jin, J., Pei, G., & Ma, Q. (2017). They are what you hear in media reports: The racial stereotypes toward Uyghurs activated by media. *Frontiers in Neuroscience, 11*, 675. doi:10.3389/fnins.2017.00675

Lippmann, W. (1922). *Public opinion*. San Diego, CA: Harcourt Brace.

Livingstone, S. M. (1998). Relationships between media and audiences: Prospects for audience reception research. In T. Liebes & J. Curran (Eds.), *Media, ritual and identity* (pp. 237–255). London: Routledge.

Mastro, D., Behm-Morawitz, E., & Ortiz, M. (2007). The cultivation of social perceptions of Latinos: A mental models approach. *Media Psychology*, *9*(2), 347–365.

MediaSmarts. (2019). *Media literacy fundamentals: Tips for integrating media literacy into the classroom (#7)*. Ottawa, ON: Canada's Centre for Digital and Media Literacy.

NBC News. (2015, January 27). Comic heroine Ms. Marvel saves San Francisco from anti-Islam ads. Retrieved from https://nbcnews.to/2Y0WBTB

Nederlandse Omroepprogramma Stichting (NOS). (1999). Hilversummary. *Broadcasting news from the Netherlands*. Hilversum: NOS.

Oniang'o, M. (2017, June 19). 10 common misconceptions and stereotypes about Africa. Retrieved from Africa.com.

Pettigrew, T. F. (1998). Intergroup contact theory. *Annual Review of Psychology*, *49*, 65–85.

Ramasubramanian, S. (2011). The impact of stereotypical versus counterstereotypical media exemplars on racial attitudes, causal attributions, and support for affirmative action. *Communication Research*, *38*(4), 497–516. https://doi.org/10.1177/0093650210384854

Sava, O., Wilson, G. W., Bollers, K., & Asselin, J. (2014, July 30). *Strides and backslides: How to tackle diversity in comics*. The A.V. Club. Retrieved from http://bit.ly/2U0z8og

Schiappa, E., Gregg, P. B., & Hewes, D. (2005). The parasocial contact hypothesis. *Communication Monographs*, *72*(1), 92–115.

Schlatter, E., & Steinback, R. (2011, February 27). 10 anti-gay myths debunked. *The Intelligence Report*. Southern Poverty Law Center.

Shares of consumers who believe that public TV has interesting programs. (2018). Statista—The Statistics Portal. Retrieved from http://bit.ly/33p6UVr

Simon, A. (1998). The relationship between stereotypes of and attitudes toward lesbians and gays. In G. M. Herek (Ed.), *Stigma and sexual orientation* (pp. 62–81). Thousand Oaks, CA: Sage.

Srull, T. K., & Wyer, R. S. (1989). Person memory and judgment. *Psychological Review, 96*(1), 58–83. http://dx.doi.org/10.1037/0033-295X.96.1.58.

Suskind, R. (2017). Why the team behind Sesame Street created a character with autism. *Smithsonian Magazine.* Retrieved from http://bit.ly/30JogdG

Tukachinsky, R., Mastro, D., & Yarchi, M. (2015). Documenting portrayals of race/ethnicity on primetime television over a 20-year span and their association with national-level racial/ethnic attitudes. *Journal of Social Issues, 71*, 17–38.

United Nations Educational Scientific and Cultural Organization. (2005). Convention for the Protection and Promotion of the Diversity of Cultural Expressions in 2005.

Williams, D., Martins, N., Consalvo, M., & Ivory, J. D. (2009). The virtual census: Representations of gender, race and age in video games. *New Media Society, 11*(5), 815–834.

8 Informing

How News Media Seek Truth, and Shape Reality

What makes something newsworthy to you? For many of us, "news" is when our bestie meets someone new and that person actually shows some promise as a significant other.

Or, news is when a family member loses their job and we want to come to their aid with memes about their stupid boss. In short, for many of us, news is personal and relevant.

Depressing or troubling headlines are often enough to keep any of us from delving into a full-length news report about the day's crises. What follows is a look at what people *are* interested in, based on the most popular Google searches of 2018 worldwide. I've also included the location in which the term was most popular during the peak time frame for the search. Search term popularity is relative to the total number of Google searches

LEARNING OBJECTIVES

Terms: Watchdog reporting, open records laws, implicit biases, gatekeeping, agenda-setting, availability heuristic, issue-attention cycle, framing, priming, citizen journalism, aggregation.

- Explain the significance of each of the fundamentals of journalism.
- Identify an example of each news value.
- Define the obstacles to excellent journalism.
- Describe the cognitive biases influencing news creation.
- Understand how media effects shape our understanding of events and issues.
- Understand the implications of "the war on truth."

- Summarize the ways technology has affected journalism, including aggregation.
- Outline the future of AI, machine learning and news.
- Know basic news literacy skills, including the illogical fallacies.

Do you regularly consume news? What sources do you use most frequently? What is your opinion of journalism today?

performed at a specific time, in a specific location.

World Cup: Nepal, which didn't even have a qualifying team, but whose native players are scattered on many WC teams.
Avicci: Sweden, the home country of the musician, who died that year.
Mac Miller: United States, with his hometown of Pittsburgh leading the searches.
Stan Lee: San Jose, Costa Rica. While a man named Stanley Lee *was* the winner of this city's two-day poker tournament in March 2018, the other, more famous Stan Lee of Marvel Comics fame, died in November. The Google search trend was for him.
Black Panther: Trinidad and Tobago, the home country of Winston Duke, who was the supervillain M'Baku in the movie.

Each of those in the top five make my point; news is what is personal and relevant. Except I still can't quite figure out why the November 12th death of Marvel Comics creator Stan Lee so captivated Costa Rica in particular. (Let me know if you figure that one out, please.)

This chapter will explore how news outlets decide that an event might be personal and relevant to you, how biases happen in the news, how to spot them, and why a balanced news diet is essential to media literacy. It will also examine the role of journalism in a society and the impact of technology and artificial intelligence on news media. It will not, sadly, explain that Stan Lee outlier in Costa Rica.

FUNDAMENTALS OF JOURNALISM

If you listen to certain world leaders, you might believe the state of journalism couldn't be in worse shape. However, it's not surprising that world leaders might not love their resident journalists. The reason? Professional journalists take seriously their job to serve as watchdogs, not lapdogs, of the people in power.

The **fundamentals** of professional journalism are the same across the globe. They include:

- Truth-seeking
- Accuracy
- Independence (such as from bribes, political influence or oversight, pressure from advocacy groups)
- Fairness and impartiality
- Accountability (to admit and publicly correct errors)
- Minimizing harm when telling others' stories, especially those of victims and children

I was a staff writer at the *Chicago Tribune* before becoming a professor. I know that news organizations are pulled in many directions, and even the most noble intentions can get off track due to the present-day pressures of the news industry. The news business is not perfect by any means, and efforts by professional journalists and reporting organizations to improve and protect the best of the profession will continue. In my experience, professional journalists are dedicated to truth-telling and serving the public (it's certainly not for the salary).

For a searchable world map of journalism codes of ethics, see The Accountable Journalism website at https://bit.ly/2ArzNmX.

Watchdog journalism is the cornerstone of the press' role in a democratic society. **Watchdog journalism** strives to ensure that public officials, public institutions and public dollars are doing what they are supposed to be doing: serving the public. Through documents, interviews and observation, watchdog journalists serve to hold public institutions accountable and transparent. One primary way watchdog journalists report on government is through **open records laws**. These laws are active in many countries, but certainly not all, and require access to public documents from any government agency. Governments have become less transparent through the erosion and narrowing of their open records laws; this makes accountability of public entities by journalists very difficult, but all the more important.

NEWS VALUES

What makes an event, issue, group or person worthy of news coverage? Common news values are:

Proximity, as in close to home; your local election results (see the graphic below and notice that people care more about national and local news than international news).

Timeliness, as in something that just happened, is happening or is about to happen; the sentencing of a convicted felon in court today.

Impact, as in the more people affected, the more newsworthy the story is; the path of the oncoming hurricane.

Relevance, as in something people relate to or care about; the new flu medicine on the market.

Conflict, as in a dispute or a clash; this covers a huge range from all-out war to a zoning dispute to ideological battles.

Prominence, as in something or someone significant, and this is relative to the size of the news outlet; a local mayor's car accident may be news for a local TV station, but not for the national cable station.

Novelty, as in news that is unusual or quirky; the duck that is palling around with the lion at the local zoo.

Usefulness, as in consumer-oriented, practical information; how to winterize your home.

Human interest, a catch-all category of interesting stories involving people; the mom reunited with her now 30-year-old daughter, whom she placed for adoption as a baby.

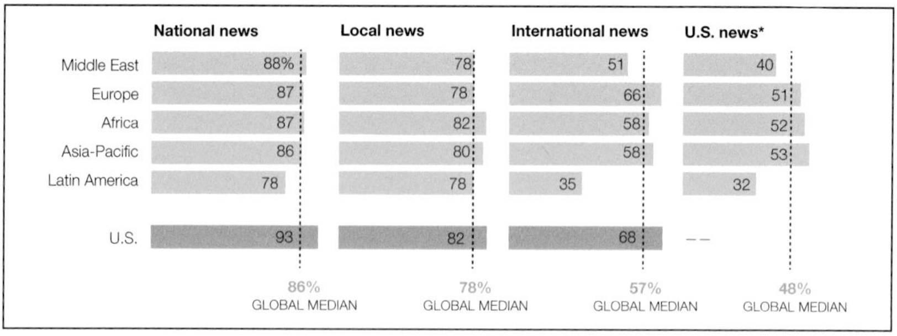

People More Closely Follow National and Local News: Regional Medians Saying They Closely Follow Each Type of News

* Question about U.S. news was not asked in the United States.

Note: Global median across 38 countries. Europe regional median excludes Russia.

Source: Mitchell, Simmons, Matsa, and Silver (2018), Pew Research Center

OBSTACLES TO EXCELLENT JOURNALISM

When friends, family, neighbors, students and the cashier at the grocery store complain about the news media, I simply offer, in an animated manner, the following seven-point lecture on the many factors that affect the neutrality and quality of news reports. You'll see that when it comes to flawless journalism, there is shared blame, and that includes news consumers. News consumers interested in being fully informed about their local communities need to decide that they are willing to pay for quality reporting and support local news operations through subscriptions and other pay-for-service models.

Time Constraints The rush to publish has accelerated to mere seconds with digitization. Beating the competition is still a priority in journalism, and the result can at times be a story that hasn't been carefully vetted for biased word choice, balanced sourcing and sufficient context. The background information to fully understand a current happening is critical to consumers' understanding of the significance of an event, but the news media's focus on breaking news is often at the expense of context.

The good news is that digital media allows for stories to be filed immediately, and updated throughout the hours after an event. Often, news outlets will then compile these instant updates into a comprehensive news story that summarizes the event. It also allows news organizations to quickly post corrections to published pieces.

VOX DISCIPULI

Sometimes I use the app called Flipboard which is a short news segment that changes daily. As far as deciding what to trust, it truly depends on the source and how able they are to back up the information that is being conveyed. I do not watch national news outlets at all or any type of national media print primarily due to lack of trust. I find the topics to be heavily focused on present trends especially with U.S. bias/politics and pop culture content rather than a general focus on necessary topics and global news.

I posted on my Instagram story asking my friends how many of them read/watched/listened to the news daily. About 150 people voted and 20 of them said they did follow news daily while the rest said they did not. Most people responded and said they chose not to because finding the content they wanted to read was too difficult, there wasn't enough time in their day, or that they felt that the information seemed of little to no purpose for them. —Nicole, 24

Story Selection Which issues get covered and which don't? Who decides what is newsworthy? See the list of common news values noted earlier in this chapter. Sometimes, news outlets follow a story simply because other outlets are following it. No one wants to get beat. But this "herd mentality" can lead to homogenized coverage that doesn't offer consumers a variety of perspectives. This can be particularly true when covering national government, as administrations can limit access to information and insist that staff don't talk to the news media.

Additionally, complicated stories require expertise, time and resources that a news outlet might not have. So shallow coverage that relies on public relations specialists and media-savvy public officials can be the result. (By the way, shallow coverage is in part the audience's fault for not supporting complex news stories with shares, likes and page views. News outlets track the analytics of their stories, and the types of stories that get audience attention tend to get covered more.)

Finally, a story needs to fit an outlet's coverage focus: Is a given story the type that this particular news organization usually covers? News outlets typically have defined geographic, topical and creative parameters that shape coverage decisions.

Lack of Diversity Journalists and editors pursue stories using news values, but what about the people, events and issues of which they aren't even aware because their staffs are not diverse? News outlets ideally have staffs that reflect the demographics of their coverage area. So, for instance, if a TV station covers a metropolitan area that is 20 percent Latino, then the goal is to have the staff be that percent as well. The idea is that journalists and staff from differing backgrounds will be more aware of the breadth of stories and issues in a region.

At the BBC in the United Kingdom, for example, the number of journalists of color (i.e., black, Asian, Latino and other minority ethnicities) was just above 12 percent of the workforce in 2015. In the United Kingdom in 2011, the year of the most recent census figures, 12.9 percent of residents identified as non-white, so that would appear to be parity. However, the minority population is higher in London, where the majority of the BBC staff work (Martinson, 2016).

In terms of BBC staff with disabilities, 733 staffers, or 3.7 percent, identified themselves as having a disability in 2015. The BBC's target was 5.3 percent by 2017.

In the United States, the majority of news staffs are white and male. Women made up one-third of news employees overall in 2017, while they are about half of the U.S. population. Journalists of color made up 16.5 percent of U.S. newsroom staff in 2017 and 24.3 percent of online-only outlets, according to the annual diversity study by the American Society of News Editors in 2017, the last year for which there was a high response rate (40 percent, or 661 outlets). Nationally, the population of people who were white and not Hispanic or Latino was 60 percent (U.S. Census Bureau, 2017). So reaching racial and ethnic parity overall is still at least 15 percentage points away.

The media literacy principle of noticing who or what is omitted from a media message is particularly relevant here. Certainly reporters are trained to seek news stories in all aspects of life, but what stories are overlooked or dismissed due to the different life experiences of staff? Further, with staff cuts, reporters have less time to dig for interesting and different news stories. As news consumers, we can offset this lack of diversity in a single outlet's content by seeking out a variety of information outlets. Ethnic media, alternative media and public media are all great options for diversifying our news diet.

Implicit Biases Journalists at all levels and of all backgrounds have implicit biases in their thinking that may inadvertently distort coverage. **Implicit biases** are attitudes or stereotypes we hold about people without our conscious knowledge. These habits of thought and shortcuts in thinking can mean that prejudices about groups of people prevent neutral and fair coverage. This is why a diverse news staff is critical, as it encourages a broader range of perspectives on the news, and greater awareness of many kinds of cultures. Also, cognitive biases are different from *ideological* biases. The latter references partisan leanings of news media, which for some outlets are purposeful and directed by the owners of a news outlet. Cognitive biases are habits of thinking that journalists don't know they have that can affect their reasoning and decision-making.

Journalists are like everyone else; they hold stereotypes and prejudices too, but professional training helps attenuate those biases. Furthermore, editors and colleagues serve to leaven the impact of implicit biases. Training and a team approach to news are important differences between professional and citizen journalists.

Story Qualities A story's inherent characteristics also dictate the way it is told and who tells it. A highly visual story is more likely to get covered by television news outlets than radio news organizations. A data-heavy story may become an infographic. A digital report will have many hyperlinks to provide evidence and background.

As we all well know by now, creating an engaging news story is essential to get noticed in our loud multimedia society. A news story in *any* medium requires choices, as you've likely experienced in your own content creation. The best quality photo may not be the most representative of a situation. The most engaging quotes may not be useable as live audio due to sound quality. The competition for attention is so strident that news outlets sometimes oversell a story to convince consumers to pay attention to their content and not the competition's.

Lack of Balance News stories can be imbalanced in many ways. Here are some ways:

- A lack of relevant and **diverse viewpoints** in a story can make it incomplete.
- The absence of **critical reporting**, such as not challenging the assertions of a source or asking for verification, can give a source too much authority in a story.
- The **placement** of the story within a newscast or website may not be commensurate with its news value, such as providing a minor story with prominent airing or treating fairly important events with a minor mention.

Imbalanced coverage can lead news consumers to think that news media are unfair and sometimes inaccurate. For example, why are news outlets so reticent to call a politician a liar?

"Many news organizations resist using the word because of the question of intent," wrote David Bauder of the Associated Press (2018). "Editors feel it's important to establish whether someone is spreading false information knowingly, intending to deceive, and it's hard to get inside a person's head."

News outlets focus on calling out the inaccuracies of statements and providing the facts. It's up to the audience to decide if a politician is lying.

Access Getting the attention of busy journalists is a critical step in getting coverage. Public relations specialists, lobbyists, spokespeople for public officials, celebrities and prominent figures all have an easier time getting the attention of journalists than everyday citizens. In turn, journalists also covet access to those same public officials, celebrities and prominent figures. Some sources want promises of only positive coverage, or of prior review of content before publication; this is why the journalistic principle of independence is so important.

New media has somewhat altered the gatekeeping function of journalists. The **gatekeeping** function describes the power of the press to decide what issues get covered, so politicians and other powerful sources seek access to journalists to endear their causes and viewpoints to them. Social media now offers another avenue to reach journalists and engage with them, or, to bypass the press altogether and tell one's own story independent of mainstream news media. In particular, political information is plentiful in the new media environment as blogs and news sites have been created to champion certain points of view.

Take a short quiz from the News Literacy Project (2019) to assess *your* news literacy smarts. This one is testing your ability to choose between a legitimate or fraudulent news site: https://newslit.org/get-smart/which-is-legit/. This one tests your news literacy smarts: http://bit.ly/32HXdB1.

COUNT TO THREE

If your time and inclination are limited, you can easily do these three things to **spot-check news credibility**:

- Count the **viewpoints**; single-perspective stories cannot possibly tell the whole story. The more differing viewpoints given with *named* sources, the more credible the story likely is.
- Count the **emotional words**, such as shocking, surprising, secret, unbelievable, forbidden, no one talks about, no one tells you. The more emotion, the less credible.
- Count on your **skepticism**, especially with visuals that don't seem plausible; they may be fake. The more doubt, the more important it is to question the content.

THE ATTACK ON TRUTH

Honest journalism serves to inform and educate citizens about their government and about issues and events in the public interest. A working democracy depends on informed citizens. After all, how else but from the media do you typically learn about people running for local or national offices? Or if the city commission is going to require local companies to pay higher than the minimum wage? Or what the national lawmakers are doing to help student debt?

The Nieman Lab's Joshua Benton (2019) summed up research on the power of a strong local press this way:

> What do strong local newspapers do? Well, past research has shown they increase voter turnout, reduce government corruption, make cities financially healthier, make citizens more knowledgeable about politics and more likely to engage with local government, force local TV to raise its game, encourage split-ticket (and thus less uniformly partisan) voting, make elected officials more responsive and efficient. . . .
>
> (para 1)

Benton (2019) showcased a recent study that demonstrated what happens when local newspapers are weakened by staff cuts. Out of 11 local California newspapers, those with sharp newsroom staffing declines also had on average significantly reduced political competition in mayoral races (Rubado & Jennings, 2019). The researchers' evidence also suggested that lower staffing levels were associated with lower voter turnout.

Wrote Benton:

> One extra candidate may not seem like much—but logically speaking, it's the difference between an uncontested reelection and a real race, or between a two-person race and a three-way battle that gives voters 50 percent more options. It's not meaningless.
>
> (2019, para 9)

Citizens need accurate and independent information in order to elect their leaders, to have a voice in shaping policies, regulations and laws, and to know if those leaders are doing their jobs ethically. This is why, for example, in the United States, the First Amendment to the Constitution guarantees the freedom of the press, which extends to digital news and information.

For a global look at public opinion about how well their country's news media covers important issues or reports fairly on politics, see this Pew Research Center interactive map: https://pewrsr.ch/2U6tRaI.

Decreasing Trust in News Media It may be difficult to feel sympathy for journalists in an era in which ideological bias and partisanship in the press are concerns across the globe. Distrust of media is high. For example, in the United States, most adults, "including more than nine in 10 Republicans, say they personally have lost trust in the news media in recent years," noted a 2018 Knight Foundation report (Opening section, para 3).

Some of the report's other key findings are worth repeating because they have resonance beyond the United States:

- "Both Republicans and Democrats were less likely to trust news sources with a partisan reputation that opposes their own. However, they did not express much greater trust in news sources that have a reputation for a partisan leaning consistent with their own" (Opening section, para 6). So even news outlets that provided agreeable content were not immune from the public's distrust.
- "Asked to describe in their own words why they trust or do not trust certain news organizations, Americans' responses largely center on matters of accuracy or bias" (Opening section, para 4).
- Across the groups, people said their decreased trust in the media can be restored. There is little difference by gender, age, education and race. "Specifically, 69% of U.S. adults who say they have lost trust in the news media over the past decade say their trust can be restored. But a rather substantial 30% of those who have lost trust—equivalent to 21% of all U.S. adults—say their trust in the media cannot be restored" (Detailed findings, para 7).

- "Attention to the news is also related to reports of declining trust. Eighty-two percent of those who indicate they pay little or no attention to national news say they have less trust in the media now" (Detailed findings, para 6).
- "Americans appear to differentiate the trustworthiness of news organizations—67 percent say they trust only some news media organizations, but not others" (Detailed findings, para 9).

Challenges to Press Freedom Many people don't realize how dangerous the occupation of journalism can be. The International Federation of Journalists listed 94 journalists and media staff killed in work-related incidents in 2018. Journalists who are uncovering government scandal and corruption, and then telling the public about it, are extremely threatening to politicians and those in power.

Countries including Great Britain, Costa Rica and Finland have relative freedom, safety and independence for the press to do their jobs, according to Reporters Without Borders' annual freedom index (2019). Other countries, including Syria, Vietnam and Saudi Arabia, are among the worst in terms of press rights. You can explore and compare various countries' levels of press freedom at www.RSF.org; look for the interactive World Press Freedom Index map.

Each year, *TIME* magazine names a Person of the Year, someone who had a major impact on the world. In 2018, the magazine named a group of journalists as their Person of the Year. Each of the people named were working to inform citizens about wrongdoing and violence—violence that was often sanctioned by governments or those in power. Journalists have been exiled, imprisoned, kidnapped and killed for telling the truth about violent and oppressive regimes, and sometimes, for telling the truth, period.

The four individuals that *TIME* honored in 2018 were slain Saudi columnist Jamal Khashoggi; Wa Lone and Kyaw Soe Oo, journalists who had been sentenced to prison in Myanmar after investigating the massacre of Rohingya Muslims; and Phillippine journalist Maria Ressa, the editor of an online news site that had been critical of the country's president and who was defending her site against what she said were trumped-up charges of tax fraud. Also honored were the staff of the *Capital Gazette* in Annapolis,

Maryland, where five people were fatally shot in June by a man who had a long-running dispute with the paper. What do you think? Why are these people worth naming as Person of the Year? In what ways were each of these people fighting a "war on truth?"

Seek out your country's stories of watchdog reporting that led to public change. For current stand-out global investigations, see the Global Investigative Journalism website at https://bit.ly/2WPstuV. In the United States, see this list by the Brookings Institution of great moments in American investigative journalism: https://brook.gs/2vPpvbB. Or, go to the Pulitzer Prize website for a list of winners in the Public Service category: http://bit.ly/2HLc9Hy.

HOW THE PRESS AFFECTS OUR THINKING

The influence of the news media on the public consciousness has been studied for decades. Here are some of the ways that the constant news cycle affects how you view the world:

Agenda-Setting The amount of attention given to an issue by the news media results in a commensurate level of importance assigned by news consumers, according to the **agenda-setting theory** first introduced by Maxwell McCombs and Donald Shaw in 1972 and further developed in many subsequent studies.

In 1963, political scientist Bernard C. Cohen wrote that the press "may not be successful much of the time in telling people what to think, but it is stunningly successful in telling its readers what to think about" (McCombs & Shaw, 1972, p. 177). This captures the essence of agenda-setting. This theory maintains that what is included in the news—what is deemed important enough for the press to give attention to—influences in turn what is perceived by the public as important. News media's concentration on a handful of topics leads the public to see those topics as more important, and in turn, these issues help shape the public policy agenda (McQuail & Windahl, 1993).

The heightened news media attention serves to make the issue more accessible in one's memory. "It is not information *about* the issue that has the effect;

it is the fact that the issue has received a certain amount of processing time and attention that carries the effect" (Scheufele & Tewksbury, 2007, p. 14).

Availability Psychologists Daniel Kahneman and Amos Tversky described people's tendency to rely on immediate examples that come to mind when evaluating topics or decisions. The pair named this cognitive phenomenon the **availability heuristic**. Relying on information that comes to mind quickly can be a handy mental shortcut, but it can also lead to inaccurate assessments. For instance, news coverage about child abductions, plane crashes or home break-ins might make these events seem more prevalent than they actually are. Just because you easily remember information doesn't mean it's complete or correct.

Indeed, a look at the first screen or two of your favorite news outlets likely paints a pretty dim picture—war, blackmail, corruption. The news these days is largely negative, and people respond to that, taking a dark view of circumstances, even though *a lot is going right in the world,* noted Steven Pinker, a cognitive psychologist at Harvard University. There's a reason for the availability of bad news, he explains.

"News is about things that happen, not things that don't happen. We never see a journalist saying to the camera, 'I'm reporting live from a country where a war has not broken out'—or a city that has not been bombed, or a school that has not been shot up," Pinker wrote (2018). "As long as bad things have not vanished from the face of the earth, there will always be enough incidents to fill the news, especially when billions of smartphones turn most of the world's population into crime reporters and war correspondents" (para 3).

Diminished Attention Once a news story plays out in the news media, the impression of the public is that the issue is resolved. Otherwise, the media would still be covering it, right? That would be great if that were true! Think of the stories that rose to peak attention and then, just. . .

disappeared.

According to political scientist Anthony Downs, an **"issue-attention" cycle** plays out for problems that are chronic and complex, such as racism, poverty or crime (Downs, 1996).

Downs' issue-attention cycle goes like this: First, there's the discovery of the problem; huge numbers of young kids in your community are living in poverty. Then, optimism follows; we can solve this with programs and attention! This is followed by a period of eventual awakening to the sacrifices required by people benefitting from existing conditions; to improve poor neighborhoods, more people with resources need to move there, for instance.

However, the public loses interest in complex issues once people grasp the immense resources or alterations needed to successfully address them, Downs noted. Audiences get bored with the problem or discouraged about what needs to be done, and thus, interest wanes. But lo and behold, another big problem comes along to claim fresh attention. The first problem moves "to a twilight realm of lesser attention" (p. 51). Think about a news story that was trending a year ago that has now largely disappeared from regular coverage; does it fit Downs' issue-attention cycle?

From the mainstream news media's point of view, once reporting has educated the public to the problem, there is nothing new to tell, so the coverage lessens until something fresh occurs on the issue. But, of course, the issue hasn't been fixed. **Solutions journalism** strives to keep these complex issues in the public eye by sharing how communities have responded to problems, what the limitations of the responses are, and proof of results. See this video explainer on solutions journalism from the Solutions Journalism Network: https://bit.ly/2Sb5pn3.

Priming Another media effect, called priming, also works on our cognitive processing. **Priming** establishes audience expectations about standards and frames of reference (Scheufele, 2000), such as what a "good" war looks like, or how a candidate with integrity behaves. The media, by choosing what to cover and how often, make certain issues seem particularly important. This media coverage primes audiences; it sets "the standards by which governments, presidents, policies, and candidates for public office are judged" (Iyengar & Kinder, 1987, p. 63).

When media focus on a few key "hot button" issues, such as abortion and immigration policy, they prime voters to assess candidates based on those issues, when in fact there are many additional issues by which to evaluate a candidate.

Framing A media effect related to agenda-setting is **framing**, which is the way that media package and present information. The angle or emphasis that a story is given is its frame. A frame can sway how the public understands and perceives issues. For instance, a familiar frame is winners and losers. Example: A news report might declare that if citizens in the downtown neighborhood get their way, the streets will be repaved this summer—but the losers will be the downtown businesses, which will likely see foot traffic lessened due to the construction.

There is less interpretation or explanation and more declaration in this sort of win-lose framing. Or, to try and get the audience's attention, a news outlet may build a story around conflicts that exist as opposed to areas of agreement on an issue. Another example of framing is the choice to negatively portray the announcement of a new public school as a drain on taxpayers because it will require an increase in taxes. A different and more positive way to frame the story could be how the new school will address severe overcrowding in existing schools. Which story would you read?

Key Differences Both agenda-setting and priming communicate to audiences that something is important through repetition; repeated and high-profile coverage creates importance and accessibility in our minds. Framing, however, communicates how we ought to think about a topic, such as from a conflict perspective or from a win-loss perspective. To differentiate among agenda-setting, priming and framing, I find helpful this pithy summary by Scheufele and Tewksbury (2007): "The primary difference on the psychological level between agenda setting and priming, on the one hand, and framing, on the other hand, is therefore the difference between *whether* we think about an issue and *how* we think about it" (p. 14).

Think about a public issue that you care deeply about; why do you care about it? How did you first find out about it? Who or what brought it to your attention, and how did that source educate you about the issue? Was media involved and if so, is it an example of priming or agenda-setting?

TECHNOLOGY AND JOURNALISM

Digitization has had, and continues to have, a profound impact on journalism worldwide. One telltale sign: the disappearance of the daily print newspaper. Ask your parents or grandparents the last time they recall getting a print newspaper delivered to their doorstep seven days a week. It's likely not too long after the internet began dominating our laptops and other screens.

So far, the digital revolution has presented both challenges and opportunities for news outlets worldwide. These impacts have implications for the quality and quantity of news that we get online.

Challenges: Falling Revenues Among the most challenging impacts of digitization has been on print newspapers and the loss of advertising revenues. Print newspapers were historically reliant on classified and display advertising for a large chunk of their revenues. News outlets, never imagining that a print paper would not always be in demand, put content online for free. The idea was to attract more subscribers to the print paper. But as you know, that plan didn't work. Newspaper publishers also didn't anticipate the wild success of Craigslist, the free classified ad service that is customizable by location. The service decimated the backbone of newspaper revenues, classified ads.

As the news product has gone online, digital advertising revenues have not kept pace. Consequently, news organizations are moving to user subscriptions and paid content. This, notes the World Association of Newspapers and News Publishers, represents a major change in the business model for newspapers. Global print and digital circulation revenue totaled $92 billion in 2014, while advertising revenues generated $86 billion. "This is a seismic shift from a strong business-to-business emphasis—publishers to advertisers—to a growing business-to-consumer emphasis, publishers to audiences" (Kilman, 2015, para 11). What might this new emphasis mean for you as a news consumer? Will you get more customized content?

Challenges: Newspaper Closures Due to falling revenues, local news operations are closing. Statistics figured by Feldman (2018) show that in the United States:

- The total number of *non-daily* U.S. newspapers fell to 5,829 in 2018 from 7,419 in 2004.
- The total number of *daily* U.S. newspapers fell to 1,283 from 1,472 in the same time period.

- The number of "news deserts"—counties where there is no newspaper at all—has risen, to the point that there were 171 counties without a newspaper in 2018.

"Unprecedented consolidation in the newspaper industry has placed the fate of local journalism into the hands of fewer companies than ever before," stated the report on which those statistics are based, a 2016 report conducted by Penelope Muse Abernathy of the Center for Innovation and Sustainability at the University of North Carolina–Chapel Hill. "The largest chains have grown so large that they necessarily have less attachment to the communities where they own newspapers. . . . The rise of the newest media owners, with their emphasis on profit benchmarks instead of civic responsibility, has added a new wrinkle" (Emerging Threat section).

Closures of newspapers in the United States and elsewhere mean one less reporter at the city government meeting, one less person keeping account of what judges are doing in court, or who is being arrested by police. It means one less reporter to ensure that public officials keep meetings public instead of meeting privately. In some areas, the newspaper reporter was the *only* person doing that work. The threat of corruption is great when the press is not active in a community.

Innovation: Machine Learning Artificial intelligence is helping journalists do their news work more efficiently, thoroughly and engagingly, and the hope is that this frees up real-life journalists to do more substantive work.

The Associated Press uses automated technology to create minor league baseball and college sports stories, among others. Bloomberg News uses AI extensively for culling key data from company quarterly earnings reports and writing a straightforward news account. The *Washington Post* has an in-house robot reporting program called Heliograf that, among other things, alerts reporters when something looks out of the ordinary in big data sets, or in athletes' winning times in the Olympics, for instance (Peiser, 2019). In the era of major document dumps, news organizations are relying on AI to sift through the data to flag where journalists should step in and spend their time and energy on reporting.

The use of AI and machine learning will continue to expand in journalism, as new uses are found. Two experts at Tattle Civic Technologies are building a tool to support fact-checkers in India, specifically focusing on misinformation on the WhatsApp social media platform. Another effort underway is by the Rochester Institute of Technology, which is working to identify the best techniques to identify fake video and audio that journalists could then use in the field. Both of these are winners of a contest to use AI in journalism (Ethics and Governance in AI Initiative, 2019).

Innovation and Challenge: Citizen Journalism An aspect of digitization with mixed impact has been the rise of **citizen journalism**. The ability for citizens and non-professionals to use websites and social media to publish their own accounts of events has provided more perspectives to news consumers. Eyewitness accounts and fresh perspectives on breaking news and hyper-local issues have contributed greatly to information available about events involving U.S. law enforcement's use of force, or about popular protests and violence in Iran, Syria and Egypt, for instance.

However, the ability for citizen journalists to post to broadly-used platforms such as YouTube has allowed for the information from breaking news events to be published without context or explanation. Also, citizen journalists can create news sites using easy-to-manage software, and not all of these sites are striving for accuracy and ethical standards.

A tip from YouTube (2019) regarding posting a video with graphic content stresses the importance of **context** when citizen journalists are posting news events:

> For example, a video posted by a citizen journalist capturing footage of protesters being beaten would likely be allowed if it includes relevant context. In this example, relevant information could be a list of tips at the beginning of the video on how to stay safe when at a protest or voice-over narration about the protest's history. The video should also have a clear title or description indicating that it is reporting on or documenting the content. (The Importance of Context, para 2).

YouTube emphasizes that citizen journalists and others posting graphic content should consider the intention of the video—"is it to inform and educate or to shock and incite?" The answer to that question should guide users as to whether or not to post potentially damaging footage.

Innovation and Challenge: Aggregation Innovations ushered in by digitization have allowed for the rise of a whole new breed of news organizations such as *The Huffington Post*, *Gawker*, BuzzFeed and *BuzzFeed News*, Yahoo! News and AOL. These digital natives are highly adept at using social media for audience engagement and audience development, and they both report their own news *and* aggregate the work of other publications.

Content aggregation is when one site takes content from other publishers and combines it to create content on its site. *How can this be legal?* There are many kinds of aggregation and the issue is still under legal debate. (For an excellent resource on the topic, see the NiemanLab article at https://bit.ly/1fNkVlb.) However, basic aggregation guidelines to stay out of legal trouble include crediting the original site—and ideally linking to it—as well as providing only a portion of the original content.

Aggregation *can* be mutually beneficial to both the original content creator and the aggregator. However, newspapers, which often post content for free to attract consumers in hopes they will commit to paid subscriptions and premium content, are losing out. According to a report for the Congressional Research Service (Whitmore, 2015) that relied on a 2009 publishers' study, in a 30-day period in 2009:

- More than 75,000 websites reused U.S. newspaper content without permission.
- Nearly 112,000 nearly exact copies of content were used.
- More than 500,000 excerpts and headlines were used.
- Stories from large national newspapers were reused up to 15 times.

This, at a time, remember, when newspapers are going out of business at a record rate.

Innovation: Choices The internet allows news consumers a huge array of content choices. Social media is the vehicle that many people use to find and access their news. People worldwide use the internet to get their news—a median of 42 percent over 38 countries in fact. Also, 35 percent of people use social media in particular to get their news (Mitchell et al., 2018).

Millennials across the globe continue to seek out the news (Kilman, 2015): seven in 10 younger adults get news on a daily basis; 40 percent pay for at

Re-Using News Content

*The legality of re-using original news content is still under debate, but for now, the practice continues. Here are three of the main types of news aggregation:

Feed Aggregators: A website that assembles material from many other websites by topic, issue or source. It contains the headline and first few lines of the original story and a link to the original website. **Examples:** Yahoo! News and Google News.

Specialty Aggregators: Are a lot like Feed Aggregators, but they are far more limited in focus, typically featuring a particular topic such as technology or politics. **Examples:** Techmeme and Everyblock.

Blog Aggregator: A website that uses third-party content as the impetus for blog posts. The posts contain links, short excerpts or summaries of original reporting. **Examples:** Huffington Post and Gawker Media.

Source: Kimberley Isbell, 2010. "The Rise of the News Aggregator: Legal Implications and Best Practices." Citizen Media Law Project, Harvard.

least one news-specific app or digital subscription; and 16 percent pay for a print newspaper subscription. The primary gateway for over half their news is Facebook.

Forty-one percent of journalists consider the potential "shareability" of a story when deciding what to write about, a 2018 study of journalists across the globe by Muck Rack and Zeno found (Joffe, 2018). At least 63 percent of journalists said they track how many times their stories are shared on social media. But what potential impact does journalists' focus on "shareability" have on what journalists write about? Are we heading toward a system in which the topics that get covered most thoroughly are those that people most "like" and share on social media?

NEWS LITERACY

How do you know if a news source is reputable? Here are some elements to watch out for in news coverage that doesn't have information and accuracy at the fore.

1. **Inflammatory content.** Is coverage being extended to a speaker or protest that does not have a clear purpose or that is primarily spewing hateful rhet-

oric? Are a source's quotes basically unfounded assumptions, and if so, is the reporting challenging those assumptions? Is a story using stereotypes to inaccurately further its angle or focus? (Ethical Journalism Network, 2019).

2. **False associations.** Are sources' names, organizations and their purposes clearly stated, or are advocates, lobbyists and special-interest groups masquerading as official-sounding sources? Are visuals juxtaposed with stories so as to suggest an association or relationship that isn't accurate or even real? Is a site of biased information disguised as a news site?
3. **Opinion-as-fact.** Is opinion clearly distinguished from news stories? Opinion pieces across all media seek to persuade consumers to a particular point of view through argument, language and biased examples. Does verifiable information get mixed in with assertions that don't come with proof or support?
4. **Missing persons.** Are the people who are most affected by a policy, regulation, proposal or conflict given prominence in the coverage? Stories that don't include those directly affected by an issue but instead are chock full of officials and authorities opining on a subject that doesn't directly impact their lives are missing the real story.
5. **The illogical fallacies.** (With credit to John Silva of *The News Literacy Project* (2018) for highlighting these common tricks of thought. The examples are mine.)
   a. The **slippery slope** fallacy: Asserts that a minor action will inevitably lead to major consequences (that are usually bad). As in: "If we approve this concession to funding maternal healthcare, soon all women will expect a free ride for *all* their medical care!"
   b. **Ad hominem** fallacy: Attacking the person making the argument rather than addressing the facts of the argument itself. As in: "How would you know what a good law looks like? You were turned down for admission at every top law school, senator."
   c. **Straw man** fallacy: Misrepresenting or oversimplifying someone's argument so it is easier to refute. As in: "Citizens who voted against the clean air referendum want us all to die of asphyxiation."
   d. **Conspiracy theory**: Asserting that a claim cannot be proven due to hidden truth or destroyed evidence. Charges that the assertion is false often lead to yet more assertions of a cover-up. As in U.S. President Donald Trump's tweet after the election in November that, "In addition to winning the Electoral College in a landslide, I won the popular vote if you deduct the millions of people who voted illegally" (Liptak & Merica, 2017).

How do you know if you're getting the full story? Ask yourself what is missing from the news you're consuming. Media literacy asks us to think about what kinds of stories we're getting around the clock—and equally if not more importantly, what news coverage we *aren't getting*. It's hard to be aware of lifestyles, points of view and values that are omitted from news coverage. That's why consuming news and information from a *variety* of reputable sources is so essential.

The honest news media are really, truly trying to help you understand the world and equip you with the information you need to be an engaged and informed citizen. Give the news habit a try if you haven't yet. The news media make mistakes, but the honest outlets correct them. Excellent journalism has supported democracy in countries worldwide. Media literate consumers need to support that kind of journalism by clicking on, sharing, posting and paying for subscriptions to the best of the truthtellers.

CHAPTER REVIEW

- Know the fundamentals of journalism.
- Explain the importance of watchdog reporting to democracy.
- Identify news values in various news stories.
- Describe the obstacles to excellent journalism.
- Differentiate among framing, priming and agenda-setting.
- Summarize the impact of digital technology on traditional journalism.
- Evaluate an example of shoddy or fraudulent news coverage.
- Apply the various fallacies to news coverage: slippery slope fallacy, ad hominem attack, straw man fallacy, conspiracy theory.

ACTIVITIES

1. Alternative news media offer a different agenda than the mainstream news media. Visit http://bit.ly/2D75V0L for global choices, or, for U.S. options, see http://bit.ly/2YzRM5m. Compare how the coverage offered

differs from mainstream news media. Who is the audience for these news sites? Why do you think they are called "alternative"? What do you think of the content they provide; would you visit them again on your own? Provide your answers in written or oral format.

2. See how you would perform on the Pew Research Center survey that asks you to sort facts from opinion; sort these statements as either fact or opinion:

   a. Spending on Social Security, Medicare and Medicaid make up the largest portion of the U.S. federal budget.

   b. Democracy is the greatest form of government.

   c. Government is almost always wasteful and inefficient.

   d. Health care costs per person in the United States are the highest in the developed world.

   e. President Barack Obama was born in the United States.

   f. Immigrants who are in the United States illegally have some rights under the Constitution.

   g. Abortion should be legal in most cases.

   h. Immigrants who are in the United States illegally are a very big problem for the country today.

   i. Increasing the federal minimum wage to $15 an hour is essential for the health of the U.S. economy.

   j. ISIS lost a significant portion of its territory in Iraq and Syria in 2017.

   When you're finished, go to https://pewrsr.ch/2TK0mdR to compare your responses with the national results.

3. Find an example of a time that the press did *not* follow ethical practice and research the incident and the fallout from it. Prepare to share your findings with the group in a short slideshow presentation that highlights the ethical principles violated.

4. To show your understanding of logical fallacies, create three mock Twitter posts that each use one of the following: slippery slope fallacy, ad hominem attack, straw man fallacy, conspiracy theory. But please don't post them; people might fall for your "logic."

5. Watch this 4-minute video featuring Dr. Claire Wardle from First Draft (www.firstdraftnews.org) to gain quick tips on verifying online media: http://bit.ly/2GlYAf7. Or, take this free one-hour, quick-start verification course from First Draft for a primer about the use of eyewitnesses in news stories, fabricated websites, memes and manipulated video: http://bit.ly/2LwwAda. After watching, summarize some key points to share with your campus community by creating a poster using a free poster maker such as Canva (http://bit.ly/2JUbMZI). Be sure to credit Dr. Claire Wardle and First Draft on your poster source credits.

REFERENCES

Abernathy, P. M. (2016). *The rise of a new media baron and the emerging threat of news deserts.* Chapel Hill, NC: UNC School of Media and Journalism, Center for Innovation and Sustainability in Local Media.

American Society of Newspaper Editors. (2017). *Newsroom diversity survey.* Retrieved from www.asne.org/diversity-survey-2017

Bauder, D. (2018, August 29). News media hesitate to use 'lie' for Trump's misstatements. *Associated Press.* Retrieved from http://bit.ly/2JPQPz8

Benton, J. (2019, April 9). When local newspapers shrink, fewer people bother to run for mayor. *Nieman Lab.* Retrieved from http://bit.ly/2XVwVg7

Center for News Literacy. *Stony Brook University School of Journalism.* Retrieved from www.centerfornewsliteracy.org

Downs, A. (1996). Up and down with ecology: The "issue-attention cycle." In P. Peretz (Ed.), *The politics of American economic policy making* (pp. 48–59). Armonk, NY: M.E. Sharpe.

Ethical Journalism Network. (2019). *Hate speech: A five-point test for Journalists.* Retrieved from ethicaljournalismnetwork.org/resources/publications/hate-speech

Ethics and Governance in AI Initiative. (2019, March 12). Announcing the winners of the AI and the News open challenge. Retrieved from aiethicsinitiative.org

Feldman, S. (2018). *Where are the news deserts in the United States*? Statista.com. Based on data from the Center for Innovation and Sustainability in Local Media via Nieman Lab.

First Draft. (2019). First Draft checklists: Getting started in verification. Firstdraft-news.org.

Joffe, J. (2018, November 20). Muck Rack says journalists want relationships with PR on social. *PR News*. Retrieved from prnewsonline.com

Knight Foundation. (2018, September 11). Indicators of news media trust. Retrieved from Knightfoundation.org

International Federation of Journalists. (2018, December 31). 2018 Reverses Downward Trend in Killings of Journalists and Media Staff with 94 Victims of Violence. IFJ.org.

Iyengar, S., & Kinder, D. R. (1987). *News that matters: Television and American opinion*. Chicago, IL: University of Chicago Press.

Kilman, L. (2015, October 5). *World press trends 2015: Facts and figures at your fingertips*. Frankfurt, Germany: World Association of Newspapers and News Publishers. Retrieved from http://bit.ly/2P1bRAF

Liptak, K., & Merica, D. (2017, January 25). Trump believes millions voted illegally, WH says—but provides no proof. Retrieved from CNN.com.

Martinson, J. (2016, March 3). BBC struggles to hit targets for staff diversity. *The Guardian*. Retrieved from http://bit.ly/2XSESCv

McCombs, M., & Shaw, D. (1972). The agenda-setting function of mass media. *The Public Opinion Quarterly, 36*(2), 176–187. doi:10.1086/267990

McQuail, D., & Windahl, S. (1993). *Communication models for the study of mass communications* (2nd ed.). London and New York, NY: Longman.

Mitchell, A., Simmons, K., Matsa, K. E., & Silver, L. (2018). *Publics globally want unbiased news coverage but are divided on whether their news media deliver*. Washington, D.C.: Pew Research Center.

News Literacy Project. (2019). Retrieved from Newslit.org. Washington, D.C.

Peiser, J. (2019, February 5). The rise of the robot reporter. *The New York Times*. Retrieved from https://nyti.ms/2LufDjr

Pinker, S. (2018, February 17). The media exaggerates negative news. This distortion has consequences. *The Guardian*. Retrieved from http://bit.ly/2JGTYT0

Reporters Without Borders. (2019). *World freedom Index*. Retrieved from RSF.org

Rubado, M. E., & Jennings, J. T. (2019). Political consequences of the endangered local watchdog: Newspaper decline and mayoral elections in the United States. *Urban Affairs Review*. https://doi.org/10.1177/1078087419838058

Scheufele, D. A. (2000). Agenda-setting, priming, and framing revisited: Another look at cognitive effects of political communication. *Mass Communication and Society*, *3*(2), 297–316.

Scheufele, D. A., & Tewksbury, D. (2007). Framing, agenda setting, and priming: The evolution of three media effects models. *Journal of Communication*, *57*, 9–20.

Silva, J. (2018, August 15). *Logical fallacies and discourse*. Washington, D.C.: The News Literacy Project. Retrieved from http://bit.ly/32DviST

U.S. Census Bureau. (2017). *QuickFacts*. Retrieved from www.census.gov/quickfacts/fact/table/US/PST045217

Whitmore, N. (2015). Extending copyright protection to combat Free-Riding by digital news aggregators and online search engines. *Catholic University Journal of Law and Technology*, *24*(1), Article 3. Retrieved from http://bit.ly/2HL2MHH

YouTube. (2019). *Help Center: The importance of context*. Retrieved from https://support.google.com/youtube/answer/6345162?hl=en

9 Protecting

How Technology Invades Your Privacy, and How to Protect It

You may well have been one of 2.32 billion monthly active users worldwide on Facebook in 2018.

If you live in Brazil, you'd be one of 90.6 million Facebook users. In Vietnam, one of 45.3 million. In India, the country with the largest percentage of Facebook use worldwide, you're a mere drop in the bucket of 294 million users. In the United States, you're one of 204 million.

Or, perhaps you're one of the 1.5 billion people who use WhatsApp. Actually, it's most likely that if you're in college, you're one of the estimated 1 billion people who use Instagram. (All the above statistics are from Statista's Facebook 2018 dossier.) Both WhatsApp and Instagram are owned by Facebook, and that means anything you do on those sites

LEARNING OBJECTIVES

Terms: Privacy, repurposed, surveillance intermediary, algorithm, data brokers, cookies, biometrics, encryption, phishing.

- Summarize the argument that privacy is a human right.
- Recognize the various ways citizens' privacy is compromised by digital media technologies.
- Explain how surveillance affects journalism.
- Describe how governments use digital data to surveille citizens.
- Explain the various responsibilities of lawmakers, governments and media companies to protect citizen privacy.
- Identify technical tools and tips for protecting your personal information.

simply feeds into the massive file of information that Facebook keeps on users of all its products. . . .

Pair up with someone to discuss one or two of the following questions on privacy. Share your observations with a larger group. Is privacy a human right? (What does *that* mean? Is it a basic freedom that should belong to all people?) Is privacy a condition that is necessary for human health and development? Do we need privacy in order to develop and maintain a healthy body and mind? On a more commonplace level, if someone relinquishes his phone to you so you can get a better look at a certain photo, is that tacit permission to swipe to see *more* photos, or is that a violation of his privacy?)

Let's see, Facebook would know your profile information, of course, plus the history of anything you've purchased—including those really iffy pants from the online "designer" warehouse. Your data file would also contain all your reactions, comments, videos, photos (including location and date taken), current location, your actions on other people's Instagram, WhatsApp and Facebook accounts, people who've liked your page, posts or who have RSVPed to an event of yours, and—

(pause for breath here)

dates, times and titles of all ads you've clicked on, all the apps you've added, all the places you've checked in to, any pages or apps you've hidden from your news feed, a whole mess of information about the devices you use to access Facebook products, including your computers, phones, connected TVs and other web-connected devices, which opens up an entirely new cache of information that extends to the apps on your laptop, its battery life (whaaa?!) and even your mouse movements.

It goes on and on and on. . . .

As I write, Facebook CEO Mark Zuckerberg announced a massive shift by the social media giant toward privacy, including encrypting messages, disappearing content and small group chats. It's ironic from a company that built its reputation and profitability on encouraging users to share their personal information.

This chapter looks at the real effects of digital technology on our personal lives and data privacy. We examine whether privacy is a basic human right. And, we'll consider the role of companies, governments and individuals in balancing the personal and practical need for connectivity with the personal and practical need for privacy. You'll likely be pleased to know that this chapter does not use hidden cameras. However, it is not above eavesdropping.

PRIVACY AND THE INTERNET

The Cambridge Dictionary (2019) says privacy is "the state of being alone, or the right to keep one's personal matters and relationships secret." Simply put, the internet was *not* built with privacy in mind. Our data travels through many hands—the internet service provider, software companies, third-party contractors—so lots of people can listen in, despite basic safeguards for data in place.

Maybe you've seen the Venn diagram that has one circle labeled "privacy" and the other circle labeled "the internet"? Those two circles do *not* overlap. We live in a society in which being online is critical to communication and commerce. So how do we manage our privacy while being digitally engaged? Add to this mix the very real human instinct to share and connect, and things get more interesting. And slightly creepy.

I find this concept from the Teaching Privacy project website (2019) helpful, as it reminds me that my online privacy takes ongoing effort: "Privacy tends to be eroded if it is not actively maintained, because others benefit more when you share more data." Actively maintain your online privacy and don't assume platforms are protecting your information.

Actively maintain your online privacy and don't assume platforms are protecting your information.

A privacy policy is just a phrase—just because a company has one doesn't mean it actually is preserving your privacy. Often, the policies are a list of all the ways the company *doesn't* maintain your privacy. (Visit the fabulously-named website "Terms of Service: Didn't Read," to see a handy reference checklist of major sites' usage terms and privacy policies.)

A reality of digital data is that information is repurposed; our information is used for reasons other than the original reason for which we gave it. So when you fill out a warranty form for your new bike, you may be asked all sorts of ancillary information, such as your income range, what kind of dwelling you live in (apartment? condo? house?) or your marital status. That information can be repurposed to target advertising to you, or even sold to other companies to build *their* files about consumers. Our digital devices collect and transmit information about us in more and more ways.

We get free online content and digital services in exchange for our information, so why complain? Tracking our data so it can be used and sold is what pays for online commerce. So where is the balance between benefits and protections? It's a constant push-and-pull to find the sweet spot between digital conveniences and personal privacy.

There are many ways that portable, digital technology tracks our whereabouts. Location tracking tools such as transit passes, toll cards, retailer loyalty cards, swipe card entrances, searches on your smartphone for restaurants or places near you are all tools that identify our locations. Privacy advocates are concerned about the growing amount of data collected by commercial and government entities. How data is stored, how it is used and who has access to it are all concerns of privacy advocates, who note the susceptibility of such data to misuse.

PRIVACY AS A HUMAN RIGHT

Throughout the world, people care about privacy a good deal. They want to know their information is safe online, and that their government has their best interests at heart. In a survey of 1,700 people ages 14 to 25 from 100 countries, Culver and Grizzle (2017) showed that:

- 74 percent strongly agree that their personal privacy is important to them.
- 60 percent disagree or strongly disagree that their government has the right to know all personal information about them.

However, while people care about privacy, they use technology daily and many likely don't understand the costs of usage when it comes to personal information. Let's face it: Most of us really don't know where our data is going, we just know that it's going, somewhere. Have you ever been the victim of identity theft? If so, you know that trying to reclaim your rightful identity is difficult, time-consuming and costly. For important lessons in managing an identity theft, read this woman's story at Forbes.com (see https://bit.ly/2ASRmN5).

Besides identity theft, another digital privacy concern is of course social media usage. While you might be careful with what you post online, your friends can tag you and post material about you without your consent. As you'll see in the graphic, some teenagers are working around privacy issues by using alternative names on Facebook.

In the immortal words of late-night comedy host Stephen Colbert: "If you're not careful your online past could destroy your offline future. But there's a solution, and it's tonight's word: control-self-delete." Posts of embarrassing moments can come back to haunt us at job-search time, so, advised Colbert, "Just don't ever make a mistake. How hard is that?" Watch his funny but true critique of social media and privacy at https://on.cc.com/2UpKWjk.

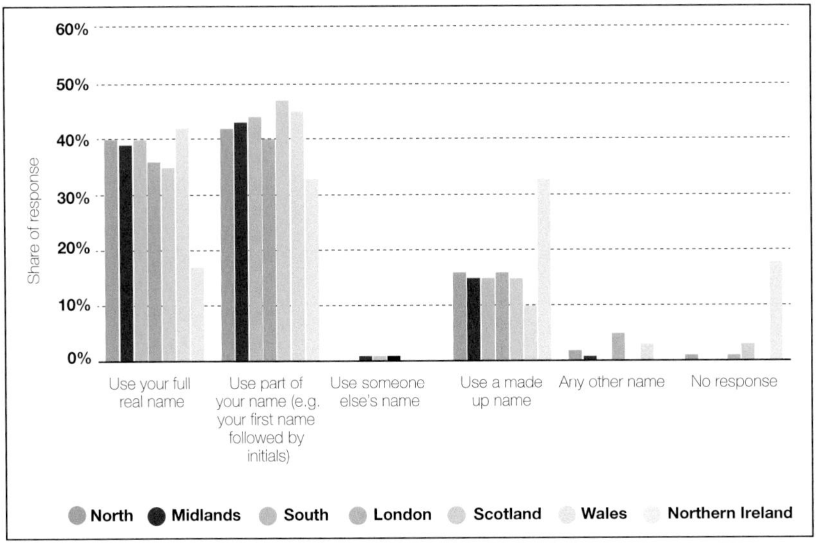

Share of Names Used by Teenagers on Facebook in the United Kingdom in January 2016

Source: BBC—Safer Internet Day Poll 2016

The Philosophy of Privacy *OK, this is a content warning. It's about to get pretty philosophical for this next section, so hang on and hang in there, as the ideas are worth serious consideration, even if they do get a bit abstract. . . .*

Luciano Floridi, a scholar on the philosophy of information, asserts that our lives are made of information—not impersonal facts and data, but "hopes and fears, passions, memories and expectations, gossip, customs and laws, languages, traditions, religions, social structures, scientific knowledge, and so forth" (Floridi, 2016, p. 309). Such information, being as it is, he says, about wondering, wanting, asking and seeking, is part of our humanness. To infringe on our private holding of that information is to violate our humanity.

> Our dignity rests in being able to be the masters of our own journeys, and keep our identities and our choices open. Any technology or policy that tends to fix and mould such openness risks dehumanising us.
>
> (p. 310)

Floridi argues that pinning down our evolving identities "onto the mounting board of a profile" robs us of our status as "informational works in progress." Potential examples of this kind of freezing of one's evolving identity might be consumer marketing data that automatically places someone in an income category because of his age, or that places limitations on the ads a person sees for college prep programs due to her ethnicity.

> Talk about the idea that your privacy is essential to your humanity. Do you ever feel that technology freezes your identity in place?

Privacy as a Choice Frederike Kaltheuner of the civil rights organization Privacy International also argues that privacy involves choice. Citizens should have the ability to choose whether or not to reveal themselves in myriad ways. Privacy is "fundamentally about human dignity and autonomy," Kaltheuner told publisher Khesrau Behroz and writers Patrick Stegemann and Milosz Paul Rosinski (2018, para 2). "People want to establish boundaries to limit who has access to their bodies, places and things, as well as their communications and information. People also want to negotiate who they are and how they want to interact with the world around them. Privacy is about enabling all of this" (Behroz, Stegemann, & Rosinski, 2018, para 2).

Algorithms (recall that **algorithms** are computerized problem-solving formulas) sort us into categories, including a high "risk score" for future criminality (Angwin, 2016). An accountability standard that gives people authority to review and challenge the data and the results of algorithms is important, say privacy advocates. People should be able to know what third-party data brokers know about you and are doing with your information, privacy advocates contend. **Data brokers** are "third parties" in online terminology; they are companies that collect information about consumers and sell that information to other companies, often without consumer knowledge. In the present reality of our digital lives, there is a tension between the convenience and efficiency of digital communication, and our comfort and safety regarding giving personal information.

Public Records Digitization of data and advent of the internet raise many concerns about privacy today, as we are mobile and carry our devices everywhere, allowing for more data collection, and digital data is mobile and easily transferrable. For example, public records on the internet seem like a good thing. Governments should be transparent and easily accessible to citizens, right? Open public records are essential to democratic society; the "sunshine" laws shed light on the hidden documents tucked away in courthouses and clerk's offices.

However, court records contain a lot of highly sensitive material and it may be inaccurate, one-sided or very dated. Many documents that are public—such as divorce proceedings, family court cases, bankruptcy filings, criminal and civil court cases—all contain information that could cause harm. A potential employer may see personal details in a messy divorce case that influences his or her opinion of a job candidate. Or, neighbors and relatives may see financial details from a bankruptcy filing that are embarrassing or better left unknown.

Online data is incremental and unforgiving; our online activity is compiled and archived, such that past lives and past errors follow us.

These documents are an example of how access to information we didn't freely disclose can freeze our lives at a point in time, as Floridi noted. Full and complete public documents that are easily searchable put people at risk of being judged based on an incident or period in life rather than placing the event within the full context of one's existence. Online data is incremental and unforgiving; our online activity is compiled and archived, such that past lives and past errors follow us.

THE STATE OF SURVEILLANCE

Your government is likely collecting *some* amount of data on its citizens on a regular basis. Similarly, the social media platforms you use are collecting your data. As are your home devices; the Internet of Things, often referenced as IoT, is the network of physical objects and everyday devices that are embedded with electronics, internet connectivity and other forms of hardware. These things communicate and interact with other devices over the internet, and they can be remotely monitored and controlled. IoT examples are a home security system, smart home devices, wearable fitness trackers or a connected car. They collect data on their surroundings.

If you were a Verizon customer in the United States in the early 2010s, you may have unknowingly had your phone records collected by the federal government. We know this because of a man with a very complex reputation named Edward Snowden.

In June, 2013, Snowden, a subcontractor for the U.S. government, leaked highly classified information about the country's National Security Agency and its surveillance of citizens. NSA was collecting the telephone records of millions of U.S. customers of Verizon without their knowledge or consent. Snowden was charged with espionage. (As of publication of this book, he was living in Russia in temporary asylum.) The revelations launched a global debate about government surveillance and citizen privacy. Another interesting figure in this realm is WikiLeaks founder Julian Assange, whose actions have prompted discussions about protecting the principles of a free press against the government's need to keep security secrets.

When, if ever, is it acceptable for the government to track your online communications and/or gather your online data without your knowledge? If you are suspected of unlawful activity? If you received communications from someone suspected of unlawful activity?

It's not just the United States that is collecting information on its citizens without citizen knowledge: The United Kingdom's laws on surveilling citizens' phone and internet data have been subject to court scrutiny. Britain's mass surveillance program, also revealed by Snowden, was ruled unlawful by the European Court of Human Rights in the fall of 2018. Other governments, from Sweden to Germany to Spain, have been implicated in global surveillance operations as well.

Surveillance and Citizen Security Our data is hardly secure. Surveys of Americans in 2016 showed nearly half said they were not confident in the federal government's ability to protect their data, and nearly one in two people said their personal data was less secure than it was five years earlier, a Pew Research Center project found (Smith, 2017). Four in ten had noticed fraudulent charges on their credit cards, and 35 percent had received notice their personal information had been compromised.

From the government point of view, surveillance of digital activity can be helpful in detecting, investigating and preventing crime, notes Joss Wright of the Oxford Internet Institute (2013). However, Wright and others, including the United Nations Human Rights Council (La Rue, 2013), have questioned the *sweeping* surveillance of citizens' online communications as a useful or legitimate crime-fighting strategy. A *ProPublica* investigative journalism project summarized it this way: "Ultimately, it's impossible to know just how successful sweeping surveillance has been, since much of the work is secret. But what has been disclosed so far suggests the programs have been of limited value" (Kirchner, 2015).

The speed and power of today's technology means that huge caches of data can be collected. Computers are faster than ever, but predictive algorithms aren't able to scale up to population-level amounts of data and deliver accurate, useful results. Basically, it is very difficult to draw authoritative conclusions from such massive amounts of data. Having all that data invites abuse such as blackmail, fraud, stalking or invasion of privacy by bad actors within the government or hackers from the outside, noted Wright. "Targeted gathering of data on well-justified grounds" must be the legal framework for surveillance (2013, p. 53).

Tech Companies as Intermediaries Major technology companies such as Google, Facebook and Apple are in the unexpected role of both **aiding and restraining** government surveillance.

These tech giants act as what Professor Alan Z. Rozenshtein dubbed "**surveillance intermediaries**" that collect massive amounts of data about users and are in turn relied on for that data by law enforcement and foreign-intelligence agencies that conduct surveillance (2018).

"By entrusting our data processing and communications to a handful of giant technology companies, we've created a new generation of surveillance intermediaries: large, powerful companies that stand between the government and our data and, in the process, help constrain government surveillance," Rozenshtein wrote in the *Stanford Law Review* (p. 105). The result is "a contentious relationship between the companies that manage our digital bodies and the government that protects our physical ones."

Technology companies have this role not by intentional design but because of their "omnipresence in our day-to-day lives," noted a 2019 article in the *Harvard Law Review* (Ch. 1, para 2). This unexpected role means that tech companies are responsible for decisions that affect national security—such as providing the cell phone records of alleged terrorists. They are also responsible for constraining the government from overreaching and collecting all manner of data on citizens' financial, travel and work activities, thus violating their privacy.

Tech companies are in the unique position of serving both as a provider and a protector of users' data.

Some tech companies offer cell phone messaging apps and social media messaging that have end-to-end encryption. **End-to-end encryption** encodes a message so only authorized parties can access it. Encryption poses problems for government surveillance, and, not surprisingly, government agencies vehemently oppose the practice. Tech companies are in the unique position of serving both as a provider and a protector of users' data. An entire body of legal and policy work is evolving to create, in effect, a governance of surveillance. In summary, for now, the law is still being made regarding issues of electronic surveillance and cybersecurity. What do you think the role of tech companies should be in providing users' data to government agencies such as the National Security Administration or the FBI?

Selling Surveillance Technologies Western technology companies and governments should block the sale of surveillance software and hardware to countries that commit human rights abuses, say the Electronic Frontier Foundation (Cohn, Timm, & York, 2012) and Reporters Without Borders (2013, 2016), among others. Such sanctions would limit authoritarian governments' ability to acquire technology that enables censoring, spying and hacking of communications by citizens and reporters.

The European Union and the United States have in the past banned the export of surveillance technology to Iran and Syria, for example. The problem is that these technologies are "dual use" and many are the same tools needed for social media and other communications by political protesters and activists worldwide, and for Western law enforcement to track criminal activities (Risen, 2015).

It's a coin with two sides: Western democracies use some of the same surveillance technologies for ostensibly more honorable purposes than oppressive regimes, but who is keeping watch on *their* ethical usage?

Surveillance Affects What You Know Activists who are working to change governments that are committing human rights violations, and the journalists who seek to cover such oppressive regimes, are subject to surveillance technologies. Their email accounts or social media exchanges may be tapped.

In late 2018, hundreds of Google employees signed a petition asking Google not to launch its new Dragonfly search engine that is specifically designed for the Chinese market. Dragonfly complies with the Communist government's censorship rules, and allows tracing of search queries back to the individual making it (Li, 2018).

This matters to you and me because, even if Dragonfly doesn't launch (and that's still in question as of this writing), it highlights the issue of online censorship and information repression by governments. China is an extreme case in that it only allows for the dissemination of state-approved news and information. According to Li's reporting, the Dragonfly version of Google would not allow many searches, including "Nobel Prize" and "human rights." It would only show air quality data from a source in Beijing as opposed to more neutral out-of-country data, for example.

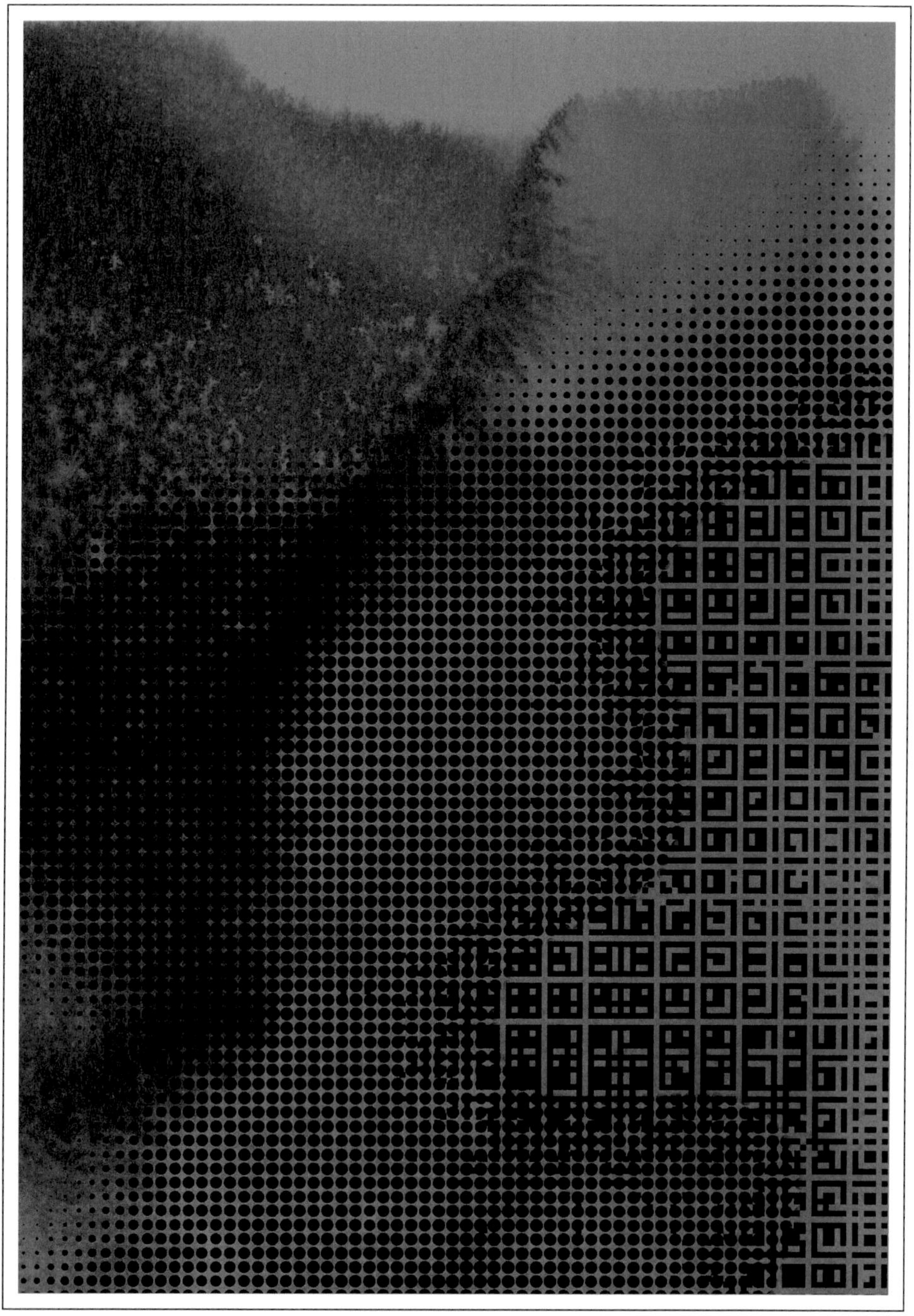

Pixelated Surveillance

Credit: Ryan Lewis

In his last column published in 2018 in the *Washington Post*, journalist Jamal Khashoggi railed against the control of information by the governments of Saudi Arabia and other authoritarian Arab regimes. Khashoggi was brutally murdered in the Saudi Arabian consulate in Istanbul, Turkey. Among the last words of his final column about the importance of free speech to a free society, Khashoggi wrote: "The Arab world needs a modern version of the old transnational media so citizens can be informed about global events. More important, we need to provide a platform for Arab voices."

SURVEILLANCE TOOLS

Digital technology has unleashed a slew of surveillance tools and techniques. These are being updated and new iterations developed each year. The legalese on privacy policies for social media and media creation sites is getting simplified and easier to understand, fortunately. (As an example of more user-friendly tools for controlling the information gathered about you, see facebook.com/ads/preferences to learn what factors influence the ads you see, and also to tighten controls on what is shared about you to advertisers.) There remains a significant lack of transparency about what technology companies do with the data they collect about users.

There remains a significant lack of transparency about what technology companies do with the data they collect about users.

Computer cookies, you'll recall from earlier discussions, are small text files stored on your computer's browser by a website you visit. Cookies track your movements within that website, and they help you remember your login, preferences and other customized functions. The original purpose of cookies has changed to now include tracking of your activity online in order to serve you customized advertisements.

Device-Related Technologies Biometrics, closed-circuit television and workplace surveillance aren't *directly* tied to media and communication. They are often connected, however, to the devices that bring us media and communication, such as our smartphones or laptops. And, the data that they collect is shared via emails and smartphones that can be hacked for content and shared on social media.

Biometrics allows recognition by means of your face, fingerprints, voice, eyes, even your gait and the way you type. Biometrics is the process of recognizing individuals through their physiological and behavioral traits or attributes. The U.S. Immigration and Naturalization Service uses biometric technologies to verify the identities of travelers and immigrants, for example.

The appeal of biometrics is that they intimately and (usually) accurately identify a subject. However, they are invasive in terms of privacy, and data storage is a concern in the event of a data breach. The signals that our bodies send about us may be one day used to determine our moods, longevity and if we're being honest (Dasgupta, Roy, & Nag, 2017). Imagine your future boss having access to *that* data.

Closed-circuit TV is at the heart of increased levels of video surveillance in public and semi-public spaces. As part of policing efforts, communities are posting closed-circuit TV (CCTV) cameras throughout their streets, parks, outside parking areas, subways, sports arenas and other public spaces. The technology is becoming more high-tech, with facial recognition capabilities, license-plate number recognition, night vision and video analysis that includes person counting and heat maps.

The rationale for CCTV is for deterring and solving crimes. Efforts are ongoing to find a balance between crime-fighting and civil liberties. An unanswered question on CCTV effectiveness for crime-deterrence is whether CCTV merely displaces crime to areas without cameras (Marković, 2018).

Workplace surveillance likely isn't top-of-the-mind when you land your first full-time job. Congratulations! Your new employers gave you a smartphone, laptop, company car and of course, an ID badge. Your employer may now track your comings and goings at work thanks to the computer chip in the ID badge; how many bathroom breaks you take and how long you stay in the loo are now company information. How fast you type and how long you talk on the phone are also recorded. Ditto on where you take the car, and whom you email and text.

This kind of monitoring helps protect trade secrets and confidential business information, not to mention embezzlement and data breaches, companies say. According to the International Human and Privacy Rights Protection Association, employees worldwide are subject to surveillance by employers. Oftentimes, surveillance is a condition of employment (2019). This is an evolving area of law, and litigation continues around the competing issues of workplace privacy and employee monitoring. A common reason for employee monitoring, said attorney V. John Ella (2016, p. 2), is "to increase productivity and dissuade cyber-slacking and social 'notworking.'" As if we would *ever* spend work time on social media. How rude.

VOX DISCIPULI

I figure I'm being watched wherever I go. It's not creepy to me, it's just the way it is. I don't do anything wrong, so I don't care if cameras see me. I know people say that their privacy is being invaded with all these cameras and that companies are spying on us online. It doesn't bother me. I don't post things I am worried about people seeing, or I just post to my friends and they don't share my stuff. Yeah, I buy a lot online but it's always with a secure site. People who are freaking out about privacy are people with something to hide. I would sue a company if they took my information illegally. —Adam, 18

DATA PRIVACY LAWS

Consumers need more protection under the law and the ability to sue a company if their information is improperly shared, according to the Council on Foreign Relations as well as legal experts. Most data breaches now don't result in any significant financial harm to companies (O'Connor, 2018).

Monitoring Children A major concern by privacy advocates and parents is the monitoring of children by technology companies. Children and teenagers are sought-after by marketers, as they represent a lucrative spending public, and potential lifetime customers. Companies such as Google that provide Chromebook computers to grade schools, for instance, are able to receive data about students' internet usage and online activities—and they are molding future adult customers by acquainting students with their products.

In the U.S, the Children's Online Privacy Protection Act requires technology companies to get parental consent to collect data on children under 13. A 2019 proposed bill would update that act through age 15, and include a way for parents to erase their children's data from certain sites. In France, strict privacy laws mean that a child could sue their parents for publishing details of their private lives without their consent (Chazan, 2016).

U.S. Law Under current U.S. law, it is extremely difficult for individual consumers to sue a company such as Facebook for damages or the imposition of fines for data breaches. Tech companies currently are fighting for a legal standard of "concrete" harm—that is, consumers whose data has been improperly shared must demonstrate physical, emotional or financial harm (Guliani, 2019). Unlike most industrialized nations, the United States does *not* have a uniform act regarding punishment for illegal sharing of personal data. Instead, individual states have passed laws, such as California's Consumer Privacy Act.

Tim Cook, the CEO of Apple, argued in early 2019 that comprehensive federal data privacy laws *should* be passed in the United States. Cook said the reforms should include stripping consumers' data of any identifying information, and informing consumers what information about them is being collected, why, and how to access and correct it. Equally important, said Cook, is requiring all data brokers to register with the Federal Trade Commission so that consumers can have the power to "delete their data on demand, freely, easily and online, once and for all" (Cook, 2019).

European Union Law The European Union has a broad law called the General Data Protection Regulation (GDPR). It affects *any* companies—even if they are not located in the EU—that collect, store and process data from EU citizens. Enacted in May 2018, the GDPR is seen as setting a global standard for basic data privacy laws. The law comes with hefty fines if consumer privacy is breached.

Specifically, the GDPR requires that companies notify consumers of data breaches, give consumers "the right to be forgotten" by allowing their data to be erased, and allow consumers to take their content from social media with them if they quit the service. You may have noticed a compliant cookie banner that pops up to alert you and ask for your consent to allow cookies to be placed on your computer—that alert and the simplified language of consent is thanks to the GDPR. Here is what one especially detailed consent looks like:

> We use cookies to personalise content and ads, to provide social media features and to analyse our traffic. We also share information about your use of our site with our social media, advertising and analytics partners who may combine it with other information that you've provided to them or that they've collected from your use of their services. You consent to our cookies if you continue to use our website.
>
> (Cookiebot, 2019)

Globally Digital media companies that are global, which are basically all the big ones—Facebook, YouTube, etc.—are following the EU's new law. And tech start-ups worldwide are also following the law because if they hope to get bought one day by a big tech firm, having the infrastructure for data privacy in place makes them more attractive purchase targets.

Elsewhere in the world, data protection is spotty. For instance, in Africa's 54 countries, *more than half* have no data privacy laws; this, in a region that has recorded the *fastest* rise in internet use in the past decade (Behroz et al., 2018).

HAVE A PRIVACY STRATEGY

As a media-literate user, you will want to develop a strategy for your online sharing. Don Tapscott, the CEO of the Blockchain Research Institute, has this advice (Where Everybody Knows Your Name, 2012):

> The fundamental problem with the case of radical personal openness is that we are a long way from a world where being an open book will not hurt us. There is the injury to individuals that arises from unauthorized disclosure of sensitive personal information, but tangible harms and damages can also occur, too, such as from blackmail, identity fraud, impersonation, and cyber-stalkers . . . the new movement toward "personal

sharing" is naïve and misguided. Transparency applies fundamentally to institutions, not to individuals.

Rather than living our lives out loud, we each need a personal privacy strategy governing what information we release and to whom. Rather than default to openness, we should default to privacy, and then choose to share information when the benefits outweigh the dangers.

Data Security Tips Much of the effort to protect your digital life must come from you. The key to data security is prevention. Here are some basic habits (Perekalin, 2018) to incorporate into your digital media use:

- Change your social media privacy settings to make your posts as limited as possible—only to friends and not the general public.
- Create a second e-mail account you only use for purchases, and refrain from sharing your true email (or cell number) on social media.
- Use messaging apps that have end-to-end encryption. WhatsApp has end-to-end encryption. Facebook Messenger does not, so use its Secret Conversations feature.
- Beware of **phishing**, which is the attempt to defraud you by posing as a trusted source. Any message asking for your personal information is suspect, as is any that starts with "Dear Customer" or some other generic greeting. Keep your browser up to date, don't click on pop-ups and use anti-virus software. Check the sender's email address, and hover over any link you're being asked to click to check that the URL actually leads to where you think it should. Look for a closed lock icon near the address in the toolbar to know a site is secure before giving personal information.
- Secure your smartphone and computer with passwords. Use a password manager to keep track of the long passwords you are going to start using for privacy purposes! Then, all you need to remember is one long password, not 24.
- Disable lock-screen notifications on your smartphone so anyone passing by your desk doesn't see your private messages.
- Avoid using a public wi-fi network when sending any sensitive data.

Advocate No single action truly prevents identity theft. It's why lawmakers, government regulators and media companies must take more steps to protect the citizens they either are elected or paid to serve, or from whom they make healthy profits. So, vote if you're old enough, let your opinion be heard by your elected representatives and advocate in your school, company and community for data security.

When asked to enroll in online activities, games or to access websites, pause to check whether your personal data can be withheld. Question where information is going and what it is used for. As more citizens become aware of their diminishing privacy, more people are advocating for opt-out measures. You can do the same.

Quitting Doesn't Work Leaving (or never starting) social media isn't a solution that prevents the sophisticated systems of technology from tracking you. As smart home technologies increase (your new washing machine collects data on you!) and retail stores use facial recognition technologies (not to mention the pervasive loyalty cards and apps), the world we move about in will continually collect and share personal data.

Said Frederike Kaltheuner of Privacy International: "It's simply not possible to opt out" (Behroz et al., 2018). Still, there are many steps you *can* take to significantly reduce your online footprint. One step is removing yourself from all social media sites. An even larger one is removing yourself from people-finder sites, from which your home address, phone number and criminal record (if you have one) are available for free or a small fee. Another fairly major move is to quit all email. One guide to minimizing your digital footprint is here: http://bit.ly/2FJyYt1.

WE'RE BUILT TO SHARE

One reason it is so hard to stay off social media is because as humans, we are built to share. Humans are *relational*. We like to be connected. It's one big reason that social media is so wildly popular. Belonging is as old as civilization, as we find *our* people and differentiate them from *others'* people. The information age has accelerated our natural instinct to relate and belong, such that each day online, we share more personal information, with more people, more quickly and more often.

Social media users and online community members say they gain in self-esteem as their social capital online increases, studies indicate (e.g., Steinfield, Ellison, & Lampe, 2008). The comments, the praise and support, the sharing of photos and videos—all this connection increases the benefits we get from relationships with others. Not only do we need to share, we *want* to share. Sharing builds our value in our own and others' eyes, it builds our knowledge and increases our networking potential for employment and advancement at work, it gives us an energy boost (physiological), a warm fuzzy (emotional) and a strategic connection (cognitive) all at once.

Sharing Shapes Identity I am going to share much more about how media shapes our identities in the next chapter, but for now, know that another reason we are built to share is that it helps us shape our sense of self. Social psychologists Henri Tajfel and John Turner (2004) proposed that the groups that people belonged to, be it a sports team or an income class, offer an important sense of social identity. Social media in particular provides a way to define our groups.

A *New York Times* Customer Insight Group study (n.d.) of 2,500 medium/heavy online sharers found that:

- 68 percent of people share to get a better sense of who they are and what they care about.
- 78 percent said they share because it helps them feel connected with other people.
- 69 percent said they share because it helps them feel more involved in the world.
- 73 percent said they share because they process information more fully and deeply when they share it.

As long as technology facilitates connection, humans will pursue it. We're built to connect, and to share. To paraphrase Kaltheuner's earlier quote, we want to establish boundaries about who has access to our communications and information. We also want to use technology to help us negotiate who we are and how we want to interact with the world around us. In short, we want our connections *and* our privacy.

CHAPTER REVIEW

- Define privacy.
- Give an example of how data given for one reason is repurposed for other uses.
- Explain how tech giants are "surveillance intermediaries."
- Discuss the pros and cons of common surveillance tools.
- Understand the significance of Edward Snowden's actions.
- Describe the state of data privacy laws in various regions of the world.
- Know the tips to maintain your internet privacy.
- Explain the reason people share so much personal information online.

ACTIVITIES

1. Google yourself and find out what information is available online about you. Dig as deeply as you can, checking public records, maps of where you've lived, Google Street View for your residence, photos, mentions of you by other people and other personal details. Write up a list of what is available about you online.
2. Create your own "personal privacy strategy," as Don Tapscott suggests. Be as specific as possible about what you will share or not share, and what sites you're willing to do business with. This should include the sorts of boundaries you will set on social media sites regarding privacy and sharing.
3. For a detailed survey of privacy laws and practice, see the Global Internet Liberty Campaign report at http://gilc.org/privacy/survey/intro.html. Assign different passages to various people who can then summarize the section and its significance to the entire group.
4. Read about the use of surveillance cameras, including the body-cams worn by police, in the alleged hate-crime hoax planned by *Empire* actor

Jussie Smollett. Consider how cameras played in the entire case. Create a short blog post about what you learned.

5. Take a walk around your downtown or your campus. Note every instance in which your information is being recorded or noted by cameras, swipe cards, computer sign-ins and other surveillance technology. Discuss the implications of this level of oversight for you as a citizen.

REFERENCES

Angwin, J. (2016, August 1). Making algorithms accountable. *ProPublica*. Retrieved from propublica.org

Behroz, K., Stegemann, P., & Rosinski, M. P. (2018, July 12). It's about human dignity and autonomy. *Privacy International*. Retrieved from privacyinternational.org

Cambridge Dictionary. (2019). *Privacy*. Retrieved from https://dictionary.cambridge.org/us/

Chazan, D. (2016, March 1). French parents "could be jailed" for posting children's photos online. *The Telegraph*. Retrieved from http://bit.ly/2O764Jg

Cohn, C., Timm, T., & York, J.C. (2012). Human rights and technology sales: How corporations can avoid assisting repressive regimes. *Electronic Frontier Foundation*. Retrieved from http://bit.ly/2OQyaZT

Cook, T. (2019). You deserve privacy online: Here's how you could actually get it. *TIME Magazine*. Retrieved from http://bit.ly/2FJO55C

Cookiebot. (2019). GDPR and cookies: What do I need to know? Is my use of cookies compliant? Retrieved from cookiebot.com/en/gdpr-cookies

Culver, S. H., & Grizzle, A. (2017). *Survey on privacy in media and information literacy with youth perspectives*. Paris: United Nations Educational, Scientific and Cultural Organization.

Dasgupta, D., Roy, A., & Nag, A. (2017). Biometric authentication: Authentication through human characteristics. In *Advances in user authentication* (pp. 37–84), Infosys Science Foundation Series. Springer International Publishing. doi:10.1007/978-3-319-58808-7_2

Ella, V. J. (2016, April 6–8). *Employee monitoring and workplace privacy law*. Section of Labor and Employment Law National Symposium on Technology in Labor & Employment Law. American Bar Association. Washington, D.C. Retrieved from http://bit.ly/2HWts7A

Floridi, L. (2016). On human dignity as a foundation for the right to privacy. *Philosophy & Technology, 29*(4), 307–312.

Guliani, N. S. (2019, January 6). We should be able to take Facebook to court. *The New York Times*. Opinion section. Retrieved from https://nyti.ms/2Sx6rLR

Harvard Law Review. (2019, May 1). Cooperation or resistance? The role of tech companies in government surveillance. *Harvard Law Review: Developments in the Law, 131*, 1722–1741.

International Human Rights and Privacy Protection Organization. (2019). *Workplace surveillance*. Retrieved from http://ihprpa.org/1-2.php

Kirchner, L. (2015, November 18). What's the evidence mass surveillance works? Not much. *ProPublica*. Retrieved from propublica.org

La Rue, F. (2013). *Report of the special rapporteur on the promotion and protection of the right to freedom of opinion and expression*. United Nations Human Rights Council. 23rd session. United Nations General Assembly.

Li, M. S. (2018, December 11) Google's dragonfly will intensify surveillance on journalists in China. *Columbia Journalism Review.* Retrieved from http://bit.ly/2M1n80F

Marković, M. (2018). Information security and privacy protection aspects of CCTV systems. *Government Europa*. Pan European Networks, Ltd., Retrieved from http://bit.ly/2WuYIyB

The New York Times (n.d.) The psychology of sharing: Why do people share online? Customer Insight Group study.

O'Connor, N. (2018). *Reforming the U.S. approach to data protection and privacy.* New York: Council on Foreign Relations.

Perekalin, A. (2018, July 11). 10 tips to improve your internet privacy. *Kaspersky Lab Daily*. Retrieved from kaspersky.com

Reporters Without Borders. (2013, 2016). Special report on internet surveillance, focusing on 5 governments and 5 companies. "Enemies of the Internet." Retrieved from http://bit.ly/31yUqZN

Risen, J. (2015, October 31). Battle heats up over exports of surveillance technology. *The New York Times.* Retrieved from https://nyti.ms/2Z3rqsa

Rozenshtein, A. Z. (2018). Surveillance intermediaries. *Stanford Law Review, 70*(1), 99–189.

Smith, A. (2017, January 26). *Americans and Cybersecurity.* Pew Research Center: Internet & Technology.

Statista. (2019). Facebook—Statistics & Facts. 2018 dossier. Retrieved from Statista.com.

Steinfield, C., Ellison, N. B., & Lampe, C. (2008). Social capital, self-esteem, and use of online social network sites: A longitudinal analysis. *Journal of Applied Developmental Psychology, 29*(6), 434–445.

Tajfel, H., & Turner, J. C. (2004). An integrative theory of intergroup conflict. In M. J. Hatch & M. Schultz (Eds.), *Organizational identity* (pp. 56–64). Oxford: Oxford University Press.

Teaching Privacy. (2019). *Privacy requires work.* Retrieved from Teachingprivacy.org

Where Everybody Knows Your Name: How to Succeed in the Post-Privacy Age. (2012, November 2). Q & A with Clay Shirky and Don Tapscott. Retrieved from The Atlantic.com

Wright, J. (2013, May 16). *Digital surveillance—Why the Snoopers' Charter is the wrong approach: A call for targeted and accountable investigatory powers.* (Excerpted portion.) Published by the Open Rights Group. Retrieved from http://bit.ly/2Ywd2cd

10 Choosing

How to Curate Your Media Use to Positively Shape Your Sense of Self

The Notebook. Fifty Shades of Grey. Blue Valentine. 500 Days of Summer. You've Got Mail. The Wedding Planner. While You Were Sleeping.

The list of romantic-themed movies is long.

A study of 294 undergraduate students (Holmes, 2007) found a connection between romance-oriented media and a belief in real-world, predestined soul mates and the idea that a person should have a complete understanding of a partner's needs and desires with little or no effort.

Uh-oh.

"Unfortunately people tend to believe the Hollywood idea of a perfect relationship," the researcher told the U.K.-based *Telegraph*

LEARNING OBJECTIVES

Terms: Social cognition theory, social identity theory, social capital, parasocial relationships.

- Examine how media contribute positively and negatively to self-esteem and identity formation.
- Identify the embedded values and points of view in various media messages.
- Explain how social cognition theory translates into real-life attitudes and behaviors.
- Apply social identity and social cognitive theories to your online media use.
- Understand how social media relies on social capital and promotes parasocial relationships.
- Consider the utility of media literacy in making media choices.

When you create content that supposedly reflects your identity, whose lifestyles, values and points of view are you using as your lens? Also, do you have distinct in-person and online identities? Knowing that different people experience the same media message differently, do you customize your media messages for different online audiences?

newspaper (Alleyne, 2008). "That is just unrealistic. People feel if their relationship is not like a Hollywood film then it is not any good." Other studies of young adults have found similar unrealistic expectations for real-life romance and marriage based on movie romance—with idealized notions that love conquers all, high expectations for intimacy, and endorsement of passionate love and perfect "chemistry" (Galloway, Engstrom, & Emmers-Sommer, 2015; Segrin & Nabi, 2002).

These are just a handful of the scores of studies on young adults' media-influenced expectations about real life. Think of the popular magazines, music and trade books that also champion this storyline of love at first sight, no bad breath and nothing-but-amazing moments together. Oh, and these couples never seem to have to go to work, either.

This chapter challenges us to consider how we use media to engage with our own identity, with others and with society as a whole. We will explore the ways that we leverage our identities and the identities of others to meet goals, and how our self-esteem and sense of self is influenced by media messages. Based on the previously mentioned research, we may also need to review what real-life couple-hood is actually about. In a double-blind study that I personally conducted, romance involved a complete understanding of when to empty the dishwasher.

MEDIA'S EMBEDDED VALUES

Consider this 2014 blog post by student "Caylee P.," and whether or not it strikes some familiar chords for you in terms of media setting expectations for real life:

> As a child, the one thing I could not wait to do was grow up. With the media's portrayals of what it was like being a high schooler, I was so dying to experience all of the things I had seen in movies and TV. With all of this media I had been led to believe that I could possibly be that one in a million and become a secret pop sensation like Miley . . . in

> "Hannah Montana," all while still maintaining a normal life. Similarly, I had believed that I would meet some amazing guy, maybe at a ski resort like in "High School Musical" and that we would have a perfect relationship, like Troy and Gabriella. I was able to hold on to these false perceptions for years until the real world slapped me in the face and showed me that life is not as easy and perfect as it is portrayed on the big screen.
>
> (Caylee P., 2014, para 1)

Media messages serve to socialize us to ways of being and thinking. It's true, isn't it? We get all sorts of ideas from media about how to behave with friends, or how to dress, deliver a joke or execute a dance move. It's commonplace to study a YouTube video or an Instagram photo for details on how to live life. It's not surprising that Caylee P. and the thousands of students involved in the research mentioned at the start of the chapter also learn from romance movies about what to expect from true love.

SOCIAL COGNITIVE THEORY

Indeed, we do learn from the media. As Albert Bandura's social cognitive theory of mass communication (2001) posits, we are not merely passive recipients of media, but we engage with it, reflect on it and learn from it. We learn about values, ideas and beliefs from the media, and this in turn affects our self-perception and self-esteem.

People learn behaviors through observation, modeling and motivation such as positive reinforcement, Bandura asserted. So, when we see others' behaviors result in reward or punishment, we learn from that, and our choice of behaviors is reinforced. So, when children see the TV hero get his way by fighting with any detractors (and always winning the fights), it wouldn't be surprising that they learn fighting solves problems and leads to success.

Social cognitive theory asserts that people learn through social modeling—by watching others in social situations; this is less tedious and hazardous than real-life trial-and-error learning. Learning from the successes and failures of others makes sense. Media easily allows for social modeling, Bandura noted, as characters showcase different personality traits, social roles and ways of being. Media consumers watch and learn from those models. We want to reproduce those models when we see them rewarded in media portrayals.

Mass media presents a behavior or a way of being, and those presentations get our *attention* through relevance, complexity, functionality and other factors. Bandura argues that we remember the media model though repeated and simplified portrayals in shows, advertisements, magazines and other representations. Once we have *retained* the model, we try to *produce* the same standard in our own lives, *motivated* by any self-satisfying responses we get when we try to reproduce the mass media models that we saw.

Bandura summarized the bewitchingly persuasive power of modeling to convince consumers that they too can get what the media promises:

> Thus, drinking a certain brand of wine or using a particular shampoo wins the loving admiration of beautiful people, enhances job performance, masculinizes self-conception, actualizes individualism and authenticity, tranquilizes irritable nerves, invites social recognition and amicable reactions from total strangers, and arouses affectionate overtures from spouses.
>
> (p. 283)

This cycle of attention, retention, production and motivation is at the heart of the social cognitive model. The threat, of course, is that too much mass media consumption leads to unhealthy goals and unrealistic aspirations in the real world, and sometimes adopting unhealthy ways of thinking. [For example, a study by van Oosten, Peter and Valkenburg (2015) stated that "viewing sexual music videos by male artists increased the acceptance of female token resistance (i.e., the notion that women say 'no' to sex when they actually mean 'yes') among adolescent girls, but not adolescent boys" (p. 986).]

We come to think the media's idealized versions are attainable, are real. However, the benefit of social cognitive theory is that by modeling positive behaviors, such as promoting anti-smoking messages in films, media representations can promote positive behaviors in real life. Many health-related public service campaigns are based on this idea that positive results from media depictions can compel audiences to try to produce the same results in their lives.

What have you learned from mass media models? Is there a TV character that has taught you something through their behavior that you either want to emulate or reject?

The Thin Ideal Bandura's theory explains the cycle of reinforcement of mass media that projects a thin ideal body type for females and a muscle-bound frame for males. Of course, we could pick any number of other celebrated traits the media has communicated, from affluence to beauty to physical fitness.

In this example, the reinforcement happens through successful, positive portrayals, such as that thin females get rewards—they "are more well liked, more likely to have romantic relationships, less likely to be bullied," reported researchers Dana Mastro and Andrea Figueroa-Caballero (2018, p. 323). Couple those rewards with media messages that pair overweight or obese characters with marginalization and negative outcomes such as "less likely to receive praise, most likely to be insulted" and the social implications are clear.

Mastro and Figueroa-Caballero examined a week's worth of U.S. television, including 1,254 characters in 89 programs. They concluded that: "Women have become increasingly thin on TV. Thinner characters were more attractive than overweight characters. The few obese and overweight characters presented were less articulate, less intelligent, and more likely to be ridiculed than thinner characters" (p. 320).

The power of media messages to serve as vehicles of socialization is real. Due to Westernized portrayals of ideal body weight for women, young females in a 2011 study of women in Pakistan were shifting their eating habits and their cultural identities to match this media ideal. "Traditionally for Pakistani females, identity had been fixed not so much in the body as in family, society, and relationships with others, in contrast to Western-cultural models that firmly fix identity in the body/self," wrote researchers Zain-Ul-Abideen and colleagues (2011). In Pakistan, the authors note, "identity is . . . experienced individually and cooperatively

The power of media messages to serve as vehicles of socialization is real.

through the well-fed bodies of others, not through one's own body" (p. 134).

A TV advertisement for Special K Chocolatey Delight cereal is an example of a media message that championed the thin ideal. "In this advertisement, a woman is watching a horror film on television, obviously frightened by what she is seeing. The omniscient voiceover then proclaims it to be that 'dangerous time of night where you fall victim to chocolate temptations lurking in the kitchen,'" wrote Vanessa Reimer and Rukhsana Ahmed (2012, p. 12). The message? The inability to maintain a slim body is, apparently, downright dangerous.

Living with Disabilities For people with disabilities, the media portrayals are generally stigmatizing and negative, dependent on health professionals for cures or society for support, noted communication researchers Lingling Zhang and Beth Haller (2013) in their review of the research. When people with disabilities *are* depicted positively in the mass media, it is as a "supercrip," or "'superhuman' because they achieve unexpected accomplishments or live a normal life just like people with no disabilities" (p. 321).

In their study on how media portrayals affect the identity formation of people with disabilities, Zhang and Haller found that even though people with disabilities found the supercrip portrayals as unrealistic and exaggerated, they were "more likely to develop positive and confident self-identity when exposed to media stories about the accomplishments of individuals with disabilities" (p. 330).

They cite previous research that suggests negative media stereotypes about people with disabilities can undermine their aspirations and performance, to the point that people in the disability community will deny their disability status or try to hide it due to fear of negative judgments. For an example of a person who choose to take her story into her own hands and create a personal blog about living with a disability, see The Squeaky Wheelchair blog (http://www.thesqueakywheelchairblog.com/).

> Review and reflect on any of the Critical Media Project media snippets that engage with various aspects of identity: age, class, disability, gender, LGBTQ, race and ethnicity and religion. They are first-rate examples and come with discussion questions. See criticalmediaproject.org.

Seeing Identity Media messages can show another view of life and offer a different lens on this crackling, constantly-changing world we live in. Seeing other identities in the media can help to educate people about those who aren't like themselves.

Media portrayals of LGBTQ people have become more common in U.S.-produced media, with a record high of 8.8 percent of TV series regulars being LGBTQ, according to the 2018–2019 report by GLAAD. Shows such as *Pose, American Horror Story, Queer as Folk, Now Apocalypse, GLOW* and *Orange is the New Black* provide a range of representations of LGBTQ people.

For the first time, LGBTQ people of color outnumbered white LGBTQ people on broadcast TV shows, and 26 trans characters were noted across all platforms. In terms of race and ethnicity, 44 percent (373 of 857) of scripted series regulars on primetime TV were people of color, GLAAD reported.

Reality TV showcases a reality most of us do not know. The shows seem scripted and contrived. But there are other options that actually do showcase reality; such as the public radio programs *Snap Judgment* or *This American Life,* both of which use dialogue, natural sound and non-fiction narratives that showcase the ambiguity and uncertainty of real life.

CONTENT CREATION AS IDENTITY FORMATION

Content creation by young people informs the shaping and expression of their identities. In fact, the process of identity formation is facilitated today through and by new media—through play, creation, trial-and-error, improvisation, feedback and reflection, as David Buckingham (2008) and others have explored.

New media is so seamlessly integrating into the daily lives of youth and young adults that soon distinctions between the "real" you and the media version of you will become invisible, noted researchers Sandra Weber and Claudia Mitchell (2008). The pair collected examples of new media content creation from a diverse range of youth in the United Kingdom, Canada and South Africa. The examples included videos and photography by youth on gender, violence and sexuality, as well as from their elaborate personal websites.

Weber and Mitchell's work showed that identity construction involves media creation in the spirit of improvisation and experimentation, free of rigid guidelines and strict adherence to genre, so that messages are created to suit various contexts and situations. Does this sound like the way you create media—not hemmed in by strict rules but free to try new ways of expressing yourself? When we create content, we are forced to think about how we want to present ourselves, and that forces us to think about who we are. Content production helps people to look at themselves and their own self-representations, and "the choices and processes that they use reveal and identify them in ways that they themselves might not even realize" (p. 41). Also, audience responses and feedback to their media messages further inform and shape people's sense of how they see themselves and how they think others see them.

> Clicking, posting, and text messaging their way through a shifting digital landscape, young people are bending and blending genres, incorporating old ideas, activities, and images into new bricolages, changing the face, if not the substance, of social interaction and altering how they see themselves and each other.
>
> (p. 44)

When we create content, we are forced to think about how we want to present ourselves, and that forces us to think about who we are.

Yet, as Buckingham notes in his writing on identity formation and new media, "the question of whose eyes we see ourselves through and whose language we use to express ourselves is not so easily answered" (Weber & Mitchell, p. 41). This is such an important idea—*who do you have in your mind's eye when creating?* Whose language and creative expression are you adopting when you create?

SOCIAL IDENTITY THEORY

A person's sense of who they are, their self-conception, as being based in part based on their membership in various groups is called **social identity theory**. The theory describes the role of self-conception and the associated thinking processes and beliefs associated with being in a group, whether it is a social class or ethnic group, or a soccer team or gaming community.

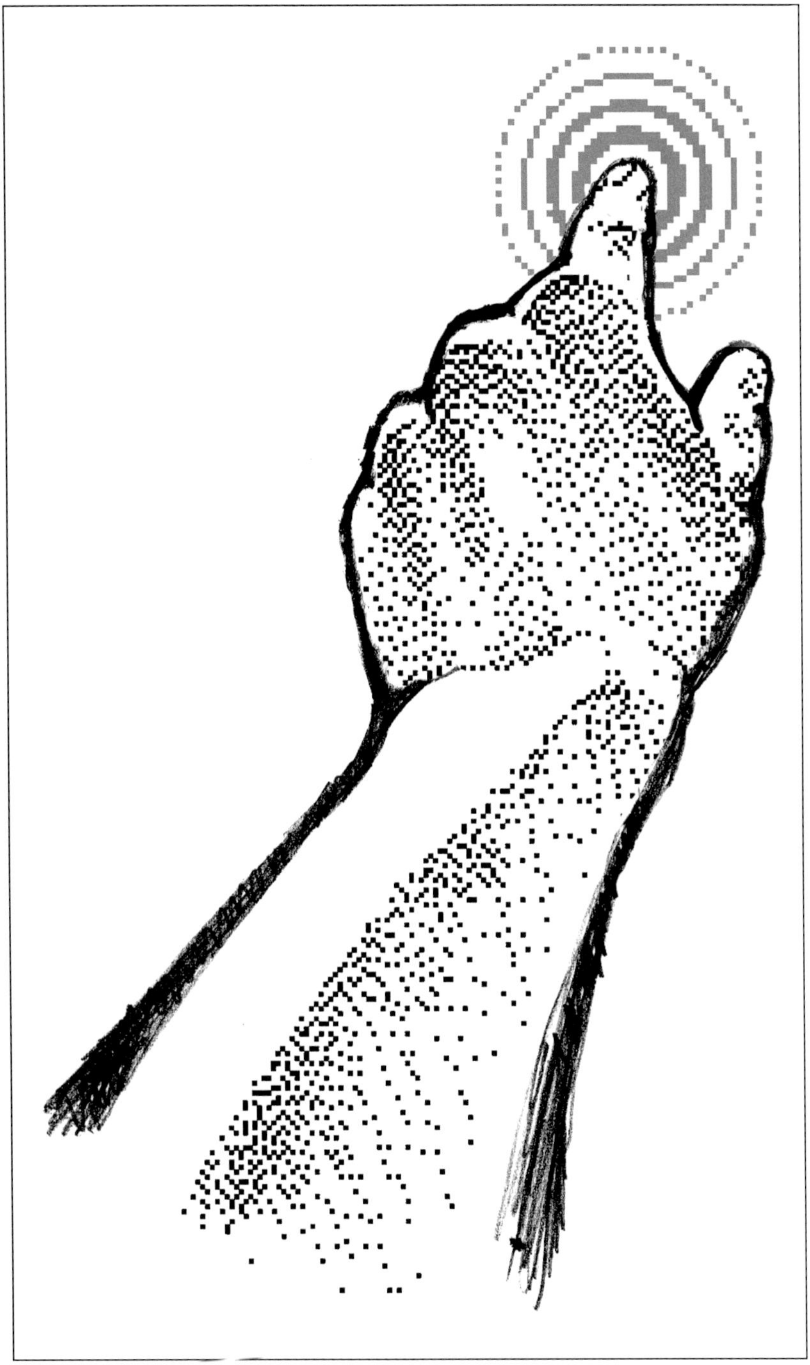

Seeking Connection

Credit: Ryan Lewis

Over the years, the theory has been extended to describe many subcategories including leadership in groups, marginalization and social protest. The important thing for digital media users to know is that we find ways to shape our identities through our online communities. For example, we may contribute to a blog that has a specific terminology and speech style that indicates membership in a group (Hogg, 2016). Partisanship is also a social identity, and it contributes to the growing divide we see in many countries between liberals and conservatives, as people find others with similar ideologies that strengthen their own viewpoints (Mason & Wronski, 2018).

VOX DISCIPULI

As far as social media goes, I follow my friends and they tend to be more like me. It strengthens my existing characteristics, and I myself become more polarized. Also, because I play basketball, I watch a lot of basketball highlights on YouTube the night after a pro or college game. I watch them for entertainment. It's nice to see someone that does what I do but 10 thousand times better than what I do. —Will, 18

Gaming Identities The world of multiplayer gaming is popular for many reasons, not the least of which is that it is highly social, as you likely well know. Being able to coordinate and play real-time games with friends and acquaintances, with each player in his or her own personal space, is convenient and fun. The fantasy world of gaming allows players to try on different personas. It's not surprising, then, that players bring their identities with them to the gaming culture, perhaps finding reinforcement of their real-life identities through their gaming. "These dynamic online environments are heavily influenced by offline dominant values and norms that players themselves carry with them while gaming" (Todd, 2012; Todd, 2015, p. 66).

Media violence is one risk factor for aggressive behavior in real life, but it is not the only factor, and it is not as big as many media critics assert. Studies are mixed on the connection between watching violence on a screen and exhibiting violence in real life. In regard to aggression and violence, there is evidence that playing violent video games is linked to increased aggression (American Psychological Association Resolution, 2015). However, as discussed in Chapter 7, a link, or correlation, is not causation. Scholars agree that exposure to violence in the media, including TV, increases hostile attitudes and the likelihood of aggressive behaviors in real life, as well as desensitizing consumers to violent content. There is a connection between violent media content and social aggression, but the extent of that connection is still unclear (for a helpful recap of the research, see Phillips, 2017).

The social aspect of gaming means society's uglier elements are also part of the culture, with sexism, rape culture and racism a real and documented part of the gaming world. For example, female characters are often depicted as hyper-sexualized, victims and submissive (e.g., Consalvo, 2012; Fox & Tang, 2014).

An example of racism in the video game community actually led to the creation of a new form of journalism. In a revelatory piece of writing, a gamer playing *Jedi Knight II: Jedi Outcast* known as "Always Black" wrote about the real-life racist whom he was playing against (Reddit user HolyTryst, circa 2012). His story, posted at 4:06 a.m. on Sept. 22, 2004, with a racial epithet in the title, launched the style of writing that is now called New Games Journalism (Bitmob, 2009). The style is highly personal and focuses on what it is like to *play* the game. It details the subjective experience of playing a particular game and includes interactions with other players and their commentary. It may even mention offline events that influence the game (Bitmob, 2009). New Games Journalism has been likened to travel journalism since it takes the audience to another world that the author got to visit.

Listen in as "Always Black" artfully puts us *in the moment* of his gaming showdown with a stranger who was somewhere in the world, taunting him with racial epithets to distract him from the game's moves and countermoves:

> You see what this has become? It's not just a trivial game to be played in an idle moment, this is a genuine battle of good versus evil. It has nothing to do with Star Wars or Jedi Knights or any of the fluff that surrounds the game's mechanics. I played by the 'rules' and he didn't, that makes me the 'good' guy and him the 'baddie', but this is real, in the sense that there's no telling who's going to win out here. There's no script or plot to determine

> the eventual triumph of the good guy (that's me, five health), there's no 'natural order' of a fictional universe or any question of an apocryphal ultimate 'balance'. There's just me and him, light and dark, in a genuine contest between the two.
>
> (HolyTryst, circa 2012, para 50)

Social Media and Self-Esteem Social media contributes greatly to our sense of self and our identities. Many people use different social media accounts for different purposes and in different ways, using one to connect with relatives, another for daily interactions with IRL friends, and a third to extend their social reach and cultivate new friendships. The existence of fake or spam Instagram accounts, shared with only users' closest friends, where users can show themselves unfiltered and un-posed, is an example of the different ways people use platforms to showcase identity.

We use social media, gaming, blogs and other new media to express our identities. In turn, our identities are influenced and shaped by feedback we get online.

New media has both nurturing and negative potential (James et al., 2009). On the one hand, new media offers unique opportunities such as virtual play that allows users to shape their identity and to express different parts of themselves in a supportive group environment. In that space, users can engage in self-reflection and get useful feedback. On the other hand, putting one's identity out for feedback runs the risk of being attacked, ridiculed or becoming so reliant on the input from others online that the result is "an unhealthy reliance on feedback and connectivity to others" (p. 33). We can become so attuned to the group feedback that we don't think for ourselves.

Our media use facilitates a continuous cycle of shaping, idealizing, championing and critiquing the process of identity creation and re-creation. As the editor of *Cyberpsychology, Behavior, and Social Networking* (a journal that didn't exist before 1998) put it, "Social media functions as a person's 'highlight reel,' rather than a true reflection of their day-to-day life" (Wiederhold, 2018).

People who spend more time on Facebook are people with lower self-esteem who are looking to compensate for inadequate in-person relationships, a study concluded (Bergagna & Tartaglia, 2018). In the study, the researchers found that both males and females with lower self-esteem were more oriented to socially comparing themselves with others, which, not surprisingly, predicted that they spent more time on Facebook. Another study (Chou & Edge, 2012) found that those who spent more time on Facebook than their peers agreed that others were happier and had better lives than they.

Social Capital One reason that people participate in social media is because it builds social relations. We increase our social capital when we successfully engage in social media. **Social capital** describes the networks of relationships we have that are built on reciprocity and sharing of identity, understanding, norms and values. We build ties that may pay off with a job lead or a letter of recommendation. We reinforce our identities through our online presentation in a personal blog or our profile. "The premise behind the notion of social capital is rather simple and straightforward: investment in social relations with expected returns," noted sociologist Nan Lin (2001, p. 30). Lin's work stresses that it is *who* you know as much as *what* you know that shapes our experience in society. With new media, our reach of connecting is all the greater, expanding our "who you know" to greater and greater lengths.

To build our social capital, we use direct and indirect social ties (such as a friend of a friend, or a follower on social media we have never met, but know through other followers). The resources of social capital include wealth, power, reputation and networks; access to these resources make social capital worth pursuing.

We increase our social capital when we successfully engage in social media.

Lin asserts that virtual networking is creating an unprecedented change in the flow of information and the ways that influence is exerted: "I suggest that indeed we are witnessing a revolutionary rise of social capital, as represented by cyber-networks. In fact, we are witnessing a new era where social capital will soon supersede personal capital in significance and effect" (p. 45).

Parasocial Relationships Twitter and other social media can be used as a form of social capital that elevates the status of the account holder as followers increase in number. Even though many social media followers may not be IRL friends, the numbers game can drive users to add anyone with the most tangential of ties. For some users, following a celebrity or famous person provides a sense of intimacy with an unreachable star that obviously isn't real. There's (of course) a term for this: **parasocial relationships**, which describe the one-sided relationships that develop between audiences and media figures (first described in 1956 by Horton and Wohl). With repeated exposure to a celebrity, sports figure or TV star, audiences develop bonds in which they extend emotional energy and attention to a star who doesn't even know they exist.

The intimacy of social media, on which celebrities are nearly required to post personal details and photos in order to cultivate fans, offers an intensification of this relationship. Also, noted Edward Schiappa and colleagues (2005) in their review of research on this topic, the human brain tends to process media experiences similarly to real life experiences. Mediated life and real life elicit the same cognitive and behavior responses.

Schiappa and colleagues wrote,

> In a media-rich environment, people may come to 'know' more people parasocially than directly through interpersonal contact. Few people have direct contact with the President of the United States, but virtually everyone in the world has strong opinions about the person holding that office. Most media users form attitudes and beliefs about many politicians, athletes, journalists, and entertainers with whom their contact has been exclusively through the mass media.
>
> (p. 95)

Anonymity Social media, blogs, video games and other online worlds allow for experimentation and exploration in one's expression of identity. Anonymity allows a user to try on and try out different personas. Anonymity also allows for discussions about potentially difficult topics such as gender or sexual identity without outing oneself. It allows users suffering from depression or other health issues to find information and others they can relate to.

But anonymity online can also cultivate an unhealthy disconnect between one's real life identity and an online persona. Bullying and harmful critique of identity happen unhindered in online environments. Also, heavy use of social media can lead to an unhealthy dependency on online feedback for affirmation of self. It can also make it easier to bully someone else. For example, one in five Swedish adolescents reported exposure to both real-life and cyber bullying (Landstedt & Persson, 2014). A non-supportive school environment and a poor body image were common among students who reported bullying, and those students were more likely to report mental health problems such as depressive symptoms.

OUR IDENTITY IN MEDIA LITERACY

Media literacy offers us a way forward through media messages and their persuasive approaches so that we can discover our own identities. Remember that YOU provide the fuel to the engine that is social media and media messaging. It is your intelligence, creativity, viewpoint and experience that makes your media creations your own. Choose to create with ethics and quality in mind, and you will not regret it.

In the postscript to his 2001 book *Media, Markets and Democracy*, author C. Edwin Baker reminds us that the internet is still a means to an end. It is a medium for messages that we seek out or create. He wrote:

> Like a printing press or plow, a typewriter or table, a telephone or airplane, the Internet and related digital computer technologies are tools. Tools can make doing some things easier, so much easier that people will now do new things. But the Internet is not ideas, not knowledge; it is not passion or values; nor is it wisdom or meaning. It may increase the creation, occurrence, or distribution of these things that it is not. But that depends on its use.
>
> (p. 285)

And so, we again hear we have a choice.

When consuming media, take time to ask yourself: *How does this message inform, challenge or support my personal system of values? What is it trying to persuade me to do or believe, either through obvious or suggested meanings?*

The Center for Media Literacy challenges media consumers to:

> Evaluate media's explicit and implicit messages against one's own ethical, moral and/or democratic principles. . . . Reflect on the media you consume and evaluate it for its inherent and implied meaning. How do these messages, be they TV shows or magazine photo shoots or music videos or Instagram posts, fulfill your needs and wants?
>
> (Uses and Gratification Theory for Instructor's Guide, 2019)

I truly am sorry to use this overused term but it really conveys a fundamental concept so well, so here goes: Media Diet. As in: Go on one. Watch the media you consume, how much of it and what kind. Get a healthy balance of entertainment, information and new perspectives in every day's intake. Be intentional about the media you use because, as we have learned in this chapter, it does affect your self-esteem and your behaviors.

(*The Food and Drug and Media Administration public service message is now over.*)

CHAPTER REVIEW

- Understand the ways that media communicate values and ideologies.
- Explain social cognitive theory and social identity theory.
- Give an example of a parasocial relationship.
- Apply the concept of social capital to a social media site.
- Describe the ways that media literacy can support positive identity formation.

ACTIVITIES

1. Tune into one of the many broadcasts by celebrity online gaming players in first-person shooter games. Note the depiction of female characters

in the game. Also note whether characters of color are depicted as lead characters or heroes. Pay attention to the storyline, the language and terms used in the game itself as well as by the players. Record two minutes of dialogue in the game. Then, use Google Docs' voice typing tool to *dictate* the video game dialogue you are hearing in your earbuds into the microphone of your computer. The text is transcribed quite accurately. Use a free word cloud maker to make a word cloud of the text. Which words are most emphasized?

2. Read Langston Hughes' "The Negro Artist and the Racial Mountain" (Hughes, 1926) about media creation as a black man in America (it's available various places online and likely accessible online through your school library). Note Hughes' references to media and identity throughout his piece. In particular, read the third paragraph of the essay. Do his sentiments apply today? How? Give examples. If you prefer, you may apply his sentiments to artists from other underrepresented ethnic groups. What surprises you about the content? What still rings true today? What can contemporary society learn from Hughes' essay?
3. Read the article "Lies Hollywood Told Us: Love and Romance Edition" (Lawson & Doll, 2012) at https://bit.ly/2GR5F8v. Then, write your own version of "Lies Hollywood Told Us: _____ Edition," focusing on just one common storyline in mass media that unrealistically glamorizes real life—crime, beauty, parenting, illness. You can draw on TV shows, movies, video games, music videos, popular magazines, songs, musicals—you name it, just as long as it is mass-produced media.
4. Use the Filter Your Identities graphic to write the various ways that you use media to both feed and transmit your on- and offline identities. Start at the top of the filter and jot down the ways you express yourself online, and what media most appeals to you in terms of informing or speaking to who you are. For example, in the upper text boxes, you might list how you play hours of first-person shooter video games and your role when playing with friends or strangers; you might mention your love of superhero action movies because of the strength and speed of the characters. You note that your social media profile picture isn't of your face but of a cool Manga character. The lowest text box synthesizes these elements to make a conclusion about your online identity at present, and how media informs your real-life identity.

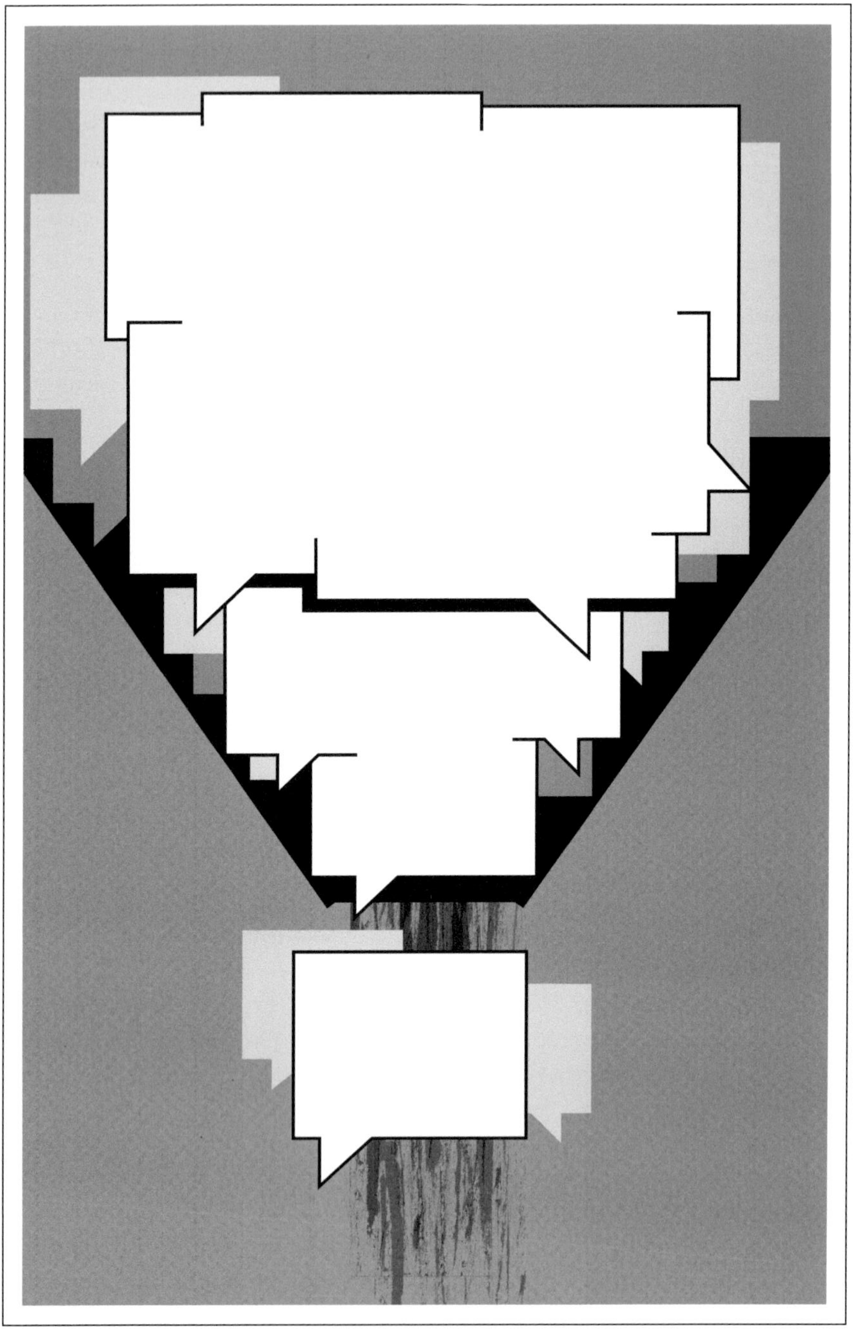

Filter Your Identities

Credit: Ryan Lewis

REFERENCES

Abideen, Z. U., Latif, A., Khan, S., & Farooq, W. (2011). Impact of media on development of eating disorders in young females of Pakistan. *International Journal of Psychological Studies, 3*(1), 122–147. doi:10.5539/ijps.v3n1p122

Alleyne, R. (2008, December 15). Romantic comedies make us 'unrealistic about relationships,' claim scientists. *The Telegraph.* Retrieved from http://bit.ly/2O9rjdt

American Psychological Association. (2015). *Resolution on violent video games.* Retrieved from www.apa.org/about/policy/violent-video-games.aspx

Baker, C. E. (2001). *Media, markets and democracy.* Cambridge: The Press Syndicate of the University of Cambridge.

Bandura, A. (2001). Social cognitive theory of mass communications. *Media Psychology, 3,* 265–299.

Bergagna, E., & Tartaglia, S. (2018). Self-esteem, social comparison, and Facebook use. *European Journal of Psychology, 14*(4), 831–845. doi:10.5964/ejop.v14i4.1592

Bitmob. (2009, July 16). The racial slur that changed games journalism. *Venture Beat.* Retrieved from venturebeat.com

Buckingham, D. (2008). Introducing identity. In D. Buckingham, D. John, & T. Catherine (Eds.), *Youth, identity, and digital media* (pp. 1–24), The John D. and Katherine T. MacArthur Foundation Series on Digital Media and Learning. Cambridge, MA: The MIT Press. doi:10.1162/dmal.9780262524834.001

Caylee P. (2014, December 8). Media gives us unrealistic expectations about life. *VoxPop blog.* Retrieved from www.Mr.Kantor.com

Center for Media Literacy. (2019). *Uses and gratification theory for instructor's guide.* Retrieved from www.medialit.org.

Chou, H. T., Edge, N. (2012). "They are happier and having better lives than I am": The impact of using Facebook on perceptions of others' lives. *Cyberpsychology Behavior and Social Networking, 15*(2), 117–121. doi:10.1089/cyber.2011.0324

Consalvo, M. (2012). Confronting toxic gamer culture: A challenge for feminist game studies scholars. *Ada: A Journal of Gender, New Media, and Technology,* #1.

Fox, J., & Tang, W. Y. (2014). Sexism in online video games: The role of conformity to masculine norms and social dominance orientation. *Computers in Human Behavior, 33,* 314–320.

Galloway, L., Engstrom, E., & Emmers-Sommer, T. M. (2015). Does movie viewing cultivate young people's unrealistic expectations about love and marriage? *Marriage & Family Review, 51*(8), 687–712. https://doi.org/10.1080/01494929.2015.1061629

GLAAD. (2018). Where we are on TV: 2018–2019. Retrieved from www.glaad.org

Hogg, M. A. (2016). Social identity theory. In S. McKeown, R. Haji, & N. Ferguson (Eds.), *Peace psychology book series: Understanding peace and conflict through social identity theory: Contemporary global perspectives* (pp. 3–17). Cham, Switzerland: Springer International Publishing.

Holmes, B. (2007). In search of my "one-and-only": Romance-related media and beliefs in romantic relationship destiny. *The Electronic Journal of Communication, 17*(3–4).

HolyTryst. (circa 2012). *Bow nigger: An new games journalism piece about a multiplayer duel in [Jedi Knight II: Jedi Outcast].* [HolyTryst is the online name of a Reddit user who posted the full text of a 2004 piece by an author known as "Always Black."] Retrieved from http://bit.ly/2HObBR3

Horton, D., & Wohl, R. R. (1956): Mass communication and para-social interaction: Observations on intimacy at a distance. *Psychiatry, 19,* 215–229.

Hughes, L. (1926, June 23). The Negro artist and the racial mountain. *The Nation, 122,* 692–694.

James, C., Davis, K., Flores, A., Francis, J. M., Pettingill, L. Rundle, M., & Gardner, H. (2009). *Young people, ethics, and the new digital media: A synthesis from the good play project.* Cambridge, MA: MIT Press.

Landstedt, E., & Persson, S. (2014). Bullying, cyberbullying, and mental health in young people. *Scandinavian Journal of Public Health, 42*(4), 393–399.

Lawson, R., & Doll, J. (2012, May 2). Lies Hollywood told us: Love and romance edition. *The Atlantic.* Retrieved from https://bit.ly/2GR5F8v

Lin, N. (2001). *Social capital: A theory of social structure and action.* Cambridge: Cambridge University Press.

Mason, L., & Wronski, J. (2018). One tribe to bind them all: How our social group attachments strengthen partisanship. *Political Psychology Supplement: Advances in Political Psychology, 39*(1), 257–277.

Mastro, D., & Figueroa-Caballero, A. (2018). Measuring extremes: A quantitative content analysis of prime time TV depictions of body type. *Journal of Broadcasting and Electronic Media, 62*(2), 320–336.

Phillips, N. (2017). Media exposure, violence, and criminology. *Oxford Research Encyclopedia of Criminology*. doi:10.1093/acrefore/9780190264079.013.189

Reimer, V., & Ahmed, R. (2012). Feeling good never looked better: Examining representations of women in Special K advertisements. In T. Carilli & J. Campbell (Eds.), *Challenging images of women in the media: Reinventing women's lives*. Chapter 1. Lanham, Maryland: Lexington Books.

Schiappa, E., Gregg, P. B., & Hewes, D. E. (2005). The parasocial contact hypothesis. *Communication Monographs, 72*(1), 92–115.

Segrin, C., & Nabi, R. L. (2002). Does television viewing cultivate unrealistic expectations about marriage? *Journal of Communication, 52*(2), 247–263.

Todd, C. (2012). "Troubling" gender in virtual gaming spaces. *New Zealand Geographer, 68*, 101–110.

Todd, C. (2015). Commentary: GamerGate and resistance to the diversification of gaming culture. *Women's Studies Journal, 29*(1), 64–67.

van Oosten, J. M. F., Peter, J., & Valkenburg, P. M. (2015). The influence of sexual music videos on adolescents' misogynistic beliefs: The role of video content, gender, and affective engagement. Communication Research, 42(7), 986–1008. http://dx.doi.org/10.1177/0093650214565893

Weber, S., & Mitchell, C. (2008). Imaging, keyboarding, and posting identities: Young people and new media technologies. In D. Buckingham (Ed.), *Youth, identity, and digital media* (pp. 25–48), The John D. and Catherine T. MacArthur Foundation Series on Digital Media and Learning. Cambridge, MA: The MIT Press. doi:10.1162/dmal.9780262524834.025

Wiederhold, B. K. (2018). The tenuous relationship between Instagram and teen self-identity. *Cyberpsychology, Behavior, and Social Networking, 21*(4), 215–216. doi:10.1089/cyber.2018.29108.bkw

Zhang, L., & Haller, B. (2013). Consuming image: How mass media impact the identity of people with disabilities. *Communication Quarterly, 61*(3), 319–334.

11 Participating

How Technology Supports and Challenges Civic Engagement and Democracy

After 17 of their classmates and teachers were killed and 17 more wounded on February 14, 2018 by a lone gunman with a legally-purchased AR-15 semi-automatic rifle, students at Marjory Stoneman Douglas High School in Parkland, Florida, took action both on- and offline.

Less than 24 hours after the shooting, surviving students gathered at a local park to grieve, talk to friends and to the media. Within three days, they had launched the Never Again MSD group with a #NeverAgain hashtag. A week after the shooting, they protested in the state capital to ask Florida lawmakers to take action to prevent more school shootings by banning assault-style rifles (Turkewitz, 2018). Using social media, they organized a march on Washington, D.C., a month later called the "March For Our Lives." Their

LEARNING OBJECTIVES

Terms: Civic engagement, slacktivism, thin and thick participation, participatory culture, collective action, contagion, digital divide.

- Recognize how digital media has changed how people engage in civic life.
- Identify examples of slacktivism.
- Explain the pros and cons of social media use for activism.
- Describe some characteristics of participatory culture.
- Understand the implications of the digital divide.
- Know the state of the world's languages online.
- Apply the media literacy principles of message format and purpose to civic engagement.

actions launched a youth-based anti-gun movement across the United States.

> Do you share your views on politics or social issues on the social media sites you use? Why or why not? Tell about a time you wish you had spoken up or promoted a civic issue but didn't, or a time you did and how it was received by your audience. Has something you read or watched on social media changed your view on a civic or political issue? Explain.

In a commentary on CNN, one of the leaders of the student movement, Cameron Kasky, said, "We can't ignore the issues of gun control that this tragedy raises. And so, I'm asking—no, demanding—we take action now" (2018).

Later in this chapter, we will look at how the Parkland students used digital media for organizing action, as well as the misinformation campaign launched against the students. Also, we look at how people across the world use media to engage with their communities on issues. Whether or not you align with the Parkland students' politics, you can still learn things from their use of media to promote a cause. We'll examine the ways that media offers us choices about how we express our civic identities, and how millions of people don't have that choice because they don't have reliable access to computers or the internet. Throughout, we will study examples of civic engagement through a media literacy lens.

CIVIC ENGAGEMENT AND CIVIC IDENTITY

It takes a while to get used to thinking about yourself as a "citizen" and as someone who is "civic minded." These labels may seem foreign to you. Most young adults don't think of themselves as having a "civic identity." Often, we think about getting involved in a community once we get a full-time job in a town, or when we buy a home. Other times, we get involved only when issues affect us, such as when the public transit system gets cut back (again) or when the river near your house is polluted, or when police actions affect loved ones. Civic engagement can range from volunteering in an after-school program to protecting the environment through a recycling campaign. It is collective and aimed at promoting the good of a community.

If you're willing to expand the way you see yourself, you might find that indeed, you do sometimes act out of a sense of civic identity. People who care about what goes on in their communities and who take action, whether politically or in non-political ways, to improve quality of life are

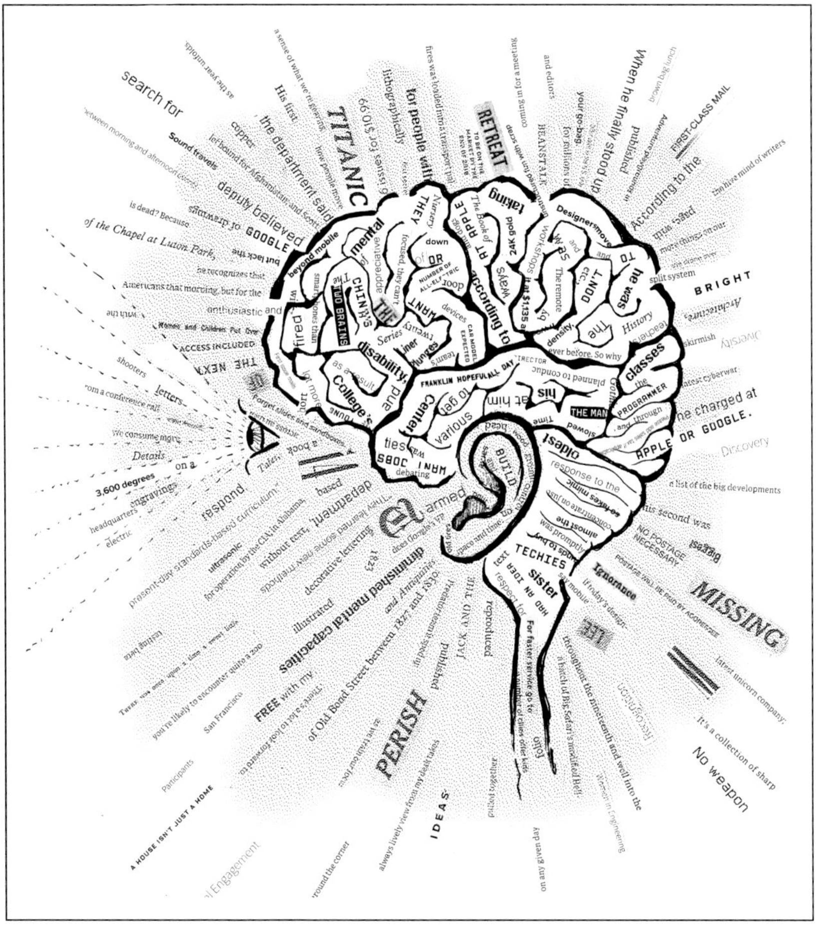

The Engaged Brain

Credit: Ryan Lewis

demonstrating **civic engagement**. American media scholar Henry Jenkins and colleagues (2006) acknowledged possible reasons for youth disengagement from civic and political life:

> Buckingham (2000) argues that young people's lack of interest in news and their disconnection from politics reflects their perception of disempowerment. "By and large, young people are not defined by society as

> political subjects, let alone as political agents. Even in the areas of social life that affect and concern them to a much greater extent than adults—most notably education—political debate is conducted almost entirely 'over their heads'" (pp. 218–219). Politics, as constructed by the news, becomes a spectator sport, something we watch but do not do.
>
> (Jenkins, 2006, p. 10)

Even though Jenkins and colleagues quote a really smart media literacy leader, British scholar David Buckingham, he said that in *2000*. That may be the year you were *born*. So it is still true today? Is politics something you "watch but do not do"? Maybe you don't even watch politics happen; some days it *can* be too much to behold. Do you think that much of the political debate about things important to you happen "over" your head? Or, do you feel empowered to make change in your community, whether that is your school or neighborhood, or a community bound by culture and ethnicity?

YOUTH AND ONLINE ACTIVISM

The potential for the internet and in particular, social media, to allow youth to connect over common concerns and in doing so, to organize for change, is evident. Youth engagement in civic and political life is easier now due to greater access to information via the internet. It's also easier now to mobilize because of social media.

However, reality has not matched the heightened hopes across the world for youth civic engagement due to digital media; the reality is more mixed. For instance, interviews and focus groups with youth in India revealed that youth were largely *apolitical* due to what they saw as corrupt politicians and youth perceptions of their own lack of money and power to bring about political change (Ilavarasan, 2013). However, using samples of young people in Australia, the United States and the United Kingdom, other researchers found a strong positive relationship between social media use and political engagement

> New media, particularly social networking sites, gives all of us, including young people, opportunities to share our civic identity and to connect with others about civic issues.

(Xenos, Vromen, & Loader, 2014). New media, particularly social networking sites, gives all of us, including young people, opportunities to share our civic identity and to connect with others about civic issues.

Elisabeth Soep is the research director and senior producer at Youth Radio, a California-based production company that teams teen reporters with professional producers. Soep noted that while young people engaging in politics is not new, what *is* new is the effect of social and digital media to reduce the costs of engagement and increase the access to collaborators far and wide (Soep, 2016). Also new, she said, is the diminishing gap between culture and politics, as the two blend more often in modern society. Oftentimes, who we are is reflected in our politics, and vice versa.

Online participation in civic or political conversations helps users develop a repertoire of skills regarding public communication about public issues, Soep explained (2016). This is significant, since civic identity is *not* something that comes naturally to many youth. As the study of young people in India found, some youth are cynical about politics and government institutions' corruption and power-hungry politics. Are you one of them?

Merging On- and Offline Civic Identity One tactic of civic engagement is to the ability *to mobilize* one's on- and offline community when the time is right. This only works if users have cultivated their community online and in person, often through shared interests. So, calling on one's community to donate to your favorite candidate for office is easier and more successful when there is a social and interest-based bond. Soep put it this way: "Just because someone's your friend, that doesn't mean he or she will necessarily take kindly to the injection of political themes when young people are just trying to hang out" (2016, p. 397).

What's your approach to injecting your political or civic self into your social media platforms?

A 21-year-old college senior who did 300 hours of service work a year, including for Habitat for Humanity and for suicide prevention efforts, said that he used Facebook "as a representation of who I am, which is someone who is involved in a lot of different things" (Weinstein, 2014, p. 218). He was among the 73 youth ages 15 to 25 interviewed by researcher Emily Weinstein and her team at the Youth Participatory Politics research network. The college senior was among the majority (53 percent) of interviewees who not only allowed, but needed, their offline activism and civic engagement to surface in their online social media presence. He continued: "I want people who are not necessarily with me all the time to see what I'm working on."

"I think people, especially my friends, look to me as someone who knows what's going on, and they sort of value what I'm putting out there," he said (p. 219).

But he's not representative of everyone: Nearly 20 percent of the youth who said they engaged actively in civic life and that it was part of their identity chose *not* to express their civic views *at all* on social network sites, while another 20 percent or so were *selective* about which sites they did share their activism or politics. Some reasons offered by the youth for this careful separation of on- and offline civic engagement included organizational policies that required members or employees to limit self-expression online, concerns about privacy, concerns about the appearance they were bragging about their involvements and potential disinterest or hostility from their online audiences. Which group do you fall in?

SLACKTIVISM

Slacktivism is the term to describe low-cost, low-risk, low- or no-commitment online activism. Examples include signing an online petition for drinkable city water in Flint, Michigan, or sharing a post condemning the denial of education to young girls in Afghanistan. Liking an organization's Facebook page or retweeting an article about a court ruling you think is unjust are other examples. Slacktivism has positive and negative aspects. It raises attention, awareness and gets people talking offline, sometimes taking real-life action by wearing a ribbon or a button (or dunking themselves with ice water as in the ALS Ice Bucket Challenge). The downside of slacktivism is that it can lead users to think that by posting online they are doing something, and that by doing *something*, they are doing enough.

An example of the upside and downside to online activism is the Save Darfur movement. The power of the internet as a means of recruitment to a cause is seen in the Save Darfur advocacy effort. Save Darfur was a coalition formed in 2004 to raise public awareness and mobilize a response to the genocide occurring in western Sudan. Facebook enabled "more than 1 million people to register their discontent with the situation in Darfur," according to researchers who studied the effort (Lewis, Gray, & Meierhenrich, 2014, p. 7). But those numbers didn't lead to sustained commitment to the work of changing the situation on the ground. Rather, the researchers' findings showed the power of the internet as a means to easily and quickly *drop* interest in a cause. In the case of Save Darfur, social media engagement was not a path to vital civic engagement. Instead, the study results showcased the stunningly fast support and even faster decline in commitment to the real work needed for change.

VOX DISCIPULI

My least favorite thing about having a smartphone is the fact that it really is taking over people's lives. I can't hang out with friends or go out to dinner without someone being on their phone, which I have to admit that I do sometimes, but I am really trying to stop it because when I am with others that I want to spend time with, I put my phone down and do just that; I spend time with them.

Constantly having your head down and looking down at your phone keeps you from seeing the beauty that you should be seeing if your head was up. It is just a waste that so many people spend so much time on their phones that they aren't able to admire the world that we still have around us, whether that be gorgeous scenery, amazing friends and family or just listening to the calming sounds. They are all amazing things and it is really a shame that people don't appreciate them because they are all more interested in what Facebook has to say. —Taylor, 21

Gauging Effort The amount of participation required by a cause is one of the things we weigh when we consider whether or not to get engaged in a civic issue, and digital media expands the options for levels of participation that much more.

"Thin forms of civic engagement are ones that require minimal effort from a participant," wrote Ethan Zuckerman, director of the Center for Civic Media at MIT (2016, p. 67). "They gain their strength through scale." **Thin forms of engagement** require lots of people to participate in order for the campaign to be effective, so organizers keep the effort factor at a minimum. An example of a thin form of civic engagement would be changing one's Facebook profile picture to include a rainbow filter to show support for same-sex marriage after the U.S. Supreme Court legalized same-sex marriage. More than 26 million Facebook members put the rainbow filter over their profile picture (Murphy, 2015).

Thick engagement, said Zuckerman, requires thinking and creativity, strategizing and time. An example of thick engagement would be the Occupy Wall Street movement in which protesters against income inequality lived in encampments for weeks and months. Unlike some others who have examined the issue, Zuckerman champions the importance of thin engagement. One potential result of people changing their Facebook profile pictures to support same-sex marriage "could have impact through the long, slow process of shaping norms" (p. 66). Also, the vast numbers showing interest in the issue mean that at least a portion, however small, will go on to participate more fully and deeply in the cause.

DIGITAL MEDIA DRAWS ATTENTION

The Arab Spring was a pro-democracy movement that involved anti-government protests, uprisings, and armed rebellions across the Middle East in early 2011. The mobilizing power of social media in the uprisings in countries including Tunisia, Egypt, Yemen, Bahrain and Libya was important to organize citizens in a unified uprising. The Arab Spring is a good example of the global use of new media in civic engagement and political protest.

"Networks formed online were crucial in organizing a core group of activists, specifically in Egypt," a Pew Research Center analysis of the movement stated (Mitchell, Brown, & Guskin, 2012). "Civil society leaders in Arab countries emphasized the role of 'the internet, mobile phones, and social media' in the protests."

But social media was also important for a different reason—to communicate the uprisings to the *rest of the world.* Without images from the uprisings, the

Western world would have been less informed, less engaged and had less pressure to respond to the pro-democracy movements in Arab countries.

"The personal decision to face rubber bullets and tear gas is only ever taken when appeals for solidarity come through social networks. Images of friends and family being beaten by security services draw people into the streets," wrote then-director of the Project on Information Technology and Political Islam Philip N. Howard (2011). "Increasingly, those appeals come digitally, as wall posts, tweets and pixilated YouTube videos hastily recorded by mobile phones."

Amid the protests in Cairo, an activist tweeted: "We use Facebook to schedule the protests, Twitter to coordinate, and YouTube to tell the world" (Howard, 2011).

Collective Action The immediate political environment is critical to understanding the role of social media in a collective action. **Collective action** describes action taken by a group of people with a common goal, usually related to improving their status in some way, such as economically or politically.

Citizens in countries in which they face hardships and inequalities (such as disrespect for human rights and corruption) often have less access to the internet. It holds that traditional media in these countries are closely monitored. However, these are the very citizens in *greatest need* of alternative communication channels such as social media.

The more difficult the political environment in a country, the higher the levels of protest activity, concluded researcher Gadi Wolfsfeld and colleagues (2013), using the Arab Spring as a case study. Further, they concluded, new media do not cause or propel protest; social media comes after local protest activity, not before.

Social media, because it spreads influence rapidly, is sometimes described as a **contagion**. Studies (e.g., Bejan, Hickman, Parkin, & Pozo, 2018) show that social media in particular can spread negative emotions, such as anger, fear or disgust, and do it quickly. One analysis of 4.1 million tweets found reposting of negative messages was 1.2 to 1.6 times that of positive or neutral messages (Tsugawa & Ohsaki, 2015).

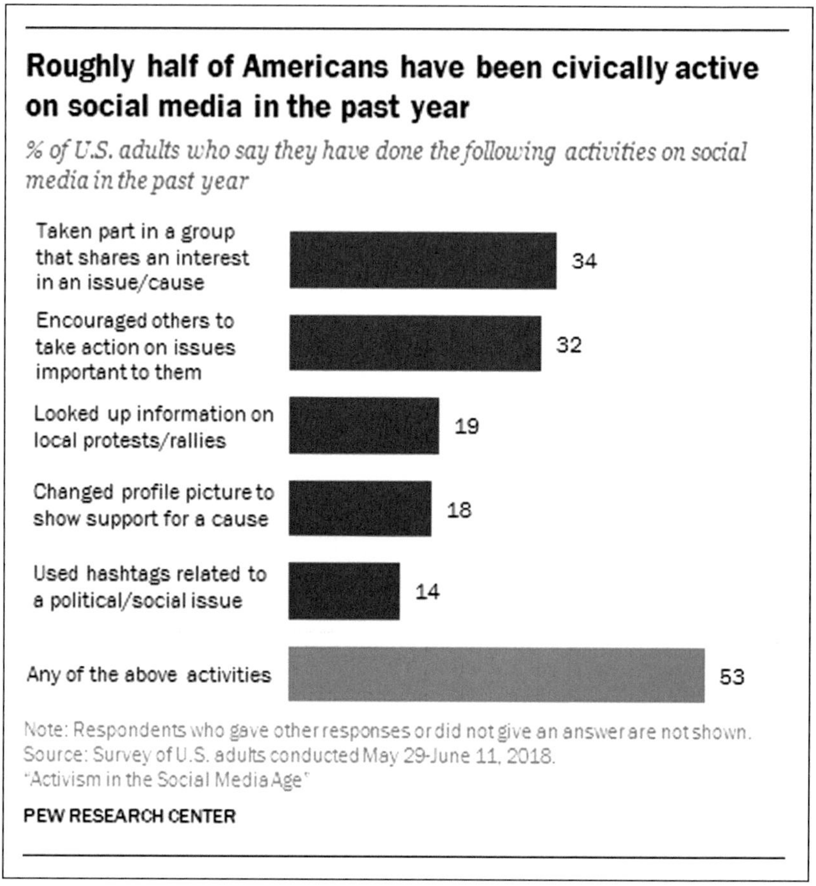

Social Media Activism

HASHTAG ACTIVISM

#Lovewins. #MAGA. #BlackLivesMatter. #JeSuisCharlie. #MeToo. #Third_debate. #Resist. #YemenInquiryNow.

These are popular Twitter hashtags. Behind them are legions of people in loosely connected movements: support for same-sex marriage; Donald Trump supporters; opposition to police lethal force against black citizens;

solidarity for freedom of speech and of press after the fatal shooting of 12 staff at the French satirical weekly magazine *Charlie Hebdo*; opposition to sexual harassment and sexual assault; critics of the high salaries of government officials in Tehran, Iran; calls for scrutiny of war crimes in Yemen. At its best, the internet promotes humans' ability to communicate real and pressing needs. "When democracies are functioning properly, people's sufferings and challenges are not entirely private matters," wrote Cass Sunstein of Harvard Law School in a 2018 Facebook Newsroom post. "Social media platforms help us alert one another to a million and one different problems. In the process, the existence of social media can prod citizens to seek solutions" (para 2).

At its best, the internet promotes humans' ability to communicate real and pressing needs.

While people have questioned the value and longevity of social media activism, a Pew Research Center analysis found that 69 percent of Americans feel these platforms are important for accomplishing a range of political goals, such as getting politicians to pay attention to issues (Anderson, Toor, Rainie, & Smith, 2018). Also, 67 percent said that social media sites create sustained movements for social change. For example, the #BlackLivesMatter hashtag launched in 2013, after a jury acquitted George Zimmerman in the shooting death of unarmed black teenager Trayvon Martin. The hashtag had been used on Twitter almost *30 million times* in the five years since the shooting, the Pew analysis found.

> Certain groups of social media users—most notably, those who are black or Hispanic—view these platforms as an especially important tool for their own political engagement. For example, roughly half of black social media users say these platforms are at least somewhat personally important to them as a venue for expressing their political views or for getting involved with issues that are important to them. Those shares fall to around a third among white social media users.
>
> (Anderson et al., 2018, para 4).

What about you—how important is it for you to express your views on issues in social media formats?

RISKS OF DIGITALLY-DRIVEN ACTIVISM

Researcher Elizabeth Soep (2016) highlights five very real risks of digitally-driven movements. You can remember them by the five S's:

- The difficulty in *sustaining* them beyond the viral moment.
- *Simplifying* complex issues so they are attention-getting but may not tackle a complex law or policy.
- *Sensationalism* that distorts truth.
- *Slippage* into universal relevance; this is the loss of focus on the conditions unique to a particular struggle, so an issue involving the rape of a college student becomes rolled into the greater issue of sexual violence.
- *Saviorism,* the idea that the movement can save people who can't save themselves.

Some of these risks are manifested in *Kony 2012,* a 30-minute documentary about the cult leader of the Ugandan Lord's Resistance Army and indicted war criminal Joseph Kony, whose Army terrorized and kidnapped children. While *Kony* is a good example of how digital media can be useful in making invisible issues undeniably visible to a greater public, it ultimately failed to achieve its lofty goals. A U.S.-based organization called Invisible Children created the slickly-produced and compelling video and followed a strategy of generating public attention and action through social media, film, events, music, T-shirts and more.

"In the first 72 hours Kony 2012 got 43 million hits. It reached 100 million views on YouTube faster than any video in history. This level of mobilisation is unprecedented," stated an analysis of *Kony 2012* by the International Broadcasting Trust (Chalk, 2012, p. 4).

"Anticipating the speed with which social media can move is crucial so campaigners aren't overwhelmed as Invisible Children were when Kony 2012 went viral," the analysis concluded (Chalk, 2012, p. 3). "The greatest challenge, which Kony 2012 failed to address, is how to make content engaging while allowing for nuance and complexity."

Invisible Children aimed for a major event called "Cover the Night," when people worldwide were to coordinate a widespread and highly visual statement about Kony, an international fugitive, by plastering his image and name on posters, stickers, buttons and other paraphernalia for sale by the non-profit. As Graham Meikle (2014) noted, if the organization had invested trust and energy in individuals *to create their own messages* in a show of collective and creative action, the Cover the Night event may have not failed so miserably.

Overall, the *Kony 2012* strategy allowed for people to engage at various levels, electing to do as little as share a *Kony 2012* post on social media to giving money to organizing locally, or still more—engaging in thin or thick levels of participation. However, the campaign failed. It oversimplified the complex political issues around delivering aid. It advocated for a military solution to the conflict. Also, the video, which features Invisible Children founder Jason Russell, who is white, among the Ugandan people, hit many as white saviorism. Teju Cole, writing in *The Atlantic*, called the movement around *Kony 2012* "a big emotional experience that validates privilege" (2012).

PARTICIPATORY CULTURE

Online communication promotes collaboration and participation in a way that analog communication does not. When we create media and post it online in some way, we enter into a culture of sharing, reaction and acknowledgement, explained Henry Jenkins and colleagues (2006). **Participatory culture** is the sum total of the digital skills of expression, collaboration and networking, skills that *complement and expand* traditional skills of writing, reading and oral literacies, Jenkins and colleagues said. These digital skills don't replace the analog ones: They add to and enhance them.

> Online communication promotes collaboration and participation in a way that analog communication does not.

This new participatory culture includes things that I suspect you often do, but you don't specifically identify, such as the use of play to problem-solve and innovate, or simulation to put yourself in another person's shoes (or in a monster's paws, depending on your video game). The list of elements of participatory culture from Jenkins and colleagues is fairly long, so I'll call out but a few here that can be used to describe what the Parkland students have done to organize and spread their agenda:

- **Networking** involves finding, combining and sharing information. The student activists organized their gun control agenda and also spread the word about their offline activities on social media.
- Using **collective intelligence** to work toward a common goal, the student activists pooled their knowledge and wrote speeches, press releases and opinion pieces to keep the focus on their agenda.
- **Distributed cognition** is an awareness of the technical tools that can deliver content real-time, like offering a phone number to text for information on the March For Our Lives cause (which they did). Distributed cognition also involves knowledge of what is needed, in what form and when. "We've protested in front of Congress, targeted influencers across the country, developed QR-coded t-shirts to register voters, filled Congressional hearing rooms with hundreds of students, and used SMS to organize supporters and drive Get Out The Vote efforts," wrote former MSD students Brendan Duff and Lauren Hogg in a press release.
- **Transmedia navigation** references managing stories and information as they travel and change across multiple formats. In an example of transmedia navigation, the students used various media for different purposes. A CNN Town Hall packed with supporters was the right media venue to pressure Florida Senator Marco Rubio to refuse further donations from the National Rifle Association (CNN Town Hall, February 22, 2018). Twitter was the appropriate place for images from the Washington, D.C., march to spread far and wide. Billboards were the obvious choice for keeping their cause in the public eye in New York City's Times Square (Duff & Hogg, 2019).

The student activism was not without opposition, however. One conspiracy theory alleged that the students were actually "crisis actors" who were using the incident to push their left-wing agenda (Yglesias, 2018). Also, a smear campaign targeting student organizer Emma Gonzales included doctored images of her ripping up the Constitution. The original image was for a photoshoot for *Teen Vogue* in which Gonzales was ripping up a paper shooting target. The fake image spread from fringe social media sites such as VOAT and 4chan to Facebook and Twitter (Storyful, 2018). The confusion caused by the images highlights the ongoing problem of disinformation. The hateful rhetoric of the postings may be one reason why some youth are reticent to go public with their civic identities.

THE DIGITAL DIVIDE

The digital divide is the term for the persistent gap between those with access to dependable technology, including high-speed internet access, and those without. It is a worldwide problem.

More than half the world's population—about 3.9 billion people—use the internet, according to the World Wide Web Foundation. That means that half the world still has unreliable, inadequate or unaffordable internet access. In particular, poor urban women in the developing world are 50 percent less likely than men to access the internet due to high access costs and lack of know-how. This offline population has less opportunity for economic and social advancement, which further deepens the inequality of the digital divide.

Throughout the year 2017, according to Internet World Stats (2019), there was a wide range of access to the internet, most likely depending on access to broadband technology, consistency of service and availability of devices. Here's a sampling of the number of people who had internet access that year:

- In Egypt, nearly one in two people
- In the European Union, nine in ten people
- In the entire continent of Africa, a little more than one in three people
- In North America, more than nine in ten people
- In Vietnam, two out of three people
- In Yemen, roughly one in five people

Not surprisingly, richer nations have higher rates of internet and smartphone use (Poushter, 2016). Across the world, there is a significant digital divide between the rich and poor, those more educated and less educated and those 18–34 years old and older than 34. "The demographic digital divide is real and pervasive," noted thc article (para 11).

The digital divide is real and unjust. It's not going away easily. The half of the world's population that is connected was the easy part—these are people with money, urbanization, resources, education. It is far harder to connect the remote villages of Africa, rural communities or low-income women worldwide. Immigrants, older people, people living in remote areas and poor people aren't connected to high-speed internet and/or aren't regularly online and able to develop tech skills.

The Opportunity Gap The digital divide has sometimes been characterized as the "opportunity gap." Those students without access to high speed internet and up-to-date computers with multimedia production capabilities may be missing out on opportunities to learn higher-level production skills and network with others through real-time media. Children in high-poverty areas in developed nations may not have dependable internet access, or schools well-equipped with technology, or educators with the training and time to teach digital skills. Unequal access to online networks and to the development of digital communication skills is a significant global problem. This unequal access will hamper the advancement of economies, health care, democratic institutions and healthy social structures.

Unequal access to online networks and to the development of digital communication skills is a significant global problem.

The Civic Engagement Gap People around the world need the internet and social networking to exercise their civic identity and connect with others on civic issues.

While many people say that they are disengaged from politics, they also said they would get politically involved if the right issues came along, a 2018 Pew Research study of nearly 15,000 people in 14 countries such as Argentina, Brazil, Israel and Nigeria, found (Wike & Castillo, 2018). What follows are some highlights of that far-reaching research. As you scan them, think critically about the link between digital access and political engagement:

- "People who use online social networking sites are particularly likely to take political action across the full range of issues included on the survey" (p. 9).

- "In 13 nations, those with more education are more likely to post their views online. In seven nations, they are more likely to have donated money to a political or social organization. And in six countries, they are more likely to participate in a political protest" (p. 8).
- "Those ages 18–29 are more likely than older adults to post comments online about social or political issues in 12 of the 14 countries surveyed. For example, 36 percent of Poles ages 18–29 have posted their views online, compared with only 4 percent of those 50 and older" (p. 5).

In a separate study by Pew, this one in India, only about one in three social media users shared their political views online compared to nine in ten people (87 percent) who shared other, non-political, views online, such as opinions about music and films (Rikhy, 2014). In India, the world's second most populous country, with 1.3 billion people, only about one in ten people have access to the internet. Just 15 percent *owned* smartphones (as opposed to having access to them, such as for work). What's the conclusion from all this data? "Clearly, lack of easy access to (the) internet and hence social media is limiting the choice of online spaces for discussion and debate for Indians" (Rikhy, 2014, para 4). In sum, the digital divide affects the opportunities for democratic dialogue and debate. It limits who gets to be engaged in the digitally-driven work of civic and political life.

The Language Divide There is also a language divide within digital media. For instance, most children's animated programming in Africa is from abroad; children don't get to see and hear themselves in cartoons. They get Western cartoons in European languages. UNESCO launched *Africa Animated!* to address this gap. (You can watch an example of an Ethiopian children's cartoon here: https://bit.ly/2CfBbtO.)

"Linguistic diversity is an integral part of cultural diversity," notes a UNESCO roadmap on safeguarding world languages (2016, Sect. 1, para 1). More than *50 percent* of about 6,700 world languages spoken today are endangered. Languages will continue to disappear in part because they are not represented on the internet. Only 5 percent of the world's languages are online.

A multilingual internet is essential for economic development as well as for meaningful cultural expression. Communities already marginalized because of language will become more so if their access to information and knowledge is limited by language and digital access. The online language divide prevents access to the vast resources for information and economic development afforded by the internet. For people who often do not find their language online, communicating and creating content in their language is obviously an obstacle. What might this mean for a woman entrepreneur in Tunisia who wants to sell her crafts to a Western market via online commerce?

See the online and interactive Atlas of the World's Languages in Danger at https://bit.ly/1JVCiLM.

"Languages are not only tools of communication, they also reflect a view of the world. Languages are vehicles of value systems and cultural expressions and are an essential component of the living heritage of humanity. Yet, many of them are in danger of disappearing," stated the UNESCO introduction to the Atlas of the World's Languages in Danger (Moseley, 2010, n.p.).

MEDIA LITERACY IN ACTION

Participation in online media should be a right available to all people, all across the globe. As the 21st century unfolds, the need to close the gap between those with digital access and those without increases. Media literacy champions the need for full participation of all people in the civic issues of the day.

Why not employ media literacy to address the issue of the digital divide in your community or region? It's a project that can involve all of the issues we've discussed in this book, from commerce to message design to audience. The world that you live in will be forever affected by media. You have a role to play.

A Message at a Time As events unfold and issues arise in your life, you can tap into your diverse media sources to stay informed and to spread legitimate information. You can also do your share of creating ethical messages to disseminate your point of view and develop expressions of your authentic self, which may well include a civic identity.

An important media literacy principle that in particular applies to civic engagement is that most media are organized to gain power or profit (Center for Media Literacy, 2019). Even in the case of grassroots media efforts such as Parkland, or the uprisings of the Arab Spring, one purpose of the messaging was power and/or profit. While there are other reasons for the messaging as well, such as information and awareness, the concept of message purpose is central to much of civic engagement using media.

Applying media literacy to a citizen-led campaign on a local community issue is a perfect way to conclude this 11-chapter analog guide to your digital life, because media literacy is all about being *active, engaged and intentional* about your media use:

- **Using** media allows your grassroots initiative to get people's **attention**.
- **Verifying** the facts of the issues at hand is essential to gaining credibility, and **analyzing** the ways that oppositional messages to the campaign are communicated helps counter the arguments.
- Also, understanding the importance of **privacy** in organizing efforts protects your campaign against unwanted interference by those who oppose your agenda.
- **Creating** messages that are interesting and exciting gain coverage by **big media** and **news outlets**.
- **Connecting** across cultural boundaries of education, demographics, geography or other divides builds momentum for the cause, and, it is hoped, allow individual users to **choose** to identify with your cause because it speaks to who they are as a socially engaged person.

This process of **participation** on- and offline—that is, in the digital world and in the analog world—is rich, nuanced and dynamic.

CHAPTER REVIEW

- Define civic engagement.
- Give an example of slacktivism.
- Describe how various media formats can be used to heighten awareness of civic issues.

- Identify the characteristics of participatory culture in an online activist campaign.
- Describe the impact of the digital divide on global development.
- Know the significance of language diversity in online media messaging.
- Apply the media literacy concept that most media messages are organized to gain profit and/or power applies to an advocacy group's activities.

ACTIVITIES

1. Spend time looking over data from the Alliance for Affordable Internet. See http://bit.ly/2HMu804. Use the themes highlighted in the data to guide your creation of a virtual or analog poster to educate others about the issue of the digital divide and its implications. Post your political message in a public place.
2. Find an example of youth-driven activism that used media to showcase its message. Develop a short presentation about the activism and use visual and/or audio examples as much as possible. Include observations about the use of media messages in terms of *format, purpose and audience.*
3. Part of being in a politically engaged audience is *what you do* with the media message you've just received and taken in. If you are able, watch this short (*warning: disturbing content*) video of harassing tweets sent to female sports journalists: http://bit.ly/1WQOTaI. Evaluate the purpose of creating this video in a one-page reaction paper or 2-minute recorded *and* prepared statement: What is the value in video recording various men, who didn't write the vile tweets, read them aloud to the actual sports journalist? What do you think we as the audience of this video are supposed to do after seeing the video? What action do you think the video producer wants us to take?
4. Each one of us makes sense of media based on our individual and collective needs. We as consumers partake of political messages all the time—whether it is presented as graffiti under a highway overpass or as an exhibit in a fine arts museum or in direct mail from political candidates. Do you think that the locations in which we find messages influence the meanings we assign to them? Take photos of political and civic messages that you see around your community. Organize them into a slideshow

with captions that provide context of where, when or how you saw the messages, and your reactions to each.

REFERENCES

Anderson, M., Toor, S., Rainie, L., & Smith, A. (2018, July 11). *Activism in the social media age*. Washington, D.C.: Pew Research Center. Internet and Technology section.

Bejan, V., Hickman, M., Parkin, W. S., & Pozo, V. F. (2018). Primed for death: Law enforcement-citizen homicides, social media, and retaliatory violence. *PLoS ONE, 13*(1), e0190571. https://doi.org/10.1371/journal.pone.0190571

Buckingham, D. (2000). *The making of citizens: Young people, news and politics*. London: Routledge.

Center for Media Literacy. (2019). *Five key questions form foundation for media inquiry*. Retrieved from www.medialit.org

Chalk, S. (2012). Kony 2012: Success or failure? *International Broadcasting Trust*. Retrieved from ibt.org.uk

CNN Town Hall. (2018, February 22). Transcript: Stoneman students' questions to lawmakers and the NRA at the CNN town hall. Retrieved from CNN.com.

Cole, T. (2012, March 21). The white savior industrial complex. *The Atlantic.com*. Retrieved from https://bit.ly/2jQo9fh

Duff, B., & Hogg, L. (2019, April). March for our Lives activism spreads to Times Square. *PR Week*. Retrieved from prweek.com.

Howard, P. N. (2011, February 23). The Arab Spring's cascading effects. *Pacific Standard*. Retrieved from psmag.com.

Ilavarasan, P. V. (2013). Community work and limited online activism among India youth. *The International Communication Gazette, 75*(3), 284–299.

Internet World Stats. (2019). *Alphabetical list of countries*. Retrieved from www.internetworldstats.com.

Jenkins, H., Clinton, K., Purushotma, R., Robinson, A., & Weigel, M. (2006). Confronting the challenges of participatory culture (Technical Rep.) Chicago.

MacArthur foundation: Media Education for the 21st century, The John D. and Catherine T. MacArthur Foundation Series on Digital Media and Learning. Cambridge, MA: MIT Press.

Kasky, C. (2018, February 20). Parkland student: My generation won't stand for this. *CNN.com*. Opinion. Retrieved from http://bit.ly/2Gq4M6o.

Lewis, K., Gray, K., & Meierhenrich, J. (2014). The structure of online activism. *Sociological Science, 1*, 1–9. doi:10.15195/v1.a1

Meikle, G. (2014). Social media, visibility, and activism: The Kony 2012 campaign. In M. Ratto & M. Boler (Eds), *DIY Citizenship* (pp. 373–384). Cambridge, MA: MIT Press.

Mitchell, A., Brown, H., & Guskin, E. (2012, November 28). *The role of social media in the Arab uprisings*. Washington, D.C.: Pew Research Center: Journalism & media.

Moseley, C. (Ed). (2010). *Atlas of the world's languages in danger* (3rd ed.). Paris: UNESCO Publishing. Online version. Retrieved from http://publishing.unesco.org/details.aspx?Code_Livre=4728

Murphy, S. (2015, June 29). Facebook says your rainbow profile pictures won't be used to sell ads. Retrieved from Mashable.com.

Poushter, J. (2016, February 22). *Smartphone ownership and internet usage continues to climb in emerging economies*. Washington, D.C.: Pew Research Center.

Rikhy, A. (2014, April 17). Only 35% of social media users use it to voice their political opinion. *The Times of India*. Retrieved from http://bit.ly/2JRilwa

Soep, E. (2016). Youth agency in public spheres: Emerging tactics, literacies, and risks. In E. Gordon & P. Mihailidis (Eds.), *Civic media: Technology/design/practice* (pp. 393–420). Cambridge, MA: MIT Press.

Storyful. (2018, March 28). Debunking the disinformation campaign against Emma Gonzales. Retrieved from storyful.com.

Sunstein, C. (2018, January 22). Is social media good or bad for democracy? *Facebook Newsroom*. Retrieved from https://newsroom.fb.com/news/2018/01/sunstein-democracy/

Tsugawa, S., & Ohsaki, H. (2015). *Negative messages spread rapidly and widely on social media*. Proceedings of the 2015 ACM Conference on online social networks, pp. 151–160. Retrieved from https://dl.acm.org/citation.cfm?id=2817962

Turkewitz, J. (2018, February 21). Florida students began with optimism: Then they spoke to lawmakers. *The New York Times*. Retrieved from https://nyti.ms/2y1vVHQ

UNESCO. (2016, February 22). Roadmap towards UNESCO's World Atlas of Languages. Executive Board, 199th session, item 4 of provisional agenda.

Weinstein, E. (2014). The personal is political on social media: Online civic expression patterns and pathways among civically engaged youth. *International Journal of Communication, 8*, 210–233.

Wike, R., & Castillo, A. (2018, October 17). *Many around the world are disengaged from politics*. Washington, D.C.: Pew Research Center: Pew Global. Retrieved from https://pewrsr.ch/2ZdyPp3

Wolfsfeld, G., Segev, E., & Sheafer, T. (2013). Social media and the Arab Spring: Politics comes first. *The International Journal of Press/Politics, 18*(2), 115–137.

Xenos, M., Vromen, A., & Loader, B. D. (2014). The great equalizer? Patterns of social media use and youth political engagement in three advanced democracies. *Information, Communication & Society, 17*(2), 151–167. Doi:10.1080/1369118X.2013.871318

Yglesias, M. (2018, February 22). The Parkland conspiracy theories, explained. *Vox*. Retrieved from vox.com.

Zuckerman, E. (2016). Effective civics. In E. Gordon & P. Mihailidis (Eds.), *Civic media: Technology/design/practice* (pp. 49–76). Cambridge, MA: MIT Press.

Index

Ferris Bueller's Conclusion

What are you doing back here?

The book is done.

It's done.

Go.